ETHICS AND
POLITICAL THEORY

Joseph Grcic

University Press of America,® Inc.
Lanham • New York • Oxford

Copyright © 2000 by
University Press of America,® Inc.
4720 Boston Way
Lanham, Maryland 20706

12 Hid's Copse Rd.
Cumnor Hill, Oxford OX2 9JJ

Library of Congress Cataloging-in-Publication Data

Grcic, Joseph.
Ethics and political theory / by Joseph Grcic.
p.   cm.
Includes bibliographical references.
1. Political ethics.   I. Title
BJ55.G73   1999   172—dc21   99-047772 CIP

ISBN 0-7618-1538-4 (cloth: alk. ppr.)
ISBN 0-7618-1539-2 (pbk: alk. ppr.)

CONTENTS

Contents

PREFACE

These essays include historical and critical discussions of ethics and political theory. Some essays deal with the foundations and historical evolution of philosophical ethics and political theory while others focus on applied ethics. Other chapters explore the historical evolution of the social contract theory of political legitimacy. In these essays I examine the contract model of obligation as it appears in Locke, Rousseau, Hobbes, Kant and Rawls.

Several of the essays deal with the philosophy of John Rawls. His work is considered by many to be one of the most significant contributions to political theory and ethics in this century. I explore the historical roots of Rawls' theory in the works of Locke, Rousseau and Kant. Some of these essays are partly critical of Rawls and others use his methodology and some of his ideas to critique existing political and social institutions. These social institutions include the family, the corporation, government, the legal profession, the university and mass media.

Some of these essays have been previously published in philosophy journals and some are new. I have revised some of the previously published articles for purposes of clarity. Most of the essays were also presented to various professional groups including the American Philosophical Association, the World Congress of Philosophy, Indiana Philosophical Association, The International Association for Philosophy of Law and Social Philosophy and other groups.

I am grateful to many people who have helped me develop my ideas through the years. I am indebted to all my teachers and especially to Professor James Sterba of the University of Notre Dame for his encouragement and guidance. Other friends and colleagues who have helped me through the years include Hank Frankel of the University of Missouri, and R. M. Hare, Robert D'Amico, and Ellen Haring of the University of Florida. Finally, I must thank my parents Ljubo and Matija Grcic and my students who have made it worthwhile.

CHAPTER 1

INTRODUCTION

Human beings are social creatures. We need others to come into existence, grow, develop, learn, love and flourish. Our social nature involves needs and presents problems which are solved by various social institutions. Social institutions are established and enduring cultural structures or patterns of activity which embody various beliefs and values of a given society to meet the needs of its members. Historically, there have been five central institutions, the family, religion, the economy, educational and government institutions, all providing for different needs of individuals. These institutions have evolved, overlapped, and been shaped by differing cultural contexts and historical circumstances. A central force in the molding of social institutions is the system of moral values that prevail in any given society. The focus of these essays is the philosophic evaluation of the moral foundations of social institutions.

To judge the validity of the moral assumptions and foundations of various institutions one must first explore the different theories of the nature of morality itself. Is morality based on religion, reason, emotion, human nature or does it have some other foundation? In the second chapter I explore various answers to this question and give a historical overview of the history of ethics. I assess the strengths and weaknesses of various theories and suggest ways of combining their strengths toward developing a more adequate ethical theory.

In the next essay, I develop my own approach to ethical theory. I argue that Western ethics has focused too exclusively on the individual agent and ignored the social functions of moral values. I survey and critique various approaches to justifying morality. My essay draws on the findings of sociologists and their research on universal values found in virtually all cultures. My own argument justifying morality is that the very possibility of community necessitates certain moral values. I discuss such classic ethical issues as the is/ought problem and present a solution to it. I also examine moral relativism and other major approaches to ethics.

In the essay on truth in ethics, I examine how truth can be attributed to ethical principles. I survey various conceptions of truth and defend the pragmatic conception as appropriate in the domain of ethics.

In my essay on errors in moral reasoning, I defend the thesis that the major theories of ethics share a basic agreement in practical moral attitudes. The theories of Aristotle, Kant and Mill are shown to agree that there are many errors in moral reasoning we must avoid. I explore the nature of prejudice, ethnocentrism, egocentrism, and other moral errors and show how the theories of Aristotle, Kant and Mill would support the view that these are indeed mistakes in moral reasoning.

Having explored ethical theory, the remaining chapters examine ethics in connection with political theory and social institutions. Political theory is concerned with the ethical and rational evaluation of political power and the institution of government. Political power is to be distinguished from other forms of power in that it is supreme in a given area and has the authority to formulate, implement and enforce rules or laws that involve the society as a whole. The laws of any society embody the values, beliefs and customs of that society at that time. Through laws and other institutions the political system maintains social order, resolves conflict and ensures protection from external enemies. Governments may also provide other services such as education, medical care and other needs of society. What services governments should provide and how political power is to be justified have been recurring issues in political philosophy.

Political philosophy must be distinguished from ideology and from purely descriptive accounts of government. An ideology is a system of ideas which seeks to justify or legitimize a given social and political system from the point of view and in the interest of a group or class. Political science and other social sciences deal with the description of how actual political systems function, not their moral evaluation. Political philosophy, on the other hand, is a normative discipline which seeks to determine the purpose, limits and nature of government. Its goal is to establish the proper ethical and rational foundations of the morally best form of government.

The philosophic evaluation of political theories must consider all relevant dimensions of these theories. All political theories exist in a wider conceptual framework. One element of this framework, whether explicit or implicit, is an epistemology or a theory of knowledge. The epistemology one holds will determine the source and limits of knowledge including the possibility of knowledge in the realm of ethics. For example, the epistemology of Plato was not that of Rawls and their differing views on this level influenced, in many ways, the shape and substance of their political theories.

Next to epistemology, the most encompassing conceptual framework is that of metaphysics or worldview. Within this framework one would find religious beliefs and claims about ultimate reality. Examples here would be Plato's Theory of Forms and Aquinas' Christian idea of God. Clearly certain theories like the divine right of kings presuppose a deity while others, like Marx's theory, explicitly deny such a being.

In addition to the frameworks of epistemology and metaphysics, political theory also assumes some conception of human nature. Since political power involves the organization of persons, some understanding of what persons are, their abilities, limits and potential is necessary. Hobbes certainly had a different view of human nature from that of Locke which played a significant role in their respective theories.

Political theory also incorporates, as already indicated, a moral theory. A moral theory seeks to understand the nature of good and specifies the rights and duties of persons and, by implication, the purpose and limits of government. For example, a democratic form of government has a different moral foundation from the political theory of someone like Plato. The philosophical evaluation of a political theory would involve the rational scrutiny of all of the above-mentioned elements. In evaluating all these elements, one would apply some basic rules of rationality. This would involve first establishing whether key terms and concepts of the theory are well defined. Ambiguity at the level of basic ideas would make the entire theory ambiguous.

Next, we must make sure the theory is consistent and follows the laws of logic. Additionally, we must determine whether all the claims are supported by sufficient evidence or true beliefs. Do scientific findings support or contradict the theory? Is the theory complete or detailed enough to account for all relevant aspects it should? Can the theory be implemented in the real world or is it simply some ideal that can never be realized as some interpreters have said of Plato's Republic? These are some of the relevant criteria for evaluating any theory, political or otherwise.

In my essay on Kant and Rawls' moral theory, I examine Rawls' claim that his political theory as expressed in his *A Theory of Justice* is Kantian in nature. I claim that Rawls' moral theory is really a synthesis of Kantian and utilitarian ideas. I critique Rawls' understanding of Kant's ethics and show the a priori nature of Kant's theory is incompatible with some elements of Rawls' theory.

In chapter seven, using the criteria for evaluating theories mentioned above, I examine the main models of political theory. This historical survey presents the main ideas of central political philosophers and evaluates their contributions. This historical overview supports the view that political power does not occur in a vacuum but is informed by the context of the prevailing worldview, moral beliefs and social realities. As worldviews and social conditions evolve, political philosophy emerges to redefine and re-evaluate the assumptions, implications and foundations of political institutions. What is the foundation of political power? How and why does it arise? What, if any, are its limits? Throughout history, different answers have been given to these questions.

As I suggest in this chapter, probably the oldest justification of political authority came from the framework of theological beliefs. Political authority was either conceived as deriving from the will of the gods or believed to be actually wielded by gods themselves. The moral legitimacy of power was seen as coming from above, from the realm of the supernatural wrapped in mystery, tradition and ritual.

The ancient Greek philosophers attempted to develop a rational and secular understanding of the world and political order. Plato's theory of political power is based on a moral and epistemological foundation elaborated in *The Republic* and other dialogues. He justified political authority as necessary for social order, moral development and happiness. Plato argued that only the Philosopher-Kings, those individuals with the highest moral and intellectual virtue, should rule and constituted the legitimacy of state power.

The dominance of Christianity in Europe revived a certain religious framework for political discourse. Although rulers were now not themselves considered to be divine, they were believed to serve by the grace of God as interpreted by the church. The divine right of kings held that monarchy was the only legitimate form of rule since rulers received their authority from God. Still, rulers were expected to rule within the framework of the moral law as revealed by God and interpreted by the church hierarchy. However, the Protestant Reformation of the 16th century, the development of nationalism, industrial capitalism and modern science all tended to weaken the secular authority of religion and provided a context for a nonreligious understanding of governmental power. The social contract theory was one such attempt at a nonreligious foundation for political authority.

The historical evolution of the social contract model of political authority is a reflection of the changing religious and philosophical ideologies and socioeconomic structures. Its origins might be traced as far back as the covenant between Abraham and Jehovah of the Old Testament. The social contract theory as defended by Locke, Rousseau, Kant and more recently, John Rawls, is a secular development of the contract idea. The social contract in this modern tradition is a type of agreement between persons used to justify and establish political institutions.

My thinking and research have been molded by these questions of political power and its moral foundations. Some of my essays deal with Rawls' discussion of the relationship of liberal democratic equality and economic liberty. My general approach is that Rawls has not paid enough attention to the difficulties for political equality raised by differences in income and wealth. I propose various means for correcting this condition and suggest ways to reform democratic societies.

Rawls states in his *A Theory of Justice* that his conception of justice is in the tradition of the social contract form of political legitimacy. I explore the historical roots of Rawls' contract theory and critically evaluate his contributions and relationship to other contract theorists, namely, Locke, Rousseau and Kant, in which tradition he claims to be working.

In my discussion of Rousseau, I show how his contract theory contrasts with that of Rawls. I attempt to show that Rousseau's theory is revolutionary in nature in contrast to that of Rawls which accepts much of the status quo as he sees it.

The issue of economic inequality and political equality is again addressed in chapter twelve. I draw on some ideas of Rawls new work, *Political Liberalism*, to argue that his attempt to reconcile the equal worth of liberty and economic inequality is inadequate. I claim that to reconcile these ideas it is necessary to implement what I call the right to political leave. This is the right of all workers to leave their place of work to run for political office and return to the place of employment after the election or term in office is over.

In addition to this theoretical aspect, I examine the practical implications of Rawls' theory and liberalism in general. Here I argue that his theory as I understand it would lead to the public financing of all election campaigns. I also argue that the legal profession must be available free of charge to all who need legal representation. I defend the idea that democracy must be extended to the corporation and the media if true democracy is to be more fully actualized.

In other essays I discuss several other current issues of social policy such as children's rights and the right to privacy. I defend the right to privacy using Locke's argument for the right to private property. Privacy and children's rights are examined in my paper on the right to have children. I analyze what it means to have a right and defend the idea that the right to have children exits only if certain conditions are met. In my essay on academic freedom and tenure I explain my understanding of the role of academic freedom for the growth of knowledge and democratic institutions. I examine the reasons for and against tenure and defend my understanding of tenure as necessary for the preservation of democracy.

These articles are an attempt to combine the theory and practice of ethics and politics. My approach draws on the findings of relevant sciences and historical facts when appropriate. I believe these essays may be found useful for philosophers and others concerned with social and political issues that impact on the quality of our lives and the opportunities we may or may not have.

CHAPTER 2

TYPES OF ETHICAL THEORY

Moral norms provide the deep structure of the human community. The nature and foundations of these moral norms have been variously understood at different times. Some believed moral norms were the will of God, others believed them to be based on human nature, or reason, or the need for social order and more recently others have judged them to be without any foundation. However, historically, the first understanding of morality was provided by religious belief systems.

Probably the oldest definitions of 'good' and 'right' come from religion. The Divine Command Theory holds that God's will and commandments define goodness. On this view, God not only defines and reveals the moral rules, but also enforces them in this life and the next. The oldest existing code of law and morality is the Babylonian Code of Hammurabi. This code, according to tradition, was given to King Hammurabi by the sun god Shamash at about 1,700 BC. It is a moral and legal code requiring the death penalty for more than thirty offenses including incest, burglary and casting an evil spell.

Though religion as a cultural phenomenon is universal, there are many incompatible and inconsistent religious belief systems. They have different ideas of god, different rituals, varying understandings of the nature of death, among other differences. However, in the midst of this theological pluralism, there is a remarkable similarity among them in their basic ethical teachings.[1] All the main world religions condemn certain acts as wrong and praise others as right. Hinduism, Judaism, Confucianism,

Taoism, Christianity, Islam, and Buddhism, reject murder, stealing, lying, hypocrisy, idleness, ignorance, selfishness, adultery and promiscuity.

The rules found in the Ten Commandments accepted by Judaism and Christianity echo many of these values. In addition to religious duties, the commandments state: "...Honor your father and your mother...You shall not kill. You shall not commit adultery. You shall not steal. You shall not bear false witness. You shall not covet your neighbor's house...or anything that is your neighbor's." (Exodus, 20. 1-17)

The religion of Islam founded by Mohammed (570-632 AD) has a moral code similar to Judaism and Christianity. The moral teachings are summarized in the Five Pillars of Islam: 1) Belief in one God, Allah, and accept Mohammed as His prophet; 2) Pray five times daily; 3) Give alms to the poor; 4) fast during the month of Ramadan; 5) Make a pilgrimage to Mecca at least once in life. The *Koran*, the holy scriptures of Islam, also states: "Be good to your parents... Approach not lewd behavior ...Take not life... Approach not the property of the orphan...Give full measure and weight in justice...If you give your word, do it justice...and fulfill your obligations before God." (*Koran*, 6.151-53)

The Hindu religion, the oldest religion still practiced today, also supports many of these same ideas. It requires: "Nonviolence, truthfulness, not stealing, purity, control of the senses." (Laws of Manu, 10.63)

The religion of Buddhism arose out of Hinduism at about the sixth century BC in India. Its founder, Siddhartha Gautama, received the title Buddha, (the Enlightened) when he grasped what he believed were the basic truths of life. This he called the Four Noble Truths: 1) Life is suffering; 2) The cause of suffering is selfish desire; 3) Desire can be overcome; 4) The Eightfold Path is the way to overcome desire. The Eightfold Path is a list of moral and meditation practices and rules: 1) Have right knowledge (especially understand the Four noble Truths and what they mean); 2) Right thought (avoid desire, envy, jealousy); 3) Right speech (no lying or boasting); 4) Right conduct (no killing of any living thing, no theft, no sexual impurity); 5) Right work (not being a butcher, alcohol seller, prostitute or slave trader); 6) Right efforts (self confidence, courage); 7) Right mindfulness (control thoughts, discipline the mind); 8) Right concentration (meditate and achieve enlightenment or Nirvana). (Sermon at Benares)

Although the divine command theory has had a long history, contemporary philosophers see its strengths and weaknesses differently. One strength often mentioned is that it provides motivation for many to be moral. The idea of divine reward and punishment, though perhaps not the highest motive, does give many a reason for acting morally. Others argue that religion provides authoritative knowledge about morality human reason alone is not capable of discovering.

Immanuel Kant, though not basing ethics on divine will, did see a vital role for religion in ethics. He realized that human moral judgments and institutions are imperfect. It seems obvious to many that, in this world, often the immoral prosper and the good suffer. Kant believed only a perfectly good and omniscient God could accurately reward and punish in this life and the next. Without God and a life after death, Kant claimed morality would not have the necessary sanctions.

Other philosophers have noted certain problems with a moral system based on religion. First, there is skepticism whether the belief in God is rationally based and which, if any, religion is true. Different religions have different ideas about God, the cosmos and the afterlife. Second, many philosophers point out that even if there is some agreement on basic values in the world religions, there is disagreement on specific applications. Issues concerning the rights of men and women, polygamy, crime, animal rights and sexual morality still persist among the religions of the world. Finally, a moral system based on religion is in practice subject to the interpretations of those individuals who have the authority to make the interpretations which introduces the human element of error, bias and other complications.

Other philosophers starting with Plato have raised questions about the logical relationship of God to morality. Does God's will define, determine, enforce and/or reveal moral values? How do we establish what is in fact God's will? What does it mean to say God is good? Why does God choose one set of values over others? Could God have chosen something like rape to be moral? Is fear of divine punishment a good reason for being moral? These questions led philosophers like Plato to the development of the attempt to formulate a purely rational and secular moral theory.

Philosophers like Plato initiated a new way of understanding the world and human experience. Philosophy didn't seek to explain the world through the traditional stories or myths, but through reason, logic, and questioning. Philosophy probes the meanings of ideas and evaluates the basis of beliefs and institutions.

Ethics is a discipline within philosophy which seeks to understand the nature, purpose and foundation of morality. It seeks a rational understanding of good and evil. Ethics is a discipline which is generally divided into normative ethics and meta-ethics. Meta-ethics deals with questions of meaning, justification and the logic of value statements, not with specific advice on how to act. Normative ethics deals with practical questions about how we should live and act.

Plato

Plato, (427-347 BC) a student of Socrates, (470-399 BC) developed an elaborate philosophic system and an ethical theory.[2]   As already mentioned, one central element of his ethics was his argument that the will of the gods could not be the foundation of morality. The question can be put this way: Is something good because the gods will it or do the gods will it because it is good? If we take the first alternative, then it is theoretically possible that the gods could will murder, rape and the like as good. Most people reject this as irrational.

If we take the second alternative, then good exists independently of the gods. This was important since the Greek gods were not morally perfect but had the same moral weaknesses humans do, they lied, cheated and fought and disagreed among themselves. They were godlike only in that most were immortal and much more powerful than humans. It is easy to see why Socrates, Plato and Aristotle could not rely on their religious tradition for a theory of right and wrong.

Plato based his theory of ethics on knowledge and reason not emotion, tradition, or myths. In short, Plato believed ethics is a branch of knowledge based on knowing what Plato called the Ideas or Forms. Plato's theory of Forms, though a complex and evolving metaphysical theory, can be briefly defined as the theory that there exists a non-physical and eternal realm of structures which are the blueprint for all things in the material world. Plato used this theory to attack moral relativism as defended by a group of philosophers called the Sophists. Plato argued against them that there was an eternal and unchanging idea of Good which exists independently of this world and which we must know in order to be good.

In Plato's allegory of the cave he tells a story about the vast majority of humanity who live as if prisoners in a cave. In this cave all they see are shadows cast on a wall which they mistake for reality. Only when humanity comes out of this cave of illusion and dreams after a long period of philosophic training, will we come to know the true nature of reality, the eternal Ideas or Forms.

Plato's Ring of Gyges story found in *The Republic* dramatizes one of the main questions of ethics. Gyges was a shepherd who found a ring that could make him invisible. Gyges would become invisible and commit all sorts of immoral and selfish acts and escape punishment for them. Wouldn't we all act this way if we could?

According to Plato, the moral life is based on the rule of reason which has been informed by knowledge of the Forms. A moral person has an inner harmony of the soul which is necessary for happiness. Plato attacks hedonism arguing that reason is superior to pleasure for without reason pleasure-seeking would lead to self-destruction. In general, Plato defends the idea that reason must rule the passions if our behavior is to be virtuous and our life, happy.

A moral life, according to Plato, includes the development of the four main virtues of wisdom, courage, moderation and justice. Without these virtues, our soul will lack harmony and will ultimately lead to disease and death. Plato goes on to argue that a society which is not ruled by reason will only destroy itself through unrestrained emotions.

Plato's theory is considered by many to be a giant step toward a rational ethic. He rejected the superstitious and myth-based morality and sought an ethical system based on human nature and a rational understanding of the cosmos. Although his contributions are many, some consider his theory problematic in places. For example, Plato could never fully explain what the Ideas or Forms really were and how they exist or relate to this world. His belief that moral virtue is a harmony in the soul is hard for many to accept because the idea of a soul seems to conflict with the scientific understanding of human nature. Many of these problems were discussed by his pupil Aristotle who borrowed some of Plato's ideas and developed his own theory.

Aristotle

Aristotle, (384-322BC) developed a theory of ethics that is influential to this day.[3] His theory is a kind of naturalism in that he claims morality is justified in terms of natural properties and processes, not the otherworldly Ideas of Plato or the gods. For Aristotle, the good is what satisfies human needs, rational desires and promotes development. The ultimate good for Aristotle is happiness or well being; everything we do, we do to be happy. Happiness is the greatest good being attained when we satisfy our needs and developed our potential to the fullest.

In Aristotle's time as in our own, there were disputes about the nature of happiness and the morally right way to live. Some defended hedonism, others defended fame, power and money as the correct goals. According to Aristotle, the question as to how we should live is answered by considering our "function." Just as a good ax is one which cuts well so a good person is one who acts as a person should. The function of something is what it does best. And what do human beings do better than any other creature? Aristotle's answer is-reason.

A truly human and therefore happy life for Aristotle is one guided by reason and which develops reason fully. And a life guided by reason will be one which has the four main virtues, wisdom, courage, moderation and justice. Wisdom is knowledge of the basic truths of reality and their

proper application in life. Courage is the rational response to fear.
Moderation is the rational control of the bodily pleasures. And justice
means treating people fairly and giving them their due. Aristotle was also
clear that the development of these virtues, which are habits, require a
proper upbringing in a home and school where these habits can be learned.

Several contemporary philosophers like Alasdair MacIntyre have argued
for a virtue theory of ethics similar to Aristotle's.[4] Virtue ethics believes
that ethics should focus on developing virtues and a good character in
persons, not trying to come up with a system of rules. Virtue theorists
claim moral rules are difficult to apply and it is not clear which rules we
should believe in. Virtues also provide the motivation to act morally
which rules do not.

Though Aristotle's theory is accepted by many who follow some version
of the virtue theory of ethics, some problems for this approach have also
been discussed. Some critics question the idea that persons have a
function at all. Is reason the only way we differ form other animals?
Maybe artistic creation is what really distinguished us from other animals?
Existentialist philosophers like Jean-Paul Sartre deny that there is a human
function arguing we must freely choose our morality and way of life.

Controversy also revolves around determining what a virtue really is.
Is it something needed by society or for the individual's happiness or both?
What is the correct set of virtues we should acquire? The virtues of
Aristotle are not the virtues of St. Paul (hope, faith, love) which are not the
virtues of Benjamin Franklin. Are virtues universal or relative to a
society? Are all virtues equal or is one dominant? Is there a reliable
method for acquiring virtue? Other critics of virtue theory see virtues as
necessary for moral behavior but not sufficient. We also need specific
rules to guide us especially in difficult situations like abortion and
euthanasia.

Aquinas

The Western religious traditions borrowed philosophical ideas from the
Greeks and combined them in various ways with theological doctrines.
Thinkers such as the Christian theologian Thomas Aquinas, (1225-1274),
formulated the Natural Law Theory of ethics.[5] This theory holds, in
essence, that God, by creating the world and humanity with reason, does
not arbitrarily define the good, but rather the good is based in nature,
God's handiwork. Thus nature is the foundation for our understanding of
morality, which divine revelation completes.

For Aquinas, 'good' is defined in relation to nature because nature is a
creation of a good God. The good is what satisfies our needs, promotes
life, our development and happiness. For example, marriage and children

are good, Aquinas argued, because they fulfill our needs for love and companionship.

Though reason can establish a minimum morality, Aquinas saw the need of divine revelation to reveal what he believed was a higher morality. As a Christian, he believed The New Testament with its ethic of love completed natural morality. Aquinas believed God enforces morality by punishing the evil and rewarding the good in this life and the next.

Natural Law theory is still accepted today, especially by conservative thinkers. Aquinas' theory upholds a traditional ethic about property, sexuality, rejects homosexuality and upholds the importance of the traditional family structure. Some critics, nevertheless, question Aquinas' notion of 'nature' as pre-scientific and simplistic. Today, Darwin's theory of evolution and science in general have shown that members of any species are more varied than previously believed. Others reject the metaphysical foundation of the theory, the existence of God, as irrational.

Kant

Although Western philosophy was initiated by the ancient Greeks, it was also profoundly influenced by the Christian religion. The 18th century German philosopher, Immanuel Kant, (1724-1804) for example, was a Christian but sought to defend an essentially Christian ethic on the basis of reason alone or a priori.[6] A priori reason is, according to Kant, pure reason or reason not limited by empirical sense data. Only a moral system founded on principles derived from reason alone could be universal and apply to all rational creatures. This is why Kant rejected happiness as the basis of ethics because he believed happiness was too subjective and therefore not universal.

Kant's ethics is deontological in structure. A deontological ethical system is one which holds that the morality of actions is determined by intent or motive, not the consequences of our actions. For Kant, our intent is the only part of action that we can control totally. We can never know with certainty or control what the total consequences of any act will be since all consequences have further consequences and so on indefinitely.

Kant saw the main problem of ethics in determining whether there was something that is absolutely good. Is there something that is good in all circumstances and at all times? Yes, Kant argued, there is such a thing, a "good will."[7] The only absolute good for Kant was "good will" or a will that is based on the pure respect for the moral law. If we act morally out of fear of punishment or to be praised by others, we are not acting from love of the moral law but love of ourselves.

For Kant, only the good will is totally good because all other things may be abused. For example, knowledge is good but, for Kant, it is not absolutely good because it can be used for an evil purpose. But how do we know we really have a good will? The answer is what Kant called the "categorical imperative."

The "categorical imperative" is the ultimate rule of Kant's ethics. According to Kant, the categorical imperative is a single principle that has two different and equivalent expressions. The first form states, "Act so that your maxim can become a universal law."[8] The maxim is the underlying principle of your volition. For example, if you decide to lie to get money from someone, then the maxim of your contemplated decision is something like 'Lie when in our own interest.' The next step is to ask whether the logic of your maxim can consistently become a universal law. Or, one must ask oneself, 'could everyone do likewise?' What would happen if everyone lied when it suited them?

Kant's answer is that there is an inherent contradiction in such a maxim as universal lying. Lying can only exist in a context where usually people tell the truth for if people knew you were lying they would not be deceived by your lie and therefore there would be no point in telling lies. Lying, therefore, could not become a consistent universal rule and is therefore immoral.

The second form of the categorical imperative states, "Act as to treat humanity, whether in thine own person or in that of any other, in every case as an end, never as a means only."[9] For Kant, to use someone as a means only is immoral because it is a violation of the person as a free and autonomous individual. Things have relative value because their value is relative or dependent on the needs of persons. Persons, on the other hand, have according to Kant absolute value because their value is independent of the needs of others. Persons have absolute value and therefore the right to autonomy because we are rational and it is reason that allows to lead our own lives. Slavery, for example, is immoral because it uses persons as things or means, and denies them their absolute value.

Another way of looking at Kant's ethics is to consider what kind of world it would be rational to live in. Would we want to live in a world where what we are intending to do were to become a universal practice? Will our future wants be consistent with such a universal practice? If not, then we should not do it. For example, is it moral for a rich person to ignore the needs of the poor? To answer this, ask yourself what Kant called the "maxim" of your decision is. If you are rich and decide not to help the poor then your maxim is: 'Ignore the poor.' Then ask yourself whether you would want your maxim to become a universal rule. Or would you want to live in a world where the rich ignored the poor? What if you were poor, would you want to be ignored? Probably not, hence your maxim is wrong since we would not want such a rule to be universal, therefore it is immoral to ignore the poor.

Kant's ethical system continues to be influential. He is credited with defending individual rights, human autonomy and a rational approach to moral values. Many praise his idea of universalizability as essential to ethical behavior. This idea holds, to put it in other words, that if something is right for me to do in some circumstances, then consistency requires one to agree that it is right for everyone to do the same in similar circumstances.

However, others find Kant's approach too rationalistic. They question his rejection of emotions like compassion as irrelevant to moral action. Compassion seems to most people a perfectly moral basis for helping others whereas Kant claimed we must act only on the basis of abstract reason.

Another problem concerns the meaning of the categorical imperative. Some actions can be universalizable as the categorical imperative requires but are not within the realm of morality. For example "Put on your left sox before the right sox" is universalizable, but it doesn't make it a moral duty. For this and other reasons, most critics believe the categorical imperative is a necessary but not a sufficient condition for moral duty.

The application of the categorical imperative is further complicated by the problem of maxim ambiguity. The problem is that one can formulate a maxim in more or less general ways. Kant believed it was always wrong to lie because lying cannot be universalized. But this depends how one articulates the problem. For example, we can formulate the maxim in a more specific way as 'Lie to save an innocent life;' this maxim seems to be universalizable. If one formulates the maxim in more general way such as, "Lie when in your self-interest," then universalizability becomes problematic. Unfortunately, Kant did not give precise instructions how to formulate the maxim.

Finally, some critics claim that Kant did not give animals any moral rights. Many animal rights people today believe animals have rights not because they are rational but because they can feel pain. Other problems have also been mentioned but it is clear that Kant's theory overall with its emphasis on the absolute value of persons and the need for consistent and rational rules in morality is a major contribution to moral theory.

Mill

An equally influential theory is that of the nineteenth century British thinker John Stuart Mill (1806-1873). His utilitarian theory of ethics is based on what he took to be the given fact that we all finally seek one thing, happiness.[10] Mill argued that being ethical simply means that in all we do we must promote happiness and reduce pain, not just for ourselves but for all involved. This is called a teleological theory in that the goodness of an action is based on the results or consequences of the act.

Mill partly based his theory on the ethics of the nineteenth century British philosopher Jeremy Bentham (1748-1832). Bentham was a colorful character who enjoyed a good joke. For example, he left his entire fortune to the University of London on the condition that his dressed and mummified body sitting in a glass case be rolled out every meeting of the board of trustees; they agreed! Bentham developed what he called the "hedonic calculus" or a set of rules for evaluating and increasing our pleasure.[11] Bentham argued we should pursue only those pleasures which score highest on the following seven criteria: 1.) intensity-how strong the pleasure is sex being more intense than a good meal; 2.) duration-how long does the pleasure last, a good concert lasts longer than a good meal; 3.) certainty-how sure are we to get the pleasure; 4.) proximity-how soon or near is the pleasure; 5.) fecundity-how many other pleasures will one pleasure produce, for example, a good friend will produce many other pleasures; 6.) purity-does the pleasure involve pain, for example, the pleasures of drugs and alcohol can lead to disease; 7.) extent-how many will experience the pleasure. Bentham's approach attempts to make happiness a scientific endeavor but many criticized him for being just a crude hedonist who did not value 'high' cultural values and sources of happiness.

Mill, following Bentham, defined 'happiness' as the increase of pleasure and the decrease of pain. But this is not a philosophy of crude hedonism or mere physical pleasure seeking through food, sex and drink as many accused Bentham of advocating. No, Mill's version of utilitarianism requires that we should pursue what he calls the "higher pleasures." These are pleasures of the mind such as knowledge, poetry, music, friendship, love and the like. Why are these the "higher pleasures"? They are higher, Mill claimed, because people who have experienced both the lower and higher pleasures judged them to be higher. We should try and develop these pleasures in ourselves and others as much as we can.

The theory of utilitarianism has two different versions. Some defend rule utilitarianism and others defend act utilitarianism. Rule utilitarianism holds that our behavior should follow rules which are based on the principle of utility. For example, the rule against murder should be obeyed, according to the rule utilitarians because the rule generally promotes happiness. Mill is generally seen as accepting the traditional moral rules against murder, stealing, lying and the others as necessary for human happiness and the reduction of pain, physical and emotional. Like Kant, he believed he was not rejecting the moral tradition that comes from Judaism and Christianity but putting them on a rational and scientific basis.

Act utilitarians accept only the principle of utility as guiding behavior. For them, we must apply the principle of utility to every contemplated act and see if it will maximize happiness. They do not see the need for any other rule. For act utilitarians, only the rule of utility is absolute, all other rules have exceptions.

Mill's theory is another major perspective with many defenders today. Many praise his theory as one that demystifies ethics and makes it clear, rational and practical. Our traditional ethical systems all seem to include the idea that moral behavior is at least in part a matter of reducing suffering and increasing happiness. Yet, Mill's theory has its detractors as well.

One problem often mentioned by critics is Mill's proposed proof for the principle of utility. His argument seems to proceed from the fact that people pursue pleasure that they ought to pursue pleasure. This is logically incorrect since one cannot deduce an 'ought' from an 'is' according to his critics.

Another problem concerns the fact that it is a theory based on consequences. As Kant argued, it is difficult to calculate all the consequences of any action. Consequences are like ripples in a pool of water, impossible to know where they will end up. Secondly, it is difficult, if not impossible, to measure pleasure and pain. How can we maximize something which we cannot measure?

Some critics claim that Mill's theory does not fully protect individual rights and justice. For example, making 1% of the population slaves could make the other 99% very happy, but this would surely be unjust. In a related criticism, others claim his theory would allow the punishment of innocent persons if such punishment would maximize social order and peace.

Others feel Mill did not defend his concept of higher and lower pleasures. There are questions whether the distinction between them is objective. Some philosophers, like R.M. Hare have sought to combine the best of Mill's theory with that of Kant's theory as the more adequate theory of ethics.[12] Debate continues about these matters, but many philosophers believe that Mill's theory is only part of what a complete ethics would look like.

Nietzsche

The philosophical movement known as Existentialism presents a very different perspective on ethics. It is a varied movement made of many different thinkers but most share some core ideas. They share a belief in the freedom of the individual and the responsibility of the individual to choose how he or she will live. With the exception of Soren Kierkegaard and some others, most Existentialists are atheists which means they do not accept any moral system based on religion.

Existentialists condemn what they see as the great masses of humanity who blindly go along with their own society's teachings. These individuals are not authentic, they are not really living in a way that reflects their true individuality. They suffer from what Jean-Paul Sartre (1905-1980) called "bad faith" since they do not accept their innate freedom.

True freedom for the Existentialists means to choose your own way of living including your morals and values. However, this choice cannot be rationally determined, hence there is always uncertainty and what Existentialists call anxiety or dread associated with life. This is why Jean-Paul Sartre said "We are condemned to be free."[13] We are free but we are also afraid of this freedom and its awesome responsibility.

Friedrich Nietzsche (1844-1900) was an Existentialist who rejected many of the beliefs, values and institutions of his day.[14] He was particularly outspoken about his hatred of the Judeo-Christian ethic as he saw it. Nietzsche accepted atheism claiming that "God is dead." He despised what he understood to be the Christian morality as a "slave morality." It was a morality fit only for slaves because its values of love, compassion, 'turn the other cheek,' forgiveness and humility are the values of the powerless. It is a morality slaves came to accept because it suited their life as oppressed people ruled by the ancient and powerful Roman Empire. Those who ruled over them, the Romans, practiced the "master morality" of ambition, arrogance, combat and conquest.

According to Nietzsche, the morality of Jesus was also contrary to nature. Nature and all reality are ruled according to Nietzsche by the "Will to Power." All things in nature seek greater power and the domination of the weak. Nature is based on 'might makes right' as the struggle for survival shows; the meek are simply eaten. Neither is nature based on equality nor democracy. People are not equal according to Nietzsche for some are clearly superior intellectually, artistically, physically, etc. For him, Christian values favor the weak, not the strong, favor mediocrity and self-denial not self-assertion or excellence. Christian morality promises an after life of happiness for those who suffer here and now. For Nietzsche, since for him there is no God or an after life, this is simply a way to control the weak so they stay weak and quietly die.

Our goal, Nietzsche maintained, should be the "Superman" (Ubermensch). The Superman is someone who has developed the full power of humanity in art, intellect, strength and will. He will be a blend of Napoleon, Caesar, Mozart and Goethe. The right moral system, then, is one which brings about the Superman in as many as possible. This should be our goal, not to help the weak but to help the strong and creative become stronger and more creative.

Nietzsche's ideas are powerful and dramatic but also puzzling to many. He claimed that there is no such thing as objective knowledge or objective truth. If there is no objective knowledge, than why should we take his view of ethics or God as true? If all beliefs are simply the interpretations of each of us, what makes his interpretation better? Why should we accept the ideal of the Superman if there can be no rational defense of ethics? Some interpreters of Nietzsche believe he was criticizing more those who claimed to be Christian not the original message of Jesus.

What kind of society would Nietzsche's ethics create if implemented? Is his theory clear enough to be implemented? Some critics believe that his philosophy of the Superman could lead to the politics of Hitler and the Nazi party who used some of his ideas to justify the holocaust and the extermination of millions of Jews and other minorities. The Nazis, like Nietzsche, also denied human equality and believed that might makes right. To be sure, Nietzsche was not a nationalist who believed Germans were the superior race, yet his views certainly do not support the democratic ideal of equal respect for all persons. Other critics point out that he did not prove his atheism but merely assumed it. Finally, it must also be said that Nietzsche wrote in a poetic and obscure style which is why many philosophers interpret him in many different ways.

Emotivism

The ideas of Nietzsche were controversial and revolutionary. His rejection of religion and the traditional understanding of morality have influenced many. A rejection of religion and traditional morality also came from those who adopted the philosophy of Emotivism. Emotivism, held by such philosophers as A. J. Ayer (1910-1989) and C. L. Stevenson (1908-1979) claims that moral judgments of right and wrong are expressions of emotions, nothing more.[15]

These philosophers came to their conclusion on ethics based on their general philosophy of Logical Positivism. Logical Positivism holds that only science makes meaningful statements about the world. These statements are meaningful because we can determine through observation and the scientific method whether they are true or not.

For Ayer, ethical statements are very different from scientific statements. They do not describe the way things are in the physical world but rather how they ought to be. How does one scientifically test the truth of a statement such as "You ought not to lie?" According to the Logical Positivists, there is no way to prove or disprove this statement scientifically. It is therefore meaningless as an objective fact. It is simply the expression of emotion. And emotions, according to the emotivists, cannot be rationally proved right or wrong.

Stevenson agreed with Ayer but added his own details. He claimed that disagreements in ethics are of two kinds, about the facts and about attitudes. Most questions about ethics assume some facts as true. For example, disputes about capital punishment include disputes about whether it deters future criminal acts. In theory, this factual level of ethical dispute can be resolved according to Stevenson. However, it is on the level of attitude, of favorable or negative appraisal of the death penalty, that the disagreement may never be resolved. Although Stevenson agrees that agreement about the facts can change attitudes it by no means necessarily does so. There is no rational way, according to Stevenson, to force an agreement about attitudes.

The theory of emotivism continues to be supported by some philosophers. It is certainly true that emotions often accompany our moral beliefs but is that all moral beliefs are? The philosophy of Logical Positivism has itself been attacked as contradictory. Logical positivism holds that only scientifically verifiable statements are meaningful but the theory of logical positivism is not itself a scientific theory; it is a philosophy. Science itself uses ideas such as atoms and sub-atomic particles which are not directly available to the senses; is the atomic theory therefore meaningless?

Some critics also claim that emotivism seems to lead to subjectivism and moral nihilism. Subjectivism is the view that there is no one right morality and that the each individual decides their own morality. Moral nihilism is the idea that moral judgments are not rational at all and must be abandoned. If they are not rational, why have them at all? Finally, emotivists do not explain why we have these emotions at all. These emotions seem to be unnecessary yet emotions connected to moral beliefs are found in all societies.

Intuitionism

Why are there so many disputes in ethics? According to G. E. Moore (1873-1958) it is due to the fact that philosophers have not paid enough attention to defining key concepts clearly.[16] Moore claims we must first define 'good' before we can do any theorizing. But, according to Moore, no definition of 'good' can in fact be given. Any definition that is offered, such as 'good-pleasure' commits what Moore calls the "naturalistic fallacy." This fallacy is committed when any natural definition is given of 'good' according to Moore. Moore believes that John Stuart Mill committed this fallacy when he defined 'good' as 'desirable' and then observed that people desire pleasure. Mill then defined 'good' as 'pleasure'. For Moore, Mill committed the naturalistic fallacy because he equated what people do desire with what they ought to desire. Mill moved from an 'is', the fact that people desire pleasure, to an 'ought', the moral claim that they should desire pleasure. This, for Moore, was a logical error. In fact, according to Moore, the "open question argument" shows it is.

Moore claimed any definition of 'good' can be refuted by what he calls the "open question argument." The open question argument holds that for any definition of 'good', we can meaningfully ask, "Is pleasure really good?" If 'pleasure' really means the same as 'good' than to deny that pleasure is the good would be self-contradictory, which it isn't. Nor is saying "good means pleasure" the same as saying "good is good." According to Moore, no definition of 'good' can in fact be given.

According to Moore, 'good' is not a complex but a simple and nonnatural property. A complex idea such as 'human' can be defined as 'rational animal'. A simple property cannot be defined because it has no parts. It is like trying to define 'yellow'; it cannot be done. How then do we know what 'good' means?

Moore's answer is by intuition. We know the good by a kind of inner mental seeing. It is like our experience of the color yellow, to know what it means we must experience it, no definition can be given. This approach to ethics is known as intuitionism.

Moore is given credit for his careful and systematic approach in ethics. His stress on the importance of logical rigor and clear definitions is what has come to be called "meta-ethics," the focus on the logic of moral statements, not offering moral advice.

But critics are puzzled by some of his other ideas. Some critics believe his conception of definition is inadequate. Others point out that perhaps 'good' is difficult to define because it is vague, ambiguous (incorporating various incompatible traditions such as Greek philosophy and Christian dogma) and context dependent. It is also not clear that Moore proved no definition of good in terms of natural properties can be given. Perhaps an acceptable definition of 'good' might be along the lines Aristotle suggested as that which satisfies a rational desire or need. Finally, many find Moore's idea of intuition puzzling. Is there such a mental power, and if so, how is it that people disagree about morality?

Kohlberg

For thousands of years, morality was the domain of religion and philosophy. Recently, however, scientific studies by Lawrence Kohlberg have shed some additional light on the nature of morality.[17] Kohlberg based on his extensive studies in many cultures, came to the conclusion that there are three stages of moral development. The first level he called the "preconventional level," this is the level of children up to about age nine. At this stage children behave morally only to avoid punishment from parents and adults.

The second level Kohlberg calls the "conventional level." This is the level of most teens and adults. At this stage one has developed a conscience or internalized or accepted the moral rules of one's society. A conscience is an internal monitor of our behavior, which, if we violate it, produces guilt.

The third level Kohlberg called the "post-conventional level." Here, one has achieved a level of moral autonomy where one does not necessarily accept the moral teachings of ones society as correct but can take a critical stand towards it. At this stage one sees all people as deserving equal moral treatment based on some moral principle such as Kant's categorical imperative. Only a few individuals reach this stage; they include historical persons such as Socrates, Martin Luther King, and Gandhi.

Most scholars agree that Kohlberg has made a significant contribution to our understanding of moral development. However feminist critics have noted that Kohlberg's research involved only men and ignored women. Feminists such as Carol Gilligan claim Kohlberg has ignored the unique moral perspectives of women.[18] Women, she argues, tend to judge moral conflicts on the basis of caring and compassion rather than on abstract rules of justice.

Rawls

The different theories of ethics we have been discussing thus far can be categorized as either cognitivist or non-cognitivist. The cognitivists such as Plato, Aristotle, and others claim ethics is a branch of knowledge. They believe that ethical statements can be known to be true just as other statements. Non-cognitivists deny this; they claim ethics is not a branch of knowledge. Emotivism would be examples of non-cognitivism.

The cognitivist theories of ethics considered so far can be broadly defined as taking the foundationalist approach to justification. That is, they build a moral theory on a foundation of some basic belief which is not justified with respect to other beliefs or is considered to be self-evidently true. For example, for Aristotle, this was his notion of function or happiness. The problem with a foundationalist perspective on ethics is that these foundational beliefs may be difficult to establish as self-evident.

The foundational view of moral theory has been challenged by those who take a coherentist approach. Coherentism holds that beliefs can only be justified by other beliefs and that there are no self-evident foundational beliefs from which other beliefs are derivable. Coherentism sees consistency among beliefs as the only possible form of justification.

John Rawls' theory of "reflective equilibrium" is a type of coherentist approach to ethics.[19] Rawls rejects the foundational approach to ethics which argues that ethics is a system of beliefs based on some self-evident basic principles. He prefers what he calls the Socratic version which is coherentist in approach. The equilibrium is a form of consistency between what Rawls calls "considered judgments" and "principles." Considered judgments are judgments made when "our moral capacities are most likely to be displayed without distortion;" after due consideration, with sufficient knowledge and impartiality. Reflective equilibrium exists "after a person has weighed various proposed conceptions and he has either revised his judgments to accord with one of them or held fast to the initial convictions (and the corresponding conception)."[20]

However, what Rawls calls "wide reflective equilibrium" (as opposed to narrow reflective equilibrium described above) goes beyond mere consistency. In this form of reflective equilibrium Rawls requires that "all possible descriptions to which one might plausibly conform one's judgments together with all relevant philosophical arguments for them."[21] However, Rawls considers the possibility of accomplishing this wide reflective equilibrium "questionable."

We may grant that consistency is a characteristic of true belief systems, but consistency alone would not be enough to establish truth in ethics. Critics see a problem in that what Rawls calls "considered judgments" may be a reflection of the society one happens to be in which may include immoral beliefs. It is also surely true that there are many different and incompatible but self-consistent ethical systems.

Relativism

It is in fact this existence of incompatible ethical systems that has lead some to accept the theory of moral relativism. Moral relativism is the view that there are no unchanging or correct and universal moral principles. They deny moral absolutism, the view that there is one right and unchanging moral code for all people. Relativists like William Graham Sumner, Karl Marx, Ruth Benedict and Gilbert Harman claim 'good' and 'evil', 'right' and 'wrong' are always defined and determined within a society's customs and traditions. We cannot judge another society's moral values, for that is 'right' for them and their circumstances.

Anthropologists like Sumner and Benedict claim that morality is a way a people adapt to their environment in order to survive and meet their needs.[22] Different circumstances and situations call for different values. For instance, if there is not a 50/50 division of men and women because, say, war kills more men, then polygyny, marrying more than one wife is 'right' for such a society.

There are in fact, several kinds of relativisms. Descriptive or cultural relativism is simply the factual claim that there is disagreement about morality across cultures and at different times even within one culture. The other main kind of relativism is usually termed ethical relativism. This view as held by noncognitivists is the claim that there is no one correct rational moral system or set of value. Some defend ethical relativism on the grounds of epistemological relativism arguing that objective knowledge in general is impossible in all areas and therefore in ethics as well. Other relativists argue that the meaning of moral terms such as 'good' and 'right' have meaning only within a given cultural framework. They claim we cannot judge another society's moral values for that is 'right' for them and their circumstances.

There are several reasons usually offered in defense of relativism. First, there is the fact of cultural relativism. We know from the study of history and sociology that different societies have had and continue to have different moral codes. There are many examples in history of moral practices we would probably find immoral-cannibalism, human sacrifice, slavery, racism, and sexism. An extreme case of sexism is shown in the ancient and now abandoned Hindu custom of sati (the obligation of widows to be burnt at their husband's cremation). Can we objectively and rationally show these are, in fact, immoral? There are many seemingly hopeless disagreements today even in our own society about abortion, euthanasia, homosexuality, capital punishment among others. Can these controversies be resolved rationally? Relativists believe not.

Another reason for relativism is the lack of an agreed upon foundation for ethics. Some use religion, other reason and still others use human nature to base ethics on. Is there a universal human nature or not? Are differences among people as great as differences among cultures? Can abstract reason supply substantive moral norms? There is even disagreement about whether ethics is a rational enterprise as emotivists and Existentialists have argued.

Some relativists argue that relativism is necessary for tolerance and respect of other cultures. Respect excludes ethnocentrism, the belief that one's culture is the best and others are inferior and have no rights. Respect and tolerance of other societies, relativists claim, require that we believe other societies are just as good as our own.

Still another argument for relativism is the argument from fairness. The view here is that most people are only aware of the moral system of their own society; to judge them by an absolute standard is unfair since they are not aware of it.

Relativism is a theory that has been subjected to many criticisms over the years. One criticism points out that many of the disagreements about moral issues come from different religious traditions. Moslems, for example, allow up to four wives, but Christianity allows only monogamy. These disagreements then flow from these other disagreements about religion and cannot be resolved without deciding which religion is correct. Many of the disagreements about moral issues come from disagreements about the "facts" not values. For example, some Eskimo tribe had the custom of abandoning its aged parents to die. Our society would condemn this as probably murder. However, the reason this tribe did this is their belief that the quality of the after life of their aged parents is related to the quality of their lives when they died. So if they died senile and seriously infirm, they would have the same weaknesses in the after life. The abandonment of their parents before this happened was their way of promoting a good after life. Here, there is no difference in respect for parents but a difference about whether there is an after life or how one assures that the after life is good.

The factual claim of cultural relativism and moral disagreements does not establish the normative claim of moral relativism. Past disagreements between the heliocentric and geocentric beliefs do not establish that there is no objectively correct view.

The question of tolerance and respect for other cultures is an important one. The problem here is that relativists contradict themselves if they hold tolerance as an absolute. Furthermore, respect does not require absolute tolerance. Can we tolerate a society that is itself not tolerant of other societies? Should we tolerate a racist and slave practicing society? Should the British have tolerated the custom of sati? Respect means to value the lives of people, not necessarily every practice and belief they happen to have at a time. Indeed, respect would imply a reasoned attempt to convince another society to give up cruel and irrational practices, difficult though this may be.

The issue of fairness is not relevant to the issue of relativism. Fairness is concerned with judging another person's behavior, not the truth of the moral code they were socialized into believing. Fairness requires we judge another based on their knowledge at the time of the action, just as we do not judge children and the insane with the same standard as the sane adult.

Relativism has been rejected by some because the facts show that although there are disagreements in morality, there are also basic agreements about universal values. Human nature and the very existence of society and social order require certain moral values and exclude others. Sociological and anthropological evidence reveals what we saw in the world religions, that all societies have a common core of basic moral values. This core consists of the prohibition of murder, violence, incest, and theft, among others. There are also rules requiring some level of care for infants and the old, the encouragement of some form of marriage and sexual mating.[23]

As I argue in the next essay, the existence of moral norms and similarities can be explained as the solution to the problem of human coexistence in a socially enduring manner. Morality is the answer to the problem of maintaining social order among members of a species which both need others and at the same time are not genetically programmed to cooperate. Moral norms channel human impulses and actions into ordered relations with the actions of others. They constitute a structure of instrumental rules or guidelines which define appropriate means for the achievement of human ends in a social environment. In other words, moral norms correspond to necessary social structures wherein a group of individuals, with some antisocial tendencies, continues to exist as a society with minimal conflict and inefficiency in meeting the needs of its members. (See ch. 3)

To determine which if any of these theories are correct requires that we consider criteria for the rational acceptability of any theory. A theory is a set of systematically related statements that explain or justify some aspect of human experience. A good theory looks for deep underlying structures and overarching patterns. It relates, synthesizes and unifies our experience. For a theory in ethics or any discipline to do this well it must first have well defined and clear concepts. Basic concepts are the building blocks of any theory; vagueness or ambiguity will contaminate the entire theory. For example, some critics believe Nietzsche's idea of the will to power is vague and poorly defined.

Second, a rational theory must be consistent and follow the rules of logic. Consistency is a fundamental requirement of logic and rationality. An inconsistent moral theory would give incompatible advice for action and thus be useless. Perhaps Kant's failure to define precisely what a maxim is would lead to similar problems.

Third, a good theory must be complete. That is, it must have sufficient scope to explain the entire domain it is a theory about. Some critics of virtue theory have argued that virtues without principles are incomplete.

Fourth, a good theory should be simple. By simple, is meant two different ideas. First the theory should be understandable to most rational adults since it is intended to guide the action of adults. Second, a good theory should not have excessive number of statements but only those required by the goal of the theory.

Fifth, a rational theory must be based on the fullest set of available and relevant evidence or facts. A theory based on limited information, and false and irrelevant claims would to that degree be irrational. These false, irrelevant or unknowable claims could be metaphysical, epistemological or empirical. Some believe, for example, that Plato's theory of Ideas is a metaphysical claim without sufficient foundation.

Different ethical theories often have different conceptions of knowledge and truth. Does the mind have direct knowledge of moral truths as Moore seems to have believed? What theory of knowledge and truth is assumed in the theory? Is truth understood as coherence or correspondence or the pragmatic view? Is knowledge based on reason or the senses?

Sixth, a rational moral theory must be capable of implementation. That is, since a moral theory is to provide guidelines for action, it must be possible to use and apply the theory in the real world. Some critics of utilitarianism claim that since pleasure cannot be measured, the theory is not useful in practical matters.

Seventh, a good moral theory must have an adequate account of human nature. It is generally agreed that 'ought implies can'; which means that no theory can require persons to do what is impossible for them to do. But 'impossible' has different meanings. There is metaphysical impossibility, such as reversing the flow of time. There is physical impossibility such as reversing the spin of the earth. There is psychological impossibility such as memorizing the content of the Encyclopedia Britannica. There is intellectual impossibility of learning all the knowledge available today. Though what human nature is capable of may vary in time and not be fully known now, a moral theory that obligated actions beyond the capability of most persons would simply be irrelevant.

Finally, a good theory must be true or be the most likely candidate for truth. There are three main theories of truth, the correspondence, coherence and pragmatic theories. Truth is a requirement of knowledge and describes, in its correspondence conception, the nature or structure of reality. In ethics, of course, truth as correspondence is problematic because ethics does not deal primarily with a description of reality but rather makes claims the way reality should be. In any case, attempts such as pragmatism, foundationalism (a form of correspondence) or coherentism (as in reflective equilibrium) have been offered as possible views of the truth of moral theory.

These criteria can help us make sense of the plurality of theories discussed here. This plurality exists at the level of meta-ethics and normative ethics. On the level of meta-ethics, it is generally agreed that emotivism and intuitionism are inadequate theories. Though relativism still has its defenders, if the argument presented in chapter two is plausible, then a complete relativism is impossible if society is to continue.

Disagreement on the level of normative or practical ethics is far less profound than many believe. With the possible exception of Nietzsche, the philosophers discussed agree on the basic values and complement one another. Aristotle, Plato, Aquinas, Kant, Mill and Rawls all agree that murder, violence, lying, stealing, ignorance, idleness and other such acts are wrong.

Where they differ are the reasons they give why these actions are wrong. But these reasons, though different, are also compatible and present just part of the whole picture. For example, lying is wrong because for Aristotle it would be an act lacking wisdom or justice, for Aquinas, contrary to God's law, for Kant, wrong because lying cannot become a universal law and for Mill because generally it causes more pain than happiness. All these are good reasons.

On the level of theory, the ethics of Aristotle, Aquinas, Kant and Mill in many ways complete one another. As I argue in the next chapter more fully, the virtue theory of Aristotle and Aquinas shows that being moral is not just a matter of discrete acts but habits of behavior that need to be developed by training and education. Secondly, their virtue theory reminds us that human nature and human needs must be at least a part of ethics because needs motivate us to act and give value to those things desired. What makes food, rest, friendship, etc. good if not because we need them? What virtue theory shows is that it is not enough to know what morality requires, we must have the motivation to act on it.

Kant and Mill's theories remind us that virtues are themselves not enough for moral action. Virtues do not offer us specific enough guidelines for moral action. For example, justice is a virtue, but it alone does not help us solve the problem of affirmative action or abortion. Virtue theory must be completed with specific moral rules.

Mill and Kant's theory complement each other in another manner. Kant's theory stresses the importance of intent, individual autonomy and human rights. What a person intends to do is important because it distinguishes an accidental killing, say, from an intentional killing or murder. The act flows from the intent which flows out from the character of the person.

As Kant argued, the intent or reason for an action is relevant in judging the person. But as critics have pointed out, Kant's categorical imperative is a necessary but not sufficient condition for moral action. As Kant himself seems to have suggested, especially in the example of the rich and poor man, we need to consider consequences (in the broad sense) and human needs and future wants when contemplating an action. The differences between Kant and Mill, then, are not as great as often presented.

The history of western ethics is a dialogue across time about the nature and foundation of a rational morality. One element that is absent is an appreciation of the social role of ethics. This approach I develop in other chapters. It is nevertheless true that all theories are to varying degrees a reflection of the historical and social conditions of the time and the experience of the writer. In addition, theories make varying assumptions based on the worldviews they accept. The rational acceptability of these worldviews will in part determine the rational validity of the ethical theory they propose.

Theories presented as complete in themselves often point out weaknesses of other theories but often fail to incorporate their valid insights. Each theory presented contributes a part of the overall mosaic of what a rational morality is about. Like the proverbial three blind men and the elephant, they all have part of the picture. The theories that have dominated western discourse presented above make reasonable contributions to the ongoing dialogue informing the picture that is still emerging.

Notes

1. See my *Moral Choices*, St. Paul. MN: West Publ. Co., 1989, for text and sources for these religious perspectives.

2. Plato's ethics is found mostly in his *The Republic* as well as his dialogue *Gorgias*.

3. Aristotle's ethics is found in his *Nicomachean Ethics* and his *Politics*.

4. MacIntyre, Alasdair. 1981. *After Virtue*, Notre Dame: Univ. of Notre Dame Press.

5. Thomas Aquinas' ethics is found mostly in his *Summa Theologica* and *Summa contra Gentiles*.

6. Immanuel Kant's ethics is in his *Foundations of the Metaphysics of Morals* and *Critique of Practical Reason.*.

7. Kant, *Foundations*, pp151-2, as excerpted in *Great Traditions in Ethics. 1999*. T. Denise, et al, eds., 9th ed., Wadsworth: Belmont, CA.

8. Ibid., pp. 157-8.

9. Ibid., pp. 160-3.

10. John Stuart Mill's ethics is found in his *Utilitarianism*.

11. Jeremy Bentham's ethics is found in his *An Introduction to the Principles of Morals and Legislation*.

12. R. M. Hare's ethics can be found in his *Moral Thinking* and other writings.

13. Jean-Paul Sartre's ethics can be found in his "Existentialism and Human Emotions," "Existentialism is a Humanism" and *Being and Nothingness*.

14. Nietzsche's ethics an be found in his *The Will to Power, Genealogy of Morals, Beyond Good and Evil* and other works.

15. A. J. Ayer's ethics is found in his *Language, Truth and Logic;* C. L. Stevenson's ethics is found in his *Ethics and Language* and other works.

16. G. E. Moore's ethics is found in his *Principia Ethica*.

17. Kohlberg, Lawrence, *Essays on Moral Development*, San Francisco: Harper and Row, 1981.

18. Gilligan, Carol, *In a Different Voice*, Cambridge: Harvard Univ. Press, 1982.

19. John Rawls' ethics is found in his *A Theory of Justice, Political Liberalism* and many essays.

20. Rawls, *Theory*, pp. 20-5.

21. Ibid., pp. 48-53.

22. William G. Sumner's theory of ethics can be found in his *Folkways;* Ruth Benedict's theory of relativism can be found in her *Patterns of Culture*.

23. This type of argument is made by Ralph Linton in his "Universal Ethical Principles: An Anthropological View" in *Moral Principles of Action*, R. Anshen, ed., New York: Harper & Bro., 1976.

CHAPTER 3

MORALITY AND COMMUNITY

Western ethical theory since the time of Plato has sought a rational foundation for moral norms. The proposed foundations have included Plato's theory of forms and his conception of the soul, Aristotle's understanding of human nature, Aquinas' theologically based natural law theory, Kant's use of a priori reason and Mill's conception of happiness. Most of these theories are based on false pre-suppositions and overlook a central fact of human existence. The first false pre-supposition is that of abstract individualism: to assume that the justification and construction of moral theory must proceed from the perspective of the a-social individual agent. The second presupposition, here termed linguistic Platonism, is committed by some philosophers who construct their theories on the moral concepts present in their culture but ignore the origins of these concepts. What they have overlooked is what is all around them, that humans are fundamentally social creatures whose interdependence permeates every aspect of their being.

As social beings, persons order their collective experience in many ways. This structuring of experience is done through various kinds of customs, institutions, belief systems and moral and non-moral norms. Although conceptions differ, it will be assumed here that moral norms have the following distinctive traits: 1) moral statements are action guiding; they are normative standards for human behavior specifying how persons should behave or act (not a description of past behavior). 2.) moral statements are overriding in nature; they have priority or precedence over other statements and considerations including self-interest (when there is a conflict), and other non-moral customs. 3.) moral statements are usually said to be universalizable. Universalizability will be understood here not in the sense that any given moral statement is universally followed (obviously many are not) but in the sense that moral statements are rules which have the highest degree of generality, i.e., they apply to all or most members (usually excluding young children, the insane) of a society. Moral norms are more general than other norms such as norms that apply only to those who are of a certain sex or perform a certain role in a given society such as a policeman, doctor, etc. (This feature will be further explained below.) 4) moral statements concern the welfare of someone other than just the person performing the action. This distinguishes moral norms from norms of prudence, or rational self-interest where the welfare of others is not involved. This last feature of morals suggests that morality is a social reality, a reality that exists only when other persons (or sentient creatures) are involved.

A complete analysis of the nature of moral norms must include not only a discussion of their formal structure but also explore their content. Cross-cultural anthropological study of the nature of society and social systems reveals aspects of moral norms that shed further light on their nature and significance.[1] A 'society' is here defined as a group of persons living in a, more or less, self-sufficient manner in a geographically defined area and in institutionally defined structures or pattern of activity. Each part of this definition needs clarification. A society is a substantially self-sufficient unit such that certain sub-groups, such as monasteries, or lesser groups are not societies since they are not self-sustaining but depend on the larger social unit for continued existence and recruitment. At the very least a society must be a group that survives the death of individual members by bringing into existence new persons. A society is usually geographically defined in that it exists in one geographic area at a time although it may migrate as nomadic societies do. And finally a society is not just a random collection of persons but a group of persons who are unified in that their behavior is defined and integrated by various kinds of norms in an institutional or ongoing manner. What norms, if any, do societies have in common?

Rules that allow and forbid certain classes of actions exist in all societies. These rules are perpetuated through the training or socialization of infants and the punishing or disapproval of those who violate the norms. It must be noted that though societies have common or core moral values, due to ethnocentrism, the scope of applicability (or universalizability) of these values varies and often, in primitive (i.e., pre-modern or pre-industrial) societies, applies only to members of their own group. Secondly, common moral values or general principles can be expressed in the more specific form of rules that vary more or less from group to group based on their differing levels of socio-economic development, beliefs, whether true or false, or differing circumstances in which they may find themselves. With these caveats clear, the evidence reveals that all societies have the following common core moral content: 1.) prohibition of murder or the killing of in-group members except within parameters specified in the group (e.g. as punishment, self--defense, or other socially accepted rituals); 2.) prohibition of random bodily violence, harm or insults (harm to prestige or self-esteem); 3.) rules requiring some degree of work from the able bodied to meet survival needs; 4.) a prohibition of theft and establishment of some degree of private property which cannot be used without permission (scope of what can be private tends to be quite restricted in hunting and gathering societies, and virtually unlimited in advanced industrial societies); 5.) rules requiring some level of care for others especially infants, the old and infirm; 6.) knowledge, truth telling and promise keeping are generally valued except in specific cases; 7.) the encouragement of some form of marriage where reproduction and nurture of children take place; 8.) some restrictions on sexual intercourse with the rule against incest being most universal. Other similarities could be mentioned but these are sufficient for present purposes.

A rational moral theory must take into account the widest body of available evidence. Like any scientific theory, it must account for the similarities as well as the differences within the realm it is trying to explain. Why are there moral norms at all and why do they have these similarities in form and content? The thesis argued here is that the existence of moral norms and similarities of their content can best be explained as constituting the solution to the problem of human co-existence in a socially enduring manner. Morality is the answer to the problem of maintaining social order among members of a species which both need others and at the same time are not genetically programmed (as, say, bees are) to cooperate. Moral norms channel human impulses and actions into ordered relations with the actions of others. They constitute a structure of instrumental rules or guidelines which define appropriate means for the achievement of human ends in a social environment. In other words, the formal features of moral norms (prescriptivity, overridingness, universalizability, impact on the welfare of others) correspond to necessary social structures wherein a group of individuals with some anti-social tendencies continue to exist as a society with minimal conflict and inefficiency in meeting the needs of its members.

Conflicts that threaten human social coexistence occur for several reasons. Without assuming any inborn instinct for aggression, human nature has certain anti-social potential. The fundamental basis for this is that, in humans, social order is necessary but not genetically specified or guaranteed. More specifically, this potential for anti-social behavior is actualized in part because human beings have limited altruism and empathy. Empathy is strongest among those who have long association and knowledge of each other as in many family units and usually attenuates the further one moves from the circle of familiarity and reciprocity. Anti-social activity is also elicited by the fact of scarcity of desired objects (food, wealth, love, status, etc.) This scarcity is partly a function of the level of availability of science, technology, partly a function of the vicissitudes of life and partly due to the nature of the desired object; status, for example, seems to require (especially in advanced societies with high degree of division of labor) a limit on availability. These conditions when combined with the fact that persons are born dependent and continue so for some years, the vulnerability of all including adults to attack by others and the fact that persons are roughly equal in physical an intellectual abilities point for rules to structure social existence. Finally, human rationality itself can be a source of conflict as illustrated in the free-rider problem.

There is an obvious advantage in enjoying the benefits of one's society without contributing one's share of labor or wealth. The aspects of the human condition mentioned above may produce conflict when individuals pursue their self-interest, i.e., the satisfaction of their needs to ensure their welfare, outside the social parameters which constitute morality. These parameters create the stability of expectations that reduce conflict and insecurity. This stability or equilibrium promotes a more efficient satisfaction of needs since the additional time and energy that would be necessary to protect one's goods, significant others and oneself in the absence or erosion of social control provided by the general compliance with moral norms can be used to satisfy needs or pursue other activities. Hence, the structuring effect of moral limits in addition to promoting survival in the extreme case by preventing chaos, also promotes greater general efficiency. Moral norms then, are the solution to persons seeking the satisfaction of their needs in a social context without producing the Hobbesian state of war of all against all; a situation, presumably, where the likelihood of satisfying one's needs are even more improbable. Moral norms constitute the 'glue' that counteracts the centrifugal forces of unlimited self-interest.

This general analysis of the nature and necessity of morality as socially based can explain the universal formal characteristics of moral norms. First, the development of rules per se has obvious efficiencies when compared with the alternative of thousands of separate commands for innumerable situations. Norms then can be seen as components of social memory and the distillation of thousands of years of cultural evolution and trial and error learning and discernment of the similarities of various problems and situations and the formulation of a general statement to cover potentially infinite number of variations. Secondly, it is clear that norms usually concern only realms of behavior where conscious control and selection are possible (reflexes are usually not morally evaluated). Again, because human behavior is not totally determined genetically and because humans have an awareness of the future and different possible courses of action, rules are necessary for choosing one of many alternatives if human behavior is to be somewhat predictable. The solution is provided by moral imperatives as rules or standards for behavior that serve as action guides.

As mentioned above, ethical norms are overriding in nature. They must be overriding or have priority for they are necessary for the continued existence of society per se and correspond to the most basic human needs (e.g. survival, security and freedom from pain and fear). The overridingness requirement is an instance of a society establishing a hierarchy among its various norms to reduce interpersonal conflict that a mere random collection of moral and non-moral norms would produce. Admittedly, these priorities are not always explicit or articulated, especially in less complex and more homogeneous cultures, but undoubtedly distinctions are made about the relative importance of traditional customs and norms.

Although all societies have various kinds of norms corresponding to different roles or social functions, the moral norms are the most general (apply across time, roles, sex, age, etc.) and as such play a unifying or integrating function. Thus, universalizability, as understood here, is necessary when interpreted as requiring that behavior be rule governed and comply with the existing moral norms. Clearly, general compliance within the group is necessary if the survival of the group is to be more probable. Universalizability can be understood as the requirementthat individual actions conform to structures and thus maintain social order.

Moral norms concern the welfare of others. This distinguishes them from norms of prudence, or technical skill because they are essentially social norms. They are norms that impact on the welfare of others and thus on the social bonds that unite individuals. Some have argued that no man is an island and that all actions and non-actions affect the well-being of others. This may be true but the effect is not of the same significance in all cases; the rule against murder is far more important for social coexistence than the rule requiring, say, personal hygiene.

Moral norms, then, as this analysis of its formal structure reveals, are social inventions which channel human impulses, needs and desires into ordered relations with the desires of others. This limits the area of the unknown and unpredictable, reducing the frustration of expectations and minimizing conflict. This analysis of the formal traits of moral norms is supported by an examination of the universal core moral content.

Persons have needs in order to maintain normal species-typical functioning. Needs are deficiencies that cannot be satisfied without interacting with others and the environment. Biological needs (e.g. food, water, sleep, etc.) are necessary for continued normal biological functioning and survival; psychological needs (companionship, intimacy, meaning, etc.) are necessary to reduce anxiety, fear, boredom, unhappiness, etc. Needs are usually consciously experienced as wants and desires. Of course, not all wants are needs in the sense that there can be false wants or wants that are objectively not in one's long term interest. Although needs are conditioned to some degree by one's culture, survival remains the most basic need. Survival is contingent upon restricting violence among group members hence the prohibition of murder and random violence (without what is socially and to a degree, variably defined as justification.) Since human infants are born in absolute dependence incapable of providing for themselves, there must be norms requiring the care and nurture of children. Hence the presence of some form of the family. Furthermore, given the vicissitudes of life, (especially in primitive and barter societies where amassing of wealth is very limited) the norm requiring aid and assistance at least to the closest relations or in-group members is also a rationally based norm. Similarly, there must be some incentives for work, the care and management of assets and the provision of food hence the corresponding rules protecting some level of private property. Sexual mating must be at least allowed for some members if the group is to replace deceased members with new persons. Since human beings are by nature sexual beings all societies consider some varieties of sexual expression good or (for more ascetic societies) at least acceptable and value offspring.

The continued existence of a society is in part decided whether the society can adopt to its environment and solve problems. Adaptation and problem solving require reliable information, decision making and cooperation to implement decisions. Truth telling is obviously a pre-condition for this. Or, put more practically, starting with the hunting and gathering stage it has become apparent that food can be acquired more efficiently if persons cooperate to meet their nutritional needs. Cooperation requires communication which in turn requires a rule favoring truth-telling in at least most collective endeavors; random lying would eliminate trust and produce social chaos.

Rules regulating sexual relations especially the general prohibition against incest (definitions vary and exceptions usually exist in some primitive societies only for royal or priestly groups) is virtually universal. Its basis rests in part on the need to integrate the society more fully by developing marital ties with other family units. In addition, prohibition of incest is advantageous for individual and family security in that having extended relations can be helpful in times of need. Although probably not apparent to pre-scientific cultures, modern science has shown the genetic benefits of exogamy. Finally, the prohibition exists to minimize possible disruptive consequences of sexual relations between parents and children. Although rules specifying pre and extra-marital relations differ more than many other norms, restrictions are always present partly to minimize disruptive emotions and partly to make ascriptions of fatherhood, and thus responsibilities for care, more reliable. This analysis of morality as the necessary solution to human collective existence can help resolve some of the classic moral disputes.

One major dispute is the conflict between deontology and teleology. Although conceptions differ, let us define deontology as the view that certain actions are wrong in themselves or by their very nature or structure of intent without regard to consequences. Kant, for example, held that lying is always wrong even when doing so might save an innocent person. Let us define teleology as the view that the morality of actions is defined by their consequences such as producing happiness, social order, pleasure or personal development. A teleologist, then, granting that lying is usually wrong, might still allow the telling of an untruth to save an innocent life. It should be clear from the above discussion that the approach taken here is broadly teleological in that morality is justified as necessary for the satisfaction of human needs without destroying the conditions for social co-existence. However, the requirements of socialization introduce deontological elements in the following manner. Socialization, the inculcation of moral norms in children, necessitates that the complex teleological nature of morality be reduced to simple easily imparted rules. These rules have a deontological form, e.g. "Don't lie," because to introduce exceptions or the consideration of consequences would complicate the enculturation process to such a degree as to weaken the sense of duty needed to ensure greater compliance in later life in general. Since almost all of us are taught moral precepts when young by our parents of whom we are in awe, the resulting moral prescriptions have a sacredness which gives them added deontological or inviolable intuitive sense. Hence the macro structure of the moral system is teleologically based but specific micro rules have a deontological weight because in fact, situations where exceptions are justified are usually rare and because without this added inviolability of norms, persons would be even more tempted to violate moral norms for self-interested reasons. Hence, the moral limits of persons and the demands of effective socialization and a stable social structure explain the deontological nature of specific moral rules within a teleological moral system that is constructed to meet the needs of persons in a social environment.

If the strength of a theory is evidenced by its ability to deal with anomalies or puzzles of another theory, then a discussion of the often cited weaknesses of Kant's deontological theory will be instructive.[2] In his attempt to articulate and justify an absolute universal moral theory he naturally had to resort to a purely a priori formulation. Such an abstract theory may be elegant but at the cost of being underdetermined in letting too much moral content slip through its net making it difficult to apply. The most often mentioned problems of Kant's theory are: 1.) that the categorical imperative (i.e "I should never act in such a way that I could not also will that my maxim should be a universal law." among other versions) is necessary but not, as Kant claims, sufficient for specifying the moral realm; 2.) given rules for applying the imperative are vague; 3.) rules for the resolution of conflict of duties are not provided or result in inconsistent and paradoxical outcomes. The universalizability criterion of the categorical imperative, in one version, is in fact nothing but the empty formal requirement that actions conform to a rule that could be consistently universalized. Hence, lying could not become a universal rule for the goal of lying being deception, if lying were to become universal no one would any longer be deceived by it since everyone would expect it. However, one could also universalize "Put on your right shoe before the left shoe" but this is clearly not a moral duty; hence universalizability is not sufficient to specify moral duty. In Kant's example of the rich man considering whether to help the poor man, the universalizability criterion becomes the question of whether we would want a rule such as "Ignore the needs of the poor" to be universal if we were to find ourselves poor in the future. Here the meaning is not just some kind of logical or structural consistency but of possible future compatibility with our needs. Hence, it is clear that not even Kant could avoid reference to human needs as he tried to do in his purely a priori theory that was to eschew any reference to human nature and happiness. To be sure, social order requires the presence of rules as its structure but the content is determined by human needs.

It will be recalled that to apply the categorical imperative one must first formulate one's maxim. The maxim is defined as the "subjective principle of volition,"[3] or the rule which captures one's intent in some moral situation. Kant's example of the person who wants to borrow money by falsely promising to pay it back is intended to explain his point. Here Kant says the maxim is "When I believe myself to be in need of money, I will borrow money and promise to repay it although I know I shall never do so."[4] He rightly points out that if this became a universal practice lying would be pointless since no one would believe anyone and hence the act the person is contemplating would be impossible thus violating the categorical imperative and is thus immoral. But, it is clear that if one formulates the maxim in a more narrow manner, such as "Lie when you need money for a worthwhile cause (medical aid for your mother) and other means have been exhausted" it could become consistently universal. Hence, Kant's notion of "maxim" is underdetermined.

From the perspective of the model defended here, the lesson is that it is impossible to organize a society with just one moral norm. No single norm can capture the complexity and myriad possibilities of circumstances persons find themselves especially when one realizes the limited rationality of persons, their tendency to selfish acts and the limited amount of time usually available to calculate and decide what is moral. Even if one interprets the categorical imperative as a criterion of the moral and not as constituting the meaning of morality, one still finds that Kant's theory is parasitic on an existing moral system which itself then must be justified in some way.

This same point is telling with respect to the conflict of duties problem. Kant at one point asks the question whether one should lie to save an innocent person; he answers that we should not lie. First, it seems to most interpreters that this is inconsistent with another formulation of the categorical imperative which reads: "Act so that you treat humanity, whether in your person or in that of another, always as an end and never as a means only."[5] Here the absolute value of persons is paramount which presumably places a higher value on the life of the innocent than telling the truth to a would be murderer. Secondly, it again shows the futility of constructing a moral system that ignores human nature and human needs for the purposes of developing a 'pure' a priori theory that, if it is a priori, must be far removed from the situations moral rules address. It should be no surprise that Kant had to import his Christian theological doctrines including the belief in a God and an after life where moral goodness is rewarded with happiness which he claimed could not be accomplished on earth. Again, theological assumptions serve as a deus ex machina to resolve problems that could have been avoided from the start if Kant did not make the arbitrary assumptions that morality must be a priori.

A similar analysis of utilitarianism can clarify the position argued here. The strengths of utilitarianism, from the present perspective, are that it makes morality more empirical and objective by accepting happiness or need satisfaction as foundational to moral systems. Its central weakness is that it approaches theory building from the abstract individual perspective virtually ignoring the social context. Specifically, the most often mentioned criticism of Mill's theory are: 1.) Mill's proposed "proof" of his theory fails; 2.) the problem of quantification and interpersonal comparison; 3.) the problem of choosing between act or rule utilitarianism; and 4.) the problem of justice.

Mill tries to prove that happiness is the only thing desirable in itself in a way that almost all agree is futile.[6] The more useful approach would be to imagine whether a society could exist for any length of time which consistently and systematically frustrated its members desire for happiness or the satisfaction of their needs. Clearly such a community would quickly cease to exist and short of that, certainly become unstable and disintegrate eventually depending to what degree natural human impulses and desires were denied.

In trying to achieve what he believed to be certainty and objectivity, Mill formulated a highly abstract theory. The advantages of such abstraction, such as elegance and simplicity, are vitiated by the difficulties implied in its actual implementation. The debate over interpersonal comparisons and quantification of utilities arises because of this abstraction and ignoring the origin of specific norms. Exact quantification or measurement is not required by moral systems because it is impossible and because, as argued herein, moral systems exist to regulate and structure human interaction so as to allow need satisfaction without producing excessive conflict that would undermine the conditions for social co-existence. Mill's distinction between higher and lower pleasures, (something Bentham's version of utilitarianism would not allow), is his attempt to add to his theory what he terms quality of pleasure and not just quantity as relevant (though probably inconsistent with his initial formulation of his theory) may be seen as an implicit concession that quantification and the abstract nature of the theory are problems because they ignored the variety of needs persons have and the impossibility of reducing them to pleasure and pain. This is another indication, as others have noted, that Mill's theory and utilitarianism generally is hopelessly abstract and a-social in formulation. Mill's eventual appeal to past social experience as a guide in deciding what norms do, in fact, maximize utility is further indication of this.

Another problem that has attended utilitarianism, is the debate between act and rule utilitarians. Simply put, act utilitarians claim that each act must be individually evaluated in terms of utility whereas rule utilitarians hold that acts must conform to rules which in turn maximize utility. Again, this controversy arose because of the abstract nature of a theory that is oblivious of the social structures that must exist if collective happiness is to be pursued. Morality understood as a social reality precludes act utilitarianism for the presence of only one rule (the principle of utility) would make social interaction unpredictable since determining what the principle of utility alone demands in any situation would lead to variable and unforeseeable results, not to mention the actual difficulty and time-consuming nature of the calculations required. Again, opportunities for bias, immoral and inaccurate decisions increases when the moral norm is so abstract as to require separate individual determinations for every moral situation.

The problem of justice is another indication of the problematic nature of Mill's abstract theory. Matters of justice concern the proper distribution of burdens and benefits in a community. Mill's utilitarianism is based on one principle, the principle of utility, which requires the maximization of happiness. The issue, simply put, is, does Mill's theory allow the increase of happiness for a society as a whole by, say, enslaving some part of that same society? Mill believed that it would not for the long term consequences of such action would be contrary to utility. Although Mill may be right, the existence of the question points to the difficulties of a normative system that has only one abstract principle which must then rely on probabilistic deductions from that principle to determine the basic normative structure of society. From the perspective of the thesis argued here, a society whose normative superstructure is incompatible with the facts of human nature and the circumstances of social interaction, is to that degree irrational and thus unstable. A society that punishes those who provide for the needs of the community and rewards those who frustrate need satisfaction and undermine the structure of norms, is an irrational and unstable society. For example, a society that enslaves or treats a group within its borders on the basis of false premises, such as the historical rationale for slavery by claiming their biological inferiority, will lack structural integrity and thus likely eventually experience internal conflict.

This analysis of the social basis of morality can also shed some light on the 'is-ought' problem. How is it possible to derive moral statements from descriptive or non-moral statements? This problem, although usually said to have been first formulated by Hume, it is a matter of dispute what Hume exactly meant.[7] The traditional interpretation is that Hume claims that ought statements cannot be entailed by any factual or 'is' statement. And since, for Hume, arguments are either deductive or defective, the logical gap between statements of fact and statements of morality is unbridgeable. Others claim that Hume, as an emotivist, identified 'ought' statement with certain 'is' statements, namely, the emotions of the speaker. Still others claim Hume makes an inference from 'ought' to 'is' on the basis of utilitarianism, although this inference is not deductive but inductive. Regardless of how this particular dispute is settled, it seems clear that the transition from 'is' to 'ought' cannot be done logically, but it can and has been done historically.

As suggested above, the facts are that the biologically and psychologically based human needs require the presence of others (society). But since human beings are not biologically programmed to cooperate it requires the development of the 'ought' of moral norms. The 'ought' arises from the 'is' of human nature in the context of social interaction. That is, the satisfaction of needs (is) must be structured by rules (ought) if society is to continue. To discuss the is/ought problem as a logical issue ignores the fact that human existence is not a logical proposition but a matter of existential fact. The moral 'ought' is in this sense analogous to its usage in non-moral practical contexts. For instance, if one wants to travel from New York to Paris in the least amount of time, then one ought or should fly (assuming the person is not afraid of flying, etc.) Here again, the 'ought' arises from the facts of the situation (distance, time) and the wants persons have. Of course, this analogy is limited but not nullified because of the asymmetry of prudential ought (fly) and moral ought. The asymmetry is simply that of the macro level (morality) and the micro level (prudence). The argument defended here, put another way, is that morality is in fact social prudence, i.e., the expression of rational self-interest of the group. Much of the is/ought debate seems to totally ignore the social existence of human beings.

Some of the same problems found in the is/ought debate are repeated in the naturalistic fallacy debate. G. E. Moore and others have claimed that any attempt to define 'good' as some natural property such as pleasure will fail because of the "open question" argument.[8] The argument holds that given any definition of 'good' it can be meaningfully asked "but is X good?" thus allegedly refuting the claim that X is the definition of good. This view has been criticized as mistaking how moral language functions (not descriptive but prescriptive), that it is ethnocentric, that the meaning of good is complex, vague, that it makes morality mysterious and does not explain the action guiding nature of moral imperatives.

We cannot enter here into a complete analysis of this problem, but a few observations are in order. Within the framework presented here and in partial agreement with Moore, it is clear that 'good' is not a completely natural property as say yellow is; something is yellow regardless of any person having a need or a desire (though not of other subjective states, i.e., adequate eyesight, etc.). Something, such as food is good because persons need it; its goodness is a product of the properties of the food (nutrition) and the fact that it is desired. The way one acquires the food (e.g. stolen, found, etc) and consumes the food (time, place, etc.) is morally right or wrong depending on whether it conforms to the social norms of that society. What is good is thus determined by human needs and desires (content) and the social context of norms and beliefs through which human needs are channeled and conditioned (form). A pork chop may be cooked, warm and juicy but it would not be considered good for an orthodox Jew or Moslem. Hence, the meaning of 'good' is not exhausted by natural properties but requires the imprimatur, as it were, of the cultural network. Hence, no definition of 'good' can be given without reference to the social context. Moore, then is partly right that 'good' is nonnatural but only in that it is, in part, social; it is partly defined in relation to a social system.

It should also be obvious form the above discussion that determining the truth of moral statements is not categorically different from determining the truth of other kinds of statements. To be sure, if the above analysis is correct and the meaning of 'good' cannot be exhausted by listing the natural properties alone, then their truth cannot be ascertained as easily as ordinary empirical or scientific proposition. The social nexus within which moral judgments are made and partly constituted can also be rationally evaluated but it is a more complex task. A statement may be rationally held even though it is not 'true' in the sense that it corresponds to actual physical states of affairs. Since moral properties cannot be fully explicated in natural properties, their truth cannot be determined in this correspondence manner alone. However, a statement may be warranted and rationally held if well informed rational persons would assent to it as necessary for the organization of collective human activity and for the accomplishment of goals. That is, in the moral realm which specifies goals and how they are to be achieved, the pragmatic meaning of truth is operative. Moral statements and systems are true if they enable the satisfaction of human needs in a social framework; they are true if they are the best means for the given ends.

This, again, is not radically different from the situation in empirical science and scientific method. Putting it rather simplistically, statements or hypotheses within science are accepted as true (or warranted) if they correspond (or increasingly approximate) to the actual structures of the physical world. But the rules and procedures of scientific method which generate hypotheses are justified in that they have been successful means to acquiring true statements and theories, not because they are a picture of the physical world. Similarly, a moral system is true or warranted if it allows for persons to meet their needs in that society in the most efficient way possible. Efficiency is here understood as achieving one's goals with the minimum of energy, time and resources. The social structure can be understood as a complex means to certain ends. These ends can be many but as already stated, usually include social survival, and all that this entails (norms limiting self-interest, truth-telling, etc.) as well as more problematic goals such ends as the greater glory of God, the dictatorship of the proletariat, actualization of the ubermensch, etc. These ends would necessitate different social norms and social structures.

One would begin to rationally assess such goals and the societal system they are a part as one would rationally assess any empirical or philosophical claim. Considerations would include: clarity of the meaning of concepts (definition), specifying evidence, reasons or facts (justification), does it explain what is required or have sufficient scope (completeness) logical analysis of the relations between claims (consistency), does it have excess claims (simplicity), comparison with other opposing views and well-established theories, (coherence), possibility and problems with institutionalization (implementation), does it actualize its stated goal or goals most effectively (efficiency) etc. Even if the ends can be agreed upon, sometimes it is difficult to determine what means are the most efficient. This difficulty is compounded when a society disagrees about the ultimate goals and the source and nature of these norms (e.g. fundamentalist Christians vs secular humanists). In addition, moral systems are usually underdetermined by the facts. The 'facts' are the past experiences of the group involved (and their interpretations of this experience) from which a norm emerges to be used in the future. Clearly, then moral norms are underdetermined because past experience is limited (if only because it is in the past) or misinterpreted and because future facts or the interpretation of these facts may not fit the norm. Finally, certain norms may be simply irrelevant as new social conditions arise. That is, moral norms are part of a groups adaptation to a particular environment and require change when the environment changes or one's understanding of the same changes.

It should be clear from the preceding that the justification of morality must be in terms of its societal function not in terms of the abstract individual outside the social context. One can look at justification from the point of view of an outsider or as a participant. An outsider looking at a society an its norms would use the criteria mentioned above (definition, consistency, etc) to evaluate a social moral system. When one looks at justification from the point of view of the individual in the system the question becomes 'Why should I be moral?'. This is clearly not a mistaken question from the position defended here is that moral systems arise as a kind of compromise between self interest and the interests of others and thus require limits on self-interest. (Of course, being moral isn't always incompatible with self-interest otherwise no one would be moral or live in society.) The rationality of the so-called 'free rider' reoccurs. Hence, if one seeks to justify morality to a would be player of the moral game, one cannot do so fully on the basis of self-interest or abstract rationality or the logic of the moral game alone because the logic of the moral system by its very nature incorporates limits on self-interest. If the free rider can be successful then it would be more rational to be such a rider.

This problem has its roots as far back as Plato's discussion of the "Ring of Gyges" in *The Republic*. The question for Plato, briefly put, is why would anyone be moral if they had a ring as Gyges did which could make them invisible thus allowing the performance of any immoral act and escaping punishment for it. Plato's answer, in short, was that an amoral person would lack inner harmony of the soul and thus be ruined even without social sanction. This answer relies on a theory of the 'soul' or human psychology that is pre-scientific and problematic. Religious answers often rely on an omnipotent and omniscient deity who will punish the evildoer in this life or the next. The problem here, of course, is to establish such a being exists and to determine what the deity in fact demands. Of course, it is important to remember that most people are not capable of being successful free riders either because they have been socialized sufficiently to feel guilt when they violate a norm, or because they are not sufficiently intelligent or lack an adequate memory to consistently avoid detection and punishment, or in short, because there is no ring of Gyges.[9] Hence, a rational morality is usually in one's long term interest because, in fact, there are no viable alternatives for most, if not all persons.

Some philosophers have attempted to prove that the self-interested egoist or free rider is somehow irrational by appeal to the idea of universalizability.[10] Rationality has at least two different meanings: 1.) as taking the most efficient means to achieving our goals; or 2.) acting and believing in a logically consistent manner. If we take the first meaning, then the amoral free rider is rational if he or she can realize his or her goals in an amoral manner without detection, i.e., ignoring morality when it suits them. From the theory argued here, morality requires to limit our self-interest at times and thus, if the amoral person can avoid this limit without detection then it would be rational for him to do so. As a matter of fact, of course, if the society the amoral agent is in has done an adequate job in socialization, the would-be amoral agent would feel guilt. Secondly, as suggested, most persons are of limited rationality such that detection is usually not avoidable forever thus some form of punishment would ensue.

Rationality as consistency employs the idea of universalizability ; if the free rider is inconsistent, then morality as a rational system is preserved. The argument goes something like this: Universalizability as consistency requires that if some act Z is right for me to perform under conditions C then it is right for all to do Z under conditions C. If I act a-morally whenever it is in my interest to do so, then it is right for a to act a-morally when it is in their self-interest. But this will lead to a Hobbesian state of nature which, presumably, no one wants. Therefore the free-rider is acting irrationally. The problem with this approach is that just because others have a right or ought to act in a way doesn't mean they will.[11] Or, put in another way, ought implies can. But, because of socialization, or insufficient rationality or the fear of God, or natural timidity, or lack of opportunity most persons cannot and do not act a-morally most of the time. (Remember, the free rider is an option only in a society that has rides, i.e., has structures that are generally obeyed.) Hence, the free-rider knows that most others will in fact not act in the same a-moral way and hence there is no inconsistency (i.e., no Hobbesian state of war) in acting a-morally.

The answer to the free rider problem from the theoretical perspective defended here focuses on the societal context and nature of moral norms. It is clear that for a society to exist and thrive, the free rider problem must be addressed for their actions weaken the social structures that are necessary for social existence. Morality, then, is partly in our interest in that we need others and thus we need society to continue in existence and partly not in our self-interest because it requires at times, a limit on our self-interest in that the interests of others or society must also be acknowledged. The answer to this dilemma consistent with the perspective taken is three-fold: socialization, education and enforcement.

Socialization, as noted above, is the process whereby a new member of a community learns the beliefs, customs and values of that community. The first agent of socialization is the family; here, informed and dedicated parents are central to the development of a conscience or the internal sense of right and wrong. Parents that are emotionally cold, ignorant of proper child rearing practices or themselves amoral would result in a weak or non-existent conscience in the child.[12] In extreme cases, this could result in the formation of a sociopath, someone who lacks a conscience or any empathy for others.

The socialization process continues throughout life. A society must ensure that socializing forces such as schools and the media are consistent and do not undermine the basic values of social co-existence. Moral training should continue throughout the educational process, difficult though this may be in a pluralistic society. The parental influence tends to be more emotional than rational; the educational institutions should reveal the rational basis of values. Here Aristotle's theory of moral development is helpful.[13] He argued, in brief, that moral behavior requires adequate training in order to develop habits called virtues. He realized that moral action requires the formation of character traits not just knowledge of moral principles. Aristotle's theory implies that every immoral action tends to weaken moral virtue thus making it increasingly difficult for the free rider to control amoral tendencies consequently making detection more likely.

However, there are clear limits to socialization and education. Human beings are morally limited and rational enough to see the possibility and desirability of pursuing their self-interest while violating social norms. This calls for the enforcement of moral norms through such modern institutions as the police and the courts. It also calls for the constant rational evaluation of moral norms to ensure that human action is not limited by arbitrary and irrational norms. This leads to the following: If a society could ensure total commitment of all to its moral norms, the rational evaluation of norms that is necessary if a society is to adapt to new circumstances and information would be impossible and thus detrimental to the survival of the society itself. That is, socialization so thorough and compelling that no norm could be questioned or abandoned would 'freeze' a society into a specific time and normative system which would be contrary to its continued social existence when new conditions called for some norms to be revised or abandoned altogether. Hence, it seems we arrive at the somewhat paradoxical but necessary conclusion namely, that though the free-rider problem must be controlled, its total elimination would in fact be detrimental to the long term survival of the community.

If the above considerations are persuasive, then the justification of moral system must be approached not from the point of view of the individual but from the point of view of society. A society that socializes its members to adhere to its rationally based norms will have a higher probability of survival and the society that does not, will not. If the socialization is adequate serious challenges will not occur and general compliance will obtain. In any case, socialization is rarely so fully successful to be sufficient to ensure compliance; other institutions, such as the courts, prisons, and other forms of punishment, must exist in all complex modern societies to complete what is left undone by socialization.

The analysis presented here can also illuminate the issue of relativism. A moral relativist is here defined as someone who holds that 'good' has meaning only within a given cultural framework and that there is no rational way to justify one moral code as superior to another. The position defended here is a modified relativism in the following sense. There are uniformities and differences in moral systems which can be explained as follows: Similarities in core values are a function of the universality of certain human needs and tendencies and the common problems and circumstances humans must confront to meet their needs. The differences arise due to the fact that moral systems emerge in different social and historical context which gives them their particular character since moral codes are in part man's attempt to adapt to an environment in order to meet his needs. However, this adaptation may be more or less adequate since human beings are not perfectly rational and thus not beyond rational evaluation and criticism. That is, a normative system may be contaminated with all kinds of vague, unwarranted, false or irrelevant beliefs which can be rationally questioned.

Religious belief systems, themselves developed in part to facilitate human adaptation, often play a major role in determining the content of the more traditional moral codes. For example, a particular Eskimo tribe may have a moral imperative to abandon their aged parents so that they die. This may seem like murder to us but given their belief about the need to enter the afterlife in more or less good mental and physical condition, precludes these Eskimos from simply allowing their parents to die of physical illness and old age. If their belief about the after life can be shown to be false, (difficult though this may be given that religious belief systems are a relatively closed system of ideas resistant to change), then their practice must be abandoned. Secondly, changing social and economic conditions necessitate the emergence of new norms. For example lending money at an interest was once considered usury and immoral. But lending money has a different meaning when it is done in a pre-industrial society where loans are usually for personal need, and when it occurs in industrial capitalist society which is based on the accumulation of large sums of capital to finance large projects requires the lending of money. Thirdly, growth in scientific knowledge and technological developments can also modify norms. Slavery for instance, and ethnocentrism or tribalism in general, were, in part based on the belief, that members of other races, or groups are radically different and inferior biologically and therefore not covered by the same moral norms as one's own kind. Most agree that modern scientific evidence refutes this belief. Another example would be marriage customs; if there is wide disparity of males to females such that one on one pairing is not possible, (perhaps because of the shortage of males due to extreme and widespread war activity or the shortage of females due to female infanticide) polygyny or polyandry may be necessary (or many divorces and re-marriages.)

However, certain value similarities already mentioned would tend to be universal since they reflect what are the more enduring elements of human nature and thus essential for group cooperation and survival. The scope of this common core is even more remarkable when one considers that widely divergent religious belief systems, from Hinduism, Buddhism, Islam, Judaism, Christianity, and others, which have such radically incompatible ontologies, theologies and rituals share these common values (life, health, knowledge, truth, friendship,). (Again, differences do exist, but they concern non-basic specifications and adaptations of core values.) Additionally, Western and Eastern philosophers, with the probable exception of Nietzsche, as different in time, place and historical context such as Confucius, Buddha, Plato, Aquinas, Mill and Kant also share the core normative values even though they justify and systematize them in radically different ways.

This concession to a modified relativism might be objected to as undermining morality itself. The present analysis seems to remove the awesome nature of duty by de-sacralizing and naturalizing morality to the extent that might weaken its effectiveness. Morality will not be undermined if it is rational morality (given the criteria defined above) i.e., one which enables its members to meet their needs, and one which is adequately internalized through socialization. To be sure, if a society encounters severe difficulties it cannot cope as in the case of acute scarcity of goods or an overwhelming enemy, with and thus begins to decay, then the moral game is off and one does one's best in Hobbesian state of nature.[12] Relativism no more destroys a moral system than the realization that language evolves and words change their meaning undermines communication among contemporaries in a society.

The problem of what is here termed linguistic Platonism is common in moral philosophy that concerns itself only with the analysis of moral concepts. Metaethics is certainly important that moral theory must clear definition of concepts and analyze the logic of normative propositions and systems, but this is merely the beginning of moral philosophy. To analyze concepts is an attempt to organize a complex epiphenomena, morality, and ignore its origin, society, and consequently achieves at best an empty certainty. This would be similar to trying to reconstruct a text by working backwards from the footnotes alone. As Wittgenstein, and others have shown, a living language is a complex reality incorporating thousands of years of remnants of vast and diffuse historical social conditions, a blend of heterogeneous cultures and beliefs. It is no surprise that metaethics is torn between cognitivists, noncognitivists, deontologists, teleologists, emotivists, prescriptivist, descriptivist, intuitionists, etc. The more removed any theoretical endeavor is from the vast domain of the empirical and social nature of persons, the more diverse, bewildering and inconsistent will be the results.

NOTES

A version of this essay originally appeared in *The Journal of Social Philosophy,* v26, N2, Fall 1995.

1. Linton, Ralph, "Universal Ethical Principles: An Anthropological View" in *Moral Principles of Action,* ed. by R.N. Anshen, V6, New York: Harper & Row, 1952, pp. 645-659.

2. Kant, Immanuel, *Foundations of the Metaphysics of Morals,* L. W. Beck, trans., Bobbs-Merrill Co.,1959.

3. Ibid., p. 17.

4. Ibid., p. 40

5. Ibid., p. 47.

6. Mill, J.S., *Utilitarianism* in *Moral Choices,* ed. by J. Grcic, West Publ. Co., 1989, p. 106.

7. Hume, David, *Treatise of Human Nature,* pp. 469-70, ed. by Selby-Bigge, Oxford, 1973.

8. Moore, G.E., *Principia Ethica,* pp.7-10.

9. Plato, *The Republic,* 2.359d.

10. For example, Kurt Baier, Alan Gewirth, et al.

11. This analysis borrows from James Sterba's *How To Make People Just,* Rowman & Littlefield, 1988, pp. 155-163.

12. Cf. Grcic, Joseph, "The Right to Have Children" in *Perspectives On the Family,* ed. by R. Moffat, J. Grcic & M. Bayles, pp. 219-232, E. Mellen Press, 1990.

13. Aristotle, *Nicomachean Ethics,* Bks. 1-2.

14. Turnbull, Colin, *The Mountain People,* New York: Simon & Schuster, 1972, p. 261.

CHAPTER 4

TRUTH IN ETHICS

Truth seems to be the first requirement for a rational belief system. Without truth, there is no knowledge and without knowledge actions seem to have no sound foundation. For the noncognitivists, this is the situation in ethics. Ethical statements do not seem to be factual statements about the way the world is but about the way it ought to be. When we say "One ought not to lie" it seems obvious that there is nothing in the physical world that corresponds to "wrong" or "ought." There seem to be no moral facts in the real world as there are physical facts. As John Mackie has argued, moral properties, if there are any, seem to be very queer sorts of things.[1] For philosophers who espouse emotivism, ethical statements are merely expressions of emotion or a subjective commitment for which there is no factual basis.

Much of the recent debate about truth in ethics has overlooked three important realities. First, philosophic debate has tended to be a priori in nature neglecting social research on the nature of moral systems. Cross-cultural empirical studies can provide useful insights and suggestions for ethical theory formation.[2]

Secondly, ethical discourse has ignored how moral systems are perpetuated. Moral norms are passed on through the process of socialization usually by parents in a societal context. It will be argued that this relationship of parent and child in a social framework fundamentally structures the nature of moral systems.

Thirdly, the debate about truth in ethics has been inconclusive because the concept of truth has not been sufficiently analyzed. Although there are several theories of truth and many versions of each theory, there are three main theories of truth, the correspondence, coherence and pragmatic theory.[3] Most debates on truth in ethics have assumed the correspondence or coherence conceptions of truth and, for the most part, ignored the pragmatic view of truth. Let us briefly consider each theory of truth as it relates to ethics.

The correspondence theory holds that truth is a relation between statements and reality. It defines a belief as true if it corresponds, pictures, describes or reflects the way reality is. To be sure, many questions arise in explicating this definition of truth, but it seems to capture what 'truth' normally means.[4] Something like the correspondence theory of truth in ethics may have been held by Plato and John S. Mill. Plato claimed that moral principles refer to Forms that exist independently of the physical world. It is generally agreed, however, that he could not prove these Forms really exist, how they exist or how they relate to the material world.

Mill attempted to prove the principle of utility as true by arguing that happiness is in fact desired by people.[5] Although it is not clear that Mill really attempted this as a proof inasmuch that he did state that first principles could not be proven, still many have pointed out that it does fail as a proof. Mill, it seems, attempted to derive an 'ought', the utility principle, from what he took to be the 'is' of the human desire for happiness. Although the correspondence view of truth has been subject to much analysis and criticism, it seems fairly clear that this view of truth is not helpful in ethics. Ethical statements in their most general form deal not with the 'is' of fact but the 'ought' or how reality and human behavior should be.

The coherence theory of truth holds that truth is not a relation between statements and reality but other statements. The coherence theory states that a statement is true if it is consistent with a system of other statements known to be true. Another version held by Brand Blanshard holds that a statement is true if it is logically implied by other true statements.[6] Although of course, criticisms and debates continue about this version of truth, it seems that this version of truth is most applicable in the realm of abstract ideas such as mathematics.

Kant may have defended a version of truth as consistency in ethics. The categorical imperative's statement of the universalizability criterion is a kind of consistency requirement.[7] Most critics of Kant as far back as Hegel agree that the categorical imperative is a necessary but not sufficient condition for moral duty.

John Rawls' theory of "reflective equilibrium" may be a type of consistency approach to truth in ethics .[8] Rawls rejects the foundational approach to ethics which argues that ethics is a system of beliefs based on some true basic principles. He prefers what he calls the Socratic version which is coherentist in approach. The equilibrium is a form of consistency between what Rawls calls "considered judgments" and "principles." Considered judgments are judgments made when "our moral capacities are most likely to be displayed without distortion."[9] after due consideration, with sufficient knowledge and impartiality. Reflective equilibrium exists "after a person has weighed various proposed conceptions and he has either revised his judgments to accord with one of them or held fast to the initial convictions (and the corresponding conception)."[10]

However, what Rawls calls "wide reflective equilibrium" (as opposed to narrow reflective equilibrium described above) goes beyond mere consistency. In this form of reflective equilibrium Rawls requires that "all possible descriptions to which one might plausibly conform one's judgments together with all relevant philosophical arguments for them."[11] However, Rawls considers the possibility of accomplishing this wide reflective equilibrium "questionable." In any case, though consistency is a characteristic of true belief systems, consistency alone would not be enough in ethics since there are many different but self-consistent ethical systems.

Different versions of the pragmatic theory of truth have been defended by William James, John Dewey, C.S. Peirce, Quine, Rorty and others. Peirce, Dewey and perhaps Rorty seem to have held a consensus view which holds that a belief is true if it is to be ultimately agreed to by all rational investigators. Peirce stated "...There is no distinction of meaning so fine as to consist in anything but a possible difference of practice."[12] And in the same article, "The opinion which is fated to be ultimately agreed to by all who investigate is what we mean by the truth."[13] The practice Peirce was discussing was the experimental practice of the community of scientists following the scientific method.

William James altered significantly the meaning of Peirce's pragmatism. James argued, in brief, that truth means what satisfies the needs and preferences of the individual, not the community of scientists.[14] This subjective approach was rejected by Peirce and Dewey. We will take the pragmatic theory to hold that a statement is true if it works in the long run and helps the community achieve some sought after rational goal. In this version beliefs are kinds of maps which help us reach our destination. Or more relevant to the thesis of this paper, beliefs are kinds of rules which guide our actions to achieve our goals.

The pragmatic theory of truth defended here is of a very limited form. Many of the criticisms of the pragmatic theory have validity because the theory is applied to areas other than the realm of morality. Some have argued that pragmatism is a form of justification or verification of true beliefs not the meaning of 'truth'. Others have argued, for example, that many false beliefs can be and were useful such as the geocentric theory of the universe. This theory worked well for a very long time and yet it is false. However, it must also be noted that the geocentric view would not work today nor does it impinge much on the day to day behavior of people as do moral rules.

It will be argued here that it is this pragmatic theory of truth that is relevant for moral statements. The argument defended here has the following structure. Persons are social beings. A 'society' is defined here not as a random collection of persons but a group of persons living in an ongoing and within institutionally defined structures or patterns of activity. Persons are social in that they need others to be conceived, born, survive, educated, loved, develop and achieve some level of the satisfaction of their needs or happiness. For various reasons discussed below, the satisfaction of needs may lead to conflict unless structured by moral norms.

For society to exist requires that individuals pursue their need satisfaction in a manner that minimizes violent resolution of conflict. Moral norms, among other norms and institutions, function to minimize conflict and allow for the peaceful resolution of disputes. Conflict is minimized when persons pursue their goals in a manner that does not destroy the preconditions for social peaceful coexistence and lead to what Hobbes called a state of nature. Peaceful social coexistence can only exist if the means used to achieve our goals and the goals we choose are restricted.

Moral norms allow for the maximization of the good, understood as the satisfaction of rational desire, in a structured manner that does not undermine the social arrangements that make a non-violent social order possible. Moral norms, it will be argued, are a form of social control which imposes certain necessary restrictions on the pursuit of goals and need satisfaction.

Moral norms are true in the pragmatic sense if rational and fully informed persons would assent to them as necessary means for the accomplishment of desired and rational individual and social goals. The goals, it will be assumed, are twofold, individual survival and happiness (satisfaction of needs) and the maintenance of social structures necessary for social cohesion and efficient use of resources. Happiness, in turn, requires the existence of personal relationships of intimacy and friendship which requires certain moral norms. In the larger social context, the continuance of social order requires that self-interest and violence be limited.

The pragmatic justification of morality requires an analysis of the nature of moral norms. An analysis of the formal traits of moral norms from a pragmatic perspective will explain why moral norms exist and why they have the formal structure they do. Although conceptions differ, it will be assumed here that moral norms have the following distinctive formal traits: 1) moral norms are learned rules. They are not inborn but acquired through the process of socialization. 2) Moral statements are action guiding. As Hare and others have argued, moral statements are normative standards for human behavior specifying how persons should act (not a description of past behavior).[15]   3.) Moral rules are overriding in nature; they have priority over other norms including self-interest (when there is a conflict), and other non-moral customs. 4.) As Kant argued, moral norms are universalizable.[16] Universalizability will be understood here in the sense that moral statements are rules which have the highest degree of generality, i.e., they apply to all or most members (usually excluding young children, the insane) of a society. 5) Moral rules concern the welfare of someone other than just the person performing the action. This distinguishes moral norms from norms of prudence, or rational self-interest where the welfare of others is not involved. 6) Moral rules have certain sanctions attached for violation. These sanctions may be simply blame and disapproval from others or more severe form of punishment. 7) Moral norms have an affective component.[17]

This description of moral rules can be pragmatically justified as necessary conditions of peaceful social cohesion. First, the development of rules per se has obvious efficiencies when compared with the alternative of thousands of separate commands for innumerable situations. Norms then can be seen as components of social memory and the distillation of thousands of years of cultural evolution and trial and error learning and discernment of the similarities of various problems and situations and the formulation of a general statement to cover potentially infinite number of variations.

Though moral rules are necessary, they are not inborn. Adults must teach their offspring to conform to the patterns of conduct of their society. Socialization is this process of social interaction whereby individuals internalize the language, customs, beliefs, and values of a society and occurs in three stages. Primary socialization is done by parents, secondary socialization occurs in schools and tertiary socialization occurs in adulthood and involves entering a profession or occupation. Primary socialization is the most important for it lays the groundwork for the other two stages.[18]

Primary socialization is the stage where parents teach the socially prevailing moral rules to their children. This fact that moral systems are perpetuated in the context of some family structure, is constitutive of any moral system. There are at least two fundamental reasons parents teach their offspring to be moral. First, as Hume claimed, there is a cross-culturally well established fact of a general natural empathy between parents and their helpless newborn children.[19] Given the work, time, expense and stress of raising children, without this innate sense of caring, there would be no good reason why parents would not simply eat or abandon their children. The parents themselves are also usually sufficiently socialized by their parents to accept essentially the same rules which preclude such treatment of children.

Secondly, the self-interest, survival and happiness of the parents alone require certain moral rules. Parents want to live and satisfy their needs so respect for life and restricting deception and violence must be taught. Parents know they may one day be sick and will get old and be in need. Consequently, children must be trained to help the sick and support the old. Parents also know that their survival and happiness as well as the happiness of their offspring as adults require similar limits on violence and deception be applied to others, so moral rules are generalized to include others in the community.

Moral rules must be action guiding for three reasons. First, human behavior is not totally determined genetically so our behavior must be defined by learned rules. Secondly, since humans have an awareness of the future and different possible courses of action, rules are necessary for choosing one of many alternatives if human behavior is to be somewhat predictable. Thirdly, in general, rules exist to further some goals, and moral rules exist to guide our actions to realize future goals such as happiness and maintain present unstable conditions such as social order.

Ethical norms are overriding in nature. They must be overriding or have priority for they are correspond to the most basic human needs (e.g., survival, security and freedom from pain and fear, happiness). The overridingness requirement is the way a society establishes a hierarchy among its various norms to maintain cohesion and reduce interpersonal conflict that a mere random collection of moral and non-moral norms would produce.

Although all societies have various kinds of norms corresponding to different roles or social functions, the moral norms are the most general. They apply across time, roles, sex, and age and, as such, play a unifying or integrating function.[20] Thus, universalizability, as understood here, is necessary when interpreted as requiring that behavior be rule governed and consistent with the conditions necessary for non-violent social order. Clearly, general compliance within the group is necessary if the survival of the group is to be more probable. Universalizability, then, can be understood as the requirement that individual actions conform to social structures and thus maintain social order.

Moral norms concern actions that affect the welfare of others. This distinguishes them from norms of prudence because they are essentially social norms. They are norms that impact on the welfare of others and thus on the social bonds that unite individuals and make society possible.

Moral norms have a sanction associated with them to motivate compliance. Some form of punishment must exist for there must be reasons for the agent not to pursue his or her self-interest without limit. Without sanctions, moral rules would weaken and a state of war result.

Closely associated with sanction is the emotive component of moral norms. Once moral norms are internalized and the conscience forms, they have an affective or emotive aspect due to the fact that moral norms are inculcated through a socialization process usually by parents to whom we have an emotional bond. Moral rules are generally not entertained in the mind in a purely intellectual manner for if they were, as Hume pointed out, moral rules would not motivate us to act.[21] The emotions may be feeling of empathy or the desire for approval from others or the avoidance of guilt and fear of punishment.

The pragmatic explanation of the formal characteristics of moral norms is not sufficient to make the argument complete. One must examine the specific contents of moral norms and show their pragmatic justification.

If the pragmatic theory of ethics is true, and if we make the reasonable, though admittedly controversial, assumption that human beings in all cultures have essentially the same basic needs, then there should be widespread agreement on the basic ethical rules. It is reasonable to hold, I believe, that persons have the same essential biological needs (survival, freedom from pain, etc.) because we are members of the same species. Moral relativism defended by Mackie and others, holds the contrary view. Let us consider the objection from relativism.[22]

Moral relativism correctly points out that there are disagreements in morality. But one must specify at what level these disagreements exist. Moral systems are a complex set of hierarchical norms of different levels of generality and importance. One may call the most general or basic norm a principle. An example would be "Human life should be preserved." Norms less general than principles one may call secondary rules. Here, one example may be "Do not lie." Even more specific is a particular judgment as how to act in a specific situation. Relativists are right that moral disagreements do exist but they tend to overlook the fact that these disagreements exist at the secondary level of rules not principles. This disagreement exists for several reasons. First, all normative rules assume some 'facts' or descriptions of the world and the situation.   Differences about beliefs about the 'facts' will lead to differences about what rules apply.

The 'facts' may also involve different worldviews, philosophies and religions. Religious belief systems in fact agree on many of the basic moral values. If the argument presented here is correct, this agreement must exist since all societies face many of the same problems of social coexistence regardless of their religious or philosophic perspective.

However, disagreements do exist about such matters as polygamy, vegetarianism, the rights of women and some sexual behavior. Since it is admittedly difficult to determine which if any metaphysical worldview or religion is true, these disagreements will likely remain for some time. But as agreement about the facts and worldviews increases, so will the convergence on moral norms.

There are disagreements about the 'facts' for two additional reasons. First, moral systems contain concepts which are difficult to define. For example, the abortion debate is exacerbated by the problem of defining 'person' precisely. There are paradigm cases of the term but certain gray areas exist which make the concept open textured to a degree.

Secondly, our knowledge of psychology, society and reality in general is incomplete. We do not know all there is to know about human nature, human needs, and the consequences of various possible social institutions and arrangements.

Finally, certain secondary moral norms may be simply irrelevant as new social conditions arise. This is where relativists usually focus their attention but they overgeneralize. As argued here, moral norms are part of a group's adaptation to a particular environment and require change when the environment changes or one's understanding of the same changes. The example of polygamy may clarify this. Anthropologists have argued that polygamy may have developed because of a lack of sufficient number of males due to deaths in war. Polygamy would be a way to ensure all females are married at least in a society that required all females to be married.

The historical tendency for moral systems to be conservative and to fail to reflect changing conditions creates another problem. Disagreements in moral norms are needlessly exacerbated due to the tendency of moral systems to incorporate within the moral domain and persist in including as morally relevant behavior that is morally neutral due to new social, scientific and technological conditions. That is, moral systems tend to overprecision or overdetermination. Moral norms may exist where there is in fact no need for a moral norm but only personal choice.

For many reasons, most primitive tradition-based societies could not sustain a significant level of pluralism in personal choices.   Modern societies, due to a more stable economic base and other factors, can tolerate substantial differences within the nine necessary moral parameters mentioned above. A rational moral system would view personal behavior which does not conflict with the necessary moral limits, as morally neutral and permissible. If moral systems were more precisely delimited, moral disagreements would be thereby reduced.

The argument here is that cross-cultural disagreements are not in the basic moral principles but in secondary rules. Contrary to relativists like Karl Marx, Ruth Benedict, J.L. Mackie, and others, there is in fact a consensus on the basic moral rules shown by cross-cultural study of the social systems. The evidence reveals that all societies have the following common basic moral content: 1.) prohibition of murder or the killing of in-group members except within parameters specified in the group (e.g., as punishment, self--defense, or other socially accepted rituals); 2.) prohibition of random bodily violence, harm or insults (harm to prestige or self-esteem); 3.) rules requiring some degree of work from the able bodied to meet survival needs; 4.) a prohibition of theft and establishment of some degree of private property which cannot be used without permission (scope of what can be private tends to be quite restricted in hunting and gathering societies, and virtually unlimited in advanced industrial societies); 5.) rules requiring some level of care for others, especially infants, the old and infirm; 6.) knowledge is valued at least to the degree it helps meet the needs of survival (food, clothing, shelter, treatment and prevention of illness); 7) truth telling and promise keeping are generally valued except in specific cases; 8.) the encouragement of some form of marriage where sexuality, reproduction and nurture of children take place; 9.) some restrictions on sexual intercourse with the rule against incest being most universal. Other similarities could be mentioned but these are sufficient for present purposes.[23]

The existence of these common basic moral principles can best be explained as constituting the pragmatic solution to the problem of human co-existence in a non-violent manner. Morality is the answer to the practical problem of maintaining social order among members of a species which both need others and at the same time are not genetically programmed to cooperate. Moral norms constitute a structure of instrumental rules or guidelines which define appropriate means for the achievement of human ends while maintaining a non-violent social environment. In other words, moral norms correspond to necessary social structures wherein a group of individuals with some anti-social tendencies continues to exist as a society with minimal violence, conflict and inefficiency in meeting the needs of its members. Let us consider these norms in their pragmatic foundation.

Persons have needs in order to maintain normal species-typical functioning. Biological needs (e.g., food, water, sleep, etc.) are necessary for continued normal biological functioning and survival. Psychological needs (security, self-esteem, companionship, intimacy, meaning, etc.) are necessary to reduce anxiety, fear, boredom, and unhappiness. Although needs are conditioned to some degree by one's culture, survival remains the most basic need. Survival is contingent upon restricting violence among group members hence the prohibition of murder and random violence. Since human infants are born in absolute dependence incapable of providing for themselves, there must be norms requiring the care and nurture of children. This explains the presence of some form of the family.

The fact that human beings are social and sexual beings has three consequences. First, persons seek sexual partners, love, companionship and friendship. Sexual and psychological intimacy, bonding and friendship require trust and caring. Without truth-telling, promise-keeping and mutual aid, intimate relations would not be possible. This would increase social alienation and insecurity, a situation most would find undesirable. Furthermore, this condition of alienation at the personal level would also make the social system extremely unstable if viable at all.

Secondly, sexual mating must be allowed if the group is to replace deceased members with new persons. Since human beings are by nature sexual beings, all societies consider some varieties of sexual expression good or at least acceptable and value offspring. Thirdly, rules regulating sexual relations, especially the general prohibition against incest, are necessary. (Exceptions usually exist in some primitive societies only for royal or priestly groups.) The basis of the incest taboo rests in part on the need to integrate the society more fully by developing marital ties with other family units. Prohibition of incest is advantageous for individual and family security in that having extended relations can be helpful in times of need. Although probably not apparent to pre-scientific cultures, modern science has shown the genetic benefits of exogamy.

Finally, the incest prohibition exists to minimize possible disruptive consequences of sexual relations between parents and children. Although rules specifying pre and extra-marital relations differ more than many other norms, restrictions are always present partly to minimize disruptive emotions and partly to make ascriptions of fatherhood, and thus responsibilities for care, more reliable.

Given the vicissitudes of life, (especially in primitive societies where the possibility for amassing of wealth is very limited) the norm requiring aid and assistance, at least to the closest relations or in-group members, is also rationally based. Similarly, there must be some incentives for work, the care and management of assets and the provision of food hence the corresponding rules protecting some level of private property.

The continued existence of a society is in part decided whether the society can adapt to its environment and solve problems. Adaptation and problem solving require knowledge, decision making and cooperation to implement decisions. Cooperation requires communication which in turn requires a rule favoring truth-telling in at least most collective endeavors; random lying would eliminate trust and produce social chaos.

In general, these moral norms exist to restrict violent conflict. Conflicts that can lead to violence that threaten peaceful social coexistence occur for several reasons. Without assuming any inborn instinct for aggression, human nature has certain anti-social potential. The potential for anti-social behavior is actualized in part because human beings have limited altruism and empathy. Empathy is strongest among those who have long association and knowledge of each other, as in many family units, and usually attenuates the further one moves from the circle of familiarity and reciprocity.

Potentially socially disruptive activity also arises from the fact of scarcity of desired goods (food, wealth, love, status, etc.) This scarcity is partly a function of the level of availability of science, technology, partly a function of the vicissitudes of life and partly due to the nature of the desired object; status, for example, seems to require (especially in advanced societies with high degree of division of labor) a limit on availability. These conditions when combined with the fact that persons are born dependent and continue so for some years and the vulnerability of all including adults to attack by others requires rules to structure social existence.

Human rationality itself can be a source of conflict as illustrated in the free-rider problem. There is an obvious advantage in enjoying the benefits of one's society without contributing one's share whether paying taxes, fighting in wars or generally observing the limits to self-interest as specified by moral norms.

For a society to exist and thrive, the free rider problem must be addressed for their actions weaken social structures. The answer to this dilemma consistent with the perspective taken here is not on the basis of individual inconsistency but on the social basis of socialization, and the institutional enforcement of norms.

The first agent of socialization is typically the family. Here, informed and dedicated parents are central to the development of a conscience or the internal sense of right and wrong. However, there are clear limits to socialization and education. Human beings are morally limited and rational enough to see the possibility and desirability of pursuing their self-interest while violating social norms. This calls for the enforcement of moral norms through judicial and penal institutions. It also calls for the constant rational evaluation of moral norms to ensure that human action is not limited by arbitrary and irrational norms. This fact leads to another important consideration about the free rider problem.

If a society could ensure total commitment of all to its moral norms, the rational evaluation of norms that is necessary if a society is to adapt to new circumstances would be impossible. This would obviously be detrimental to the survival of the society itself. That is, socialization so thorough and compelling that no norm could be questioned or abandoned would 'freeze' a society into a specific time and normative system which would be contrary to its continued social existence when new conditions called for some norms to be revised or abandoned altogether. Hence, it seems we arrive at the somewhat paradoxical but necessary conclusion namely, that though the free-rider problem must be controlled, its total elimination would in fact be detrimental to the long term survival of the community.

Not all goals of a given society at a given time are necessarily rational or promote the efficient satisfaction of needs. One would begin to rationally assess such goals and the societal system they are a part as one would rationally assess any claim. Considerations would include: clarity of the meaning of concepts (definition), specifying sufficient evidence, reasons or facts for claims (justification), does it assume a correct worldview and conception of human nature (foundation); does it explain what is required or have sufficient scope (completeness) logical analysis of the relations between claims (consistency), does it have excess claims (simplicity), comparison with other opposing views and well-established theories, (compatibility with established knowledge), possibility and problems with institutionalization (implementation), does it actualize its stated goal or goals most effectively (efficiency) etc. Complications arise in times of incomplete knowledge and worldview and religious pluralism.

A society that socializes its members to adhere to its rationally based norms will have a higher probability of survival than one that does not. If the socialization is adequate, serious challenges will not occur and general compliance will obtain.

However, this argument for the pragmatic necessity of morality only applies to a certain ethical systems, namely a form of naturalism. Naturalism, as understood here, means that moral statements require the maximization of certain natural properties such as happiness, welfare or the satisfaction of human needs.

This I take was the view of philosophers like Aristotle, Mill, and Hume, among others. Though Hume is often quoted about his emotivism, his remarks about social utility of morality are often overlooked. Hume said, "The use and tendency of that virtue [justice] is to procure happiness and security, by preserving order in society."[24]

It should also be clear that the pragmatic approach takes a broadly teleological view of ethics with deontological secondary elements. That is, in a teleological view, moral norms require the maximization of certain states conducive to happiness and social harmony. Deontology, such as defended by Kant, holds that morality is defined by certain intrinsic facts about the intention, not on the consequences. For example, Kant claimed it was always wrong to lie while a teleologist would allow lying in some cases if it maximized happiness.

As Rawls has argued, one must distinguish social practices from actions that fall under those practices.[25] Social practices such as punishment for violation of social norms are teleologically based since they are necessary for general compliance with moral norms. However, any specific instance of punishment must not involve punishing the innocent simply because it is believed it may promote social utility or order in some special set of circumstances. Here, on the level of rules, the deontological elements are necessary. From the perspective defended here, deontological rules are necessary because they provide the necessary rigidity that social structure require. Without a system of essentially inviolable rules, social uncertainty and unpredictability of the behavior of others would undermine social cohesion.

The view defended here is also a form of realism. That is, moral norms correspond to objective conditions necessary for individual needs satisfaction in a non-violent social system. Mackie's argument for non-realism in ethics is based on two claims, moral relativism and what he calls the "queerness" of moral concepts. The relativism claim was discussed above and rejected as factually false when it concerns the basic principles of social existence. We must explore his second claim about the queerness of moral terms.

By moral realism Mackie means the view that there are objective moral facts just as there are objective facts about the physical world.[26] The queerness comes according to Mackie when we accept the thesis of materialism, that only material objects exist. Now, clearly, moral terms are not physical objects. Mackie then suggests that moral properties somehow supervene on physical properties. That is, physical properties must in some way be transformed to become moral properties. Mackie believes this makes no logical sense. But it does make sense when one introduces human needs, desires and the social context.

The pragmatic view of ethics explains how supervenience is possible. Moral properties can be explained as those physical properties which satisfy human needs and desires in such a manner that allows necessary social structures of non-violence and group survival. The supervenience is due to the fact, as stated above, that persons are social in that they need others to survive and flourish but are not genetically programmed to necessarily act in such a manner. They must construct the web of rules that constitute moral norms. [27]

The same argument can be made against Gilbert Harman theory of moral nihilism.[28] Moral nihilism as held by logical positivism and Harman claim that moral norms do not apply at all and have no objective foundation as do scientific claims. Harman rejects the attempt, such as that presented here, to explain moral facts as sociologically and psychologically based. He claims any such attempt "would have to be complex, vague and difficult to specify."[29] Surprisingly, the terms he uses as indicative of the difficulties involved in such an explanation are not as categorical as one might expect given Harman's theoretical perspective of nihilism.

Contrary to Harman, there is an analogy between scientific method and moral theory. Just as the rules of scientific method do not correspond to objective facts about the world but are rules necessary to bring forth scientific truth, so moral rules do not correspond to some physical facts but to rules necessary for the satisfaction of human needs while preserving a social context.

Harman's error and the error of much contemporary ethics, as suggested, is the neglect of the social nature of human beings. Moral norms, as has been argued, are based on the fact of human needs and the requisite conditions for an efficient social system. It is not complex or vague or difficult to specify what would happen to a society that did not allow sexual mating, knowledge, the care of infants, and truth-telling or forbid random killing, pain and injury infliction. If survival is preferable to death, and happiness is preferable to misery and peace is preferable to war, then moral norms have sufficient objectivity and foundation.

To sum up, a moral system is true from the pragmatic perspective if it allows for persons to meet their needs in that society with minimal conflict and in the most efficient way possible. Moral rules are an efficient means to certain ends. These ends can be many but as already stated, include individual and social survival, and all that this entails.

Moral norms constitute the gravity that counteracts the centrifugal forces of uncontrolled self-interest. Moral norms perform this function by channeling human needs and desires into ordered relations with the needs and desires of others. This ordering is efficient because it limits the area of the unknown and unpredictable, reducing the frustration of expectations and minimizing conflict and violence.

Efficiency is here understood as achieving one's goals with the minimum of energy, time and resources. Without trust or promise keeping, insecurity would be increased and necessitate measures for self-defense requiring additional time and energy needed to protect one's goods and significant others. This would entail depleting resources that could be used to satisfy other needs more fully or pursue other activities. Hence, the structuring effect of moral limits, in addition to promoting survival in the extreme case by preventing chaos, also promotes greater general efficiency. This would be especially relevant in circumstances where a society faced external enemies. Moral norms are the solution to persons seeking the satisfaction of their needs without producing the Hobbesian state of war of all against all. This would seem to be a state of affairs where, presumably, the likelihood of satisfying one's needs is even more improbable.

NOTES

1. Mackie, J.L., *Ethics: Inventing Right and Wrong*, (Penguin, 1977.)

2. Linton, Ralph, "Universal Ethical Principles: An Anthropological View" in *Moral Principles of Action*, ed. R. Anshen, Harper & Bros.; May Edel & Abraham Edel, *Anthropology and Ethics*, Case Western Reserve Press, 1968; Marion J. Levy, *The Structure of Society*,(Princeton UP, 1952); Clyde Kluchhohn, et al. "Values and Value-Orientations in the Theory of Action" in Talcott Parsons and A. Shils., eds., *Toward a General theory of Action*, Cambridge: Harvard UP, 1951, pp. 388-433.

3. Chisholm, Roderick, *Theory of Knowledge*, Englewood Cliffs, NJ: Prentice-Hall, 1976, pp 103-111.

4. Ibid, p. 107.

5. Mill, John Stuart, *Utilitarianism*, Bobbs-Merril, pp. 12-13.

6. Blanshard, Brand, *The Nature of Thought*, London: George Allen & Unwin, 1939, p. 68.

7. Kant, I., *Foundations of the Metaphysics of Morals*, tr. L. W. Beck, New York: The Liberal Arts Press, 1959, p. 19.

8. Rawls, John, *A Theory of Justice*, Cambridge: Harvard UP, 1971, pp. 20f, and *Political Liberalism*, New York: Columbia University Press, 1993, pp. 8, 28, 45, 72.

9. *Theory of Justice*, p. 47.

10. Ibid., p. 48.

11. Ibid., p. 49.

12. Peirce, C.S. "How To Make Our Ideas Clear" in *Introducing Philosophy*, ed. by Robert C. Solomon, New York: Harcourt Brace & Co., 1997, p. 204.

13. Ibid, p. 205.

14. James, William, *Pragmatism*, in Solomon, op. cit., p. 207.

15. Hare, R.M., *Moral Thinking*, Oxford: Oxford UP, 1981, pp. 23-32.

16. Kant, op. cit., p. 19.

17. Frankena, William K., *Ethics*, Second Edition, Englewood Cliffs, NJ: Prentice-Hall, 1973, pp.4-9.

18. Moore, Stephen, *Sociology*, Chicago: NTC Publishing, 1995, pp. 23-5.

19. Hume, David, *An Enquiry Concerning The Principles of Morals*, excerpted in *Great Traditions in Ethics*, Denise & Peterfreund, eds. p.20.   20.) Parsons, Talcott, op. cit., pp. 390-5.

21. Hume, op. cit., p. 23.

22. Mackie, J.L., *Ethics: Inventing Right and Wrong*, New York: Penguin Books, 1977, pp. 34-54; Robert M. Stewart & Lynn L. Thomas, "Recent Work on Ethical Relativism," American Philosophical Quarterly, V28, N2, April 1991.

23. Linton, op. cit.,p. 34.

24. Hume, op. cit. p. 20.

25. Rawls, John, "Two Concepts of Rules," Philosophical Review, 64, 1955, pp. 3-32.

26. Mackie, op. cit. pp. 24-6.

27. Cf. Brink, David, "Moral Realism and the Skeptical Arguments from Disagreement and Queerness" Australasian Journal of Philosophy, 62, 1984, pp. 111-25.

28. Harman, Gilbert, *The Nature of Morality*, Oxford: Oxford UP, 1977, pp. 35-7.

29. Ibid., p. 36.

CHAPTER 5

ERRORS IN MORAL REASONING

Most philosophical discussions on ethics usually focus on such theoretical issues as the nature of 'good' and the foundation of moral norms. Typically, they tend to focus on the disagreements between the theories rather than the agreements and often ignore what the theories imply as to what we should not do. This discussion of moral fallacies reveals an underlying consensus in the ethics of Aristotle, Immanuel Kant and John Stuart Mill.[1] The theories of these three philosophers were chosen for several reasons. First, they are widely considered to be among the most important theorists in the Western tradition. They also represent three very distinct theoretical approaches in ethics. If, as is claimed here, all three theories would consider certain moral fallacies as indeed errors, then their plausibility as moral fallacies would be enhanced.

Of course, there are other theories of ethics besides that of Aristotle, Kant and Mill. These three share a perspective now called cognitivism, the view that ethics is a field where objective knowledge is possible. Others, the non-cognitivists, who hold emotivism, existentialism and the like would not find all of the listed fallacies as fallacies. Philosophers will not agree on errors in practical ethics until they agree on the theoretical foundations of ethics, so, to this extent, this is a limited proposal. To those who share the cognitvist perspective, the following may be a useful endeavor.

Errors in moral reasoning must be distinguished from immorality and amorality. Immorality means accepting morality in general as binding but performing the wrong action by simply refusing the moral principle or rule that applies. Instances of this would be acts such as stealing and cheating by persons who know these are immoral. An amoral person, by contrast, simply rejects morality in general and acts on the basis of pure self interest. Errors in moral reasoning do result in immoral acts but due to some mental confusion, irrationality, ignorance or error of fact or logic rather than conscious rejection of an accepted moral standard.

A brief summary of the main points of the three theories will be helpful.

Aristotle

Aristotle's theory can be briefly summarized as holding that happiness is the ultimate goal for all persons.[2] But what constitutes happiness or right living for humans? Happiness means the actualization of our essential nature as defined by our "function" or what we do best. The function of a knife, for instance, is to cut and that is how a knife should be used. Man's function, according to Aristotle, is reasoning, what he does better than any other being on this planet. Hence happiness for Aristotle is the virtuous activity of the soul (mind, life) in conformity to reason.

Aristotle goes on to define "virtues" as those traits that enable us to perform our function well. They are habits such as wisdom, justice, courage and moderation which help us achieve happiness. His analysis of virtue as the mean between extremes relative to the individual requires that we know the relevant facts about the person before we can determine the mean for them. That is, the moderate amount of food would not be the same for an adult as for a child, a laborer as compared to a sedentary individual.

Mill

Mill's theory of utilitarianism is founded on his desire to formulate an objective rational moral theory.[3] His goal, as that of his predecessor, Jeremy Bentham, was to develop a theoretical framework that is not corrupted by the obfuscations of custom, opinion and emotion. The foundation of Mill's theory is the principle of utility which states that an act is right to the degree it maximizes happiness for the greatest number. Happiness means pleasure and/or the absence of pain. His theory, like that of Aristotle's, is grounded in the belief that happiness is the ultimate human goal which can be rationally understood and achieved in principle.

Mill did not consider his theory to be one which promoted a crass hedonism or pleasure seeking. He argued that there were "higher pleasures" such as those of the mind, art, love and friendship which are superior to the "lower pleasures" of food, drink and sex. His theory requires that we consider the consequences of our actions on the satisfactions and pleasures, higher and lower, not just on our self but on all parties affected.

Kant

Kant's theory holds that the only absolute good is the "good will."[4] A good will acts from duty, i.e., from pure respect for the moral law. We are acting from pure respect for the moral law if our intention conforms to the categorical imperative. The first form of the categorical imperative requires us to act only on that basis whereby the maxim (principle we are thinking of putting into action) can become a universal law. This universalizability criterion has at least two dimensions: first, there is the logical consistency sense of universalizability so that lying could not become universal for then no one would be deceived by lies and hence no one would tell them. Thus, lying can exist only as an exception to the rule or general practice.

There is another sense of universalizability that brings out another element of the categorical imperative. This sense is revealed in Kant's treatment of the rich man example when he asks whether one can universalize the maxim "The rich should not help the poor." Kant answers that it is indeed logically possible to make that maxim universal but that no rational being would will such a maxim be universal because we might find ourselves poor one day and in need of help from others.[5]

Kant's second form of the categorical imperative introduces another important element in his theory. This version of the imperative requires that we not use persons as a means only.[6] Persons, Kant maintains, have the right to autonomy, to lead their own lives and make their own decisions because they are rational. To use a person for our own means treats them as things, not as beings capable of controlling their own lives.

Theoretical Agreement

These three great moral theories, although very different, share more than might at first be suspected. First, as mentioned, all three are cognitivists, they hold that ethics is a realm of knowledge not just opinion or tradition. For Aristotle, this knowledge is based on his conception of human nature, for Mill, the nature of happiness and Kant on the nature of reason itself. They all reject emotivism, that moral judgments express only emotions and attitudes. Similarly, they avoid any appeal to any form of intuitionism or the belief that morality is based on some direct mental insight not subject to rational defense. Subjectivism, the view that each person defines his or her own morality, is also repudiated. Aristotle, Kant and Mill held that morality is an essentially social institution, an institution that governs the relations of persons and makes community possible.

They also subscribe to a form of naturalism. Naturalism is the view that moral properties are found in nature and human experience and not derived from divine commands. They, to various degrees and in different ways, saw the necessity of using human nature to found moral imperatives. Kant may be a partial exception to this in that he held that God and an after life are necessary presuppositions or ideals of morality. That is, he believed that the good are not always rewarded nor are the evil always punished in this life. Only an omniscient and omnibenevolent God can perfectly reward justice with happiness and punish injustice in the life hereafter. For Kant, then, God is the ultimate enforcer of morality not its source since Kant believed that even God was subject to moral principles.

Fallacies
1.) Prejudice - to make a negative judgment about a person or a group before considering all the relevant evidence and other possible interpretations or judgments.

This is probably the most common error in moral reasoning. There are innumerable examples of it but most fall in the category of racism, sexism, snobbery and xenophobia. Prejudice involves the conscious or unconscious negative appraisal or pre-judgment of those that are perceived as 'other' or significantly different from 'us' in customs, beliefs, appearance or background. Racism even in the justice system is evidenced by recent research into the use of capital punishment on African-Americans and whites.[7] Racial prejudice judges the members of other races as somehow inferior and less worthy than members of the dominant group. Sexism is a form of prejudice that treats all women as passive, weak, emotional and therefore fit only for work in the home. Prejudice de-personalizes the 'other' and denies them equal dignity as persons.

Prejudice is the unfair treatment of minorities, women and others who are relatively weak and dominated by those in power. It may manifest itself in one individual making an unwarranted negative judgment of another or in an institutional and social framework where the prejudicial beliefs are formalized into law and social custom. Gender roles, the cultural expectations that only certain positions are open to women, denies them the equal opportunity to develop and express themselves. Language itself reflects and promotes prejudicial attitudes. Examples of this would be the practice where only women give up their last name upon marriage. Prejudice may result in the forced assimilation of the minority into the dominant culture resulting in the loss of an irretrievable cultural heritage and some of the rich diversity of human expression.

Prejudice overlooks our common humanity and misinterprets the differences that exist among members of a group and between groups and the obstacles they have had and may still have in achieving equality and respect.

Prejudice would be clearly deemed a fallacy by Aristotle who held wisdom to be the foundation of ethics. For Aristotle, to have a prejudice is to hold an opinion without sufficient evidence or reflection, a clear violation of the basic requirement of morality, rationality itself.

Mill's theory requires that our actions maximize happiness and minimize pain. Clearly, consequences call for knowledge of the facts of the situation and how the action will affect other situations and persons and thus requires rationality not prejudice.

Kant's theory explicitly holds that we must not rely on emotion or personal likes and dislikes when moral action is called for. The categorical imperative is a rational principle which precludes the irrational emotion of prejudice.

2.) Emotionalism- using emotion or strong feelings to support a moral claim.[8]

It is a commonplace of our experience that persons are emotional beings. But, emotions without the guidance of reason can be destructive as witnessed by the consequences of panic in groups facing some real or imagined danger. Emotional manipulation is common in politics, advertising and personal relations. The skillful use of images and music often seen in political campaign ads can lead viewers to the intended opinion almost unconsciously. Fanaticism, the overzealous pursuit of some ideal to the detriment of other values, is permeated by emotive power. Similarly, the right use of certain emotion-laden words can also influence opinion. One can give a negative or positive connotation to situations through the choice of the right word as in public servant/bureaucrat.

Emotions are in fact far more complex than they may at first seem. It is commonly believed that emotions arise spontaneously as a response to some experience. In fact, psychological studies show that every emotion is preceded by some interpretation of the experience which then triggers an emotional response.[9] The interpretation, may be a result of mistaken beliefs and hidden assumptions.

Aristotle's theory rejects any form of emotionalism. His list of virtues are not emotions but the rationally guided habits of action.[10] Aristotle comments that youths are not fit for politics because they often react emotionally which is to react immaturely and without wisdom, the supreme virtue.[11] Emotion not guided by wisdom is blind and may lead to a hedonism that, for Aristotle, restricts the development of human potential and is ultimately self-destructive.

Kant would surely agree as he is adamant that inclination or personal feelings and preferences must not be a factor in determining the will to action.[12] They cannot be a factor because they are unreliable and vary from person to person and from time to time. Reason alone is the sole criterion of morality for Kant.

Mill's theory would also reject emotionalism. Although he, unlike Kant, did not exclude happiness or inclination as morally irrelevant, he did require reason. Mill saw the necessity of using reason to determine the morality of an action because the evaluation of all the circumstances and the consequences requires a long range view which emotions usually exclude.

3.) Egocentrism- the inability or unwillingness to imaginatively put oneself in another's situation and attempt to see things from their perspective; the absence of empathy.

We all start life as egocentrics. The newborn does not distinguish itself from the world or its parents and sees all as a oneness of undifferentiated experience and a sense of omnipotence. It has no guilt or concern for the feelings and needs of others. The findings of the Swiss psychologist Jean Piaget and others show that through about the age of two, the infant is totally immersed in her mental world.[13] As the normal child is socialized it begins to realize others exist and have needs and feelings similar to her own. Lack of proper socialization, whether due to the absence of parents or cold and abusive parenting, can result in a weak conscience or what Freud called an underdeveloped superego.[14] In extreme cases this could result in the adult sociopath who lacks all sense of empathy for others and in milder forms this is manifested as egoism and selfishness or the lack of regard or concern for others. It implicitly denies the equal humanity of others.

Aristotle clearly saw the need of proper parenting, education and training for the development of virtuous habits. The virtues can become part of one's character only after repeated actions guided by those already in possession of the virtues. His endorsement of friendship as essential to happiness and the highest form of friendship, described as a relationship wherein friends help each other live the best life possible, would constitute the supreme conquest over egocentrism.[15]

Kant would view the egocentric perspective as a perspective wherein one fails to universalize the maxim or underlying principle of one's action. The second form of the categorical imperative would also be violated for egocentrism would imply using others as merely a means to one's own well being. As such, the egocentric is amoral and outside the realm of the kingdom of ends.

Mill's higher pleasures are in fact the pleasures of friendship, virtue and concern for others. He considered selfishness a major source of unhappiness and immorality. Utilitarianism specifies that pain and pleasure are of equal moral value regardless of who is experiencing it. It requires that we see things from the perspectives of all involved and equally empathize with them; a difficult task to be sure but one that is assumed by the Golden Rule: Do to others as you would wish they do to you.

4.) Ethnocentrism- assuming one's society or group is infallible or the best and other groups are inferior and thus do not have the same rights as one's own group; to interpret the behavior of other groups with the categories and conceptual framework of our own society when this is inappropriate.

This is a version of the double standard in that the moral principles one applies to one's own group does not apply to others. Extreme nationalism and groupthink are instances of this mental attitude. Other examples would be the treatment of Native Americans by the early explorers and settlers and the interment of Japanese-Americans during World War II. Ethnocentrism reinforces group solidarity and loyalty but at a very high price. The de-personalization it involves is often a prelude to war and other forms of violence. It usually implicitly assume a form of moral relativism as well as some factual errors.

Moral relativism, put briefly, is the view that moral norms are not universal or unchanging for all persons but only apply to a particular society at a given time. It also usually holds that morality is not a rational enterprise and that the moral practices of other cultures cannot be objectively criticized. If moral norms do not apply across cultures then there are no norms that limit our behavior with respect to other cultures; they are outside the moral realm and thus fair game for any action at all. Although Aristotle was ethnocentric, his belief was inconsistent with his own theory. His theory precludes relativism for the simple reason that human nature, the basis of his ethics, is in fact universal and cross cultural, even though he himself seems to have denied this.

Kant's categorical imperative requires that a moral act must be an act which can be consistently universalized over all rational beings. In ethnocentrism, the scope of universalization is too narrow since it only covers one's own group.

Mill would similarly reject ethnocentrism by arguing that the desire for happiness is a universal property of humanity. Mills' efforts to extend equal treatment for women is an instance of this.

Other errors of ethnocentrism concern the belief that one's group is morally perfect. Historical evidence is unanimous against this in that no community has been found to have complete knowledge yet this attitude inhibits change and learning from other cultures. Lawrence Kohlberg's studies of moral development support this.[16] His research shows that moral development consists of three levels: 1.) Pre-conventional-this is the level of children prior to the age of about eight years of age. Since the moral values have not been internalized, the motive for moral behavior is the avoidance of punishment; 2.) Conventional-at this point most of the societal values have been internalized and approval and avoiding guilt feelings are the primary motives for morality; 3.) Post-conventional-morally correct action is determined by abstract universal principles that are equally applied to all persons of all cultures. It is clear from this schema that ethnocentrism is part of the conventional level of development; a level that has not yet reached the critical rational awareness of the highest level of moral thinking.

5.) Specieism- to deny non-human species any moral worth or to consider them as unfeeling automatons.

The moral status of lower animals is a controversial arena. Traditionally, the moral status of animals was not given much thought with the possible exception of the Buddha and St. Francis. Descartes considered them "thoughtless brutes"[17] while Spinoza granted they had feelings but of a different nature and concluded we may "use them as we please."[18] Some philosophers reject this attitude which they call anthropocentric ethics, i.e., an ethic which places man at the center of the universe and denigrates other life forms. They argue that animals should be considered as having rights similar to that of humans. Others argue for a more modest concern for animals. The extreme animal rights advocates demand vegetarianism while the more moderate advocate only the prevention of unnecessary cruelty towards other species.

Modern scientific findings show that the there is no sharp or absolute dividing line between homo sapiens and other life forms. There are signs of rationality in the higher primates and mammals. These findings would tend to support at least the moderate view of concern for the suffering of all life forms.

Aristotle is not known to have expressed an opinion on the issue of animal suffering. He did believe them to have 'souls' but to him this was just a principle of life not a spiritual essence we normally associate with the word today. However, it may be plausible to argue based on his comments on virtues as habits that cruelty to other animals would be precluded simply because as habits virtues would be weakened if not practiced uniformly.

Kant argued for the moderate view that a moral person could not be cruel to animals and moral toward persons.[19]

The utilitarian Jeremy Bentham, Mill's predecessor, states "The question is not can they reason? nor can they talk? but can they suffer?"[20] In general, utilitarian theory is congenial to the animal rights advocates because it is based not on reason but on the capacity to feel pain and pleasure; a trait we obviously share with all animals. Human history has witnessed an expanding circle of moral concern; the rejection of specieism is one example.

6.) Stereotypical thinking–using stereotypes (false or oversimplified beliefs usually about a minority) to argue for or against a position; sexism, racism and ageism are instances of this.

Stereotypical thinking means the use of certain oversimplified mental constructs or schemas by which to interpret experience. These mental filters are based on false beliefs, exclude relevant information and disregard other possible interpretations of the experience. This form of thinking combines the fallacies of hasty generalization (generalizing without sufficient evidence) and oversimplification (reducing a complex matter to such a degree as to distort it). Such thinking would include labeling blacks as lazy, the Irish as drunkards, women as passive and senior citizens as senile. To commit this fallacy is not to judge persons on an individual basis but to assume that all persons of a certain group share the same traits, which is patently false. Labeling others in this blanket manner encourages polarization and upholds our own belief in our superiority.

Aristotle, Kant and Mill would all judge stereotypical thinking as an instance of irrationality. It is irrational because it makes unwarranted assumptions about people. Mill was clear about his belief in the diversity of persons as he uses this fact for the limitation of government in his essay *On Liberty*.[21]

Aristotle's discussion of virtue requires that the mean be determined relative to the individual not in general. This clearly means that we must know the other persons needs, way of life, etc. before we can judge them morally. Although it is true Aristotle accepted the prevailing view of his time that women were inferior and thus he too lapsed into stereotypical thinking, in this he was simply not true to his general empirical and critical method.

Kant also defends the individuality and differences among persons. He argues, for example, against using happiness as a basis for ethics by claiming different persons have a different opinion about what makes them happy.[22]

Human beings are extremely diverse. This diversity originates from our genetic inheritance which is further differentiated by environment, both natural and cultural. Stereotypical thinking is a form of hardening of the categories, of rigidly maintaining traditional beliefs in spite of new data. It is a form of selective perception that reveals an intellectual laziness and a lack of self-knowledge.

7.) Weakness of Will-believing that some act is wrong but voluntarily doing the very act.

Weakness of will is a common human experience. St. Paul said "That which I will, I do not, that which I will not, I do."[23] For example, a cashier may give us ten dollars too much in change accidentally and knowing we should tell her, we nevertheless say nothing and keep the money. Weakness of will usually involves three elements: 1.) A judgment that some act is immoral; 2.) a desire to do the act in any case; 3.) Acting on the desire without external compulsion.[24] Here, one seems to know what one is doing is wrong and does it anyway without threats or coercion. Some instances of lack of will power can be explained as Aristotle did by holding that while under the influence of drugs or alcohol which heighten emotion and weaken rationality, we are overcome by the desire for a present pleasure or a novel experience and thus ignore the morality of the situation and long term consequences.[25]

The more difficult examples of weakness of will consist of acting contrary to what we believe is right but not being under the influence of mind altering chemicals. Plato dismissed the possibility of this and argued that no one does wrong knowing that it is wrong.[26] Yet, contrary to Plato, there does seem to be such phenomena. The reasonable answer seems to rest on the realization that value judgments are commitments not beliefs and thus a matter of degree rather than either/or propositions in the case of truth or knowledge. Aristotle's conception of virtue as habit clearly implies virtue is a matter of degree. Weakness of will occurs when our value commitments lack the sufficient force to forego an immoral present pleasure or experience.[27]

The experience of weakness of will is instructive in several senses. It supports Aristotle's claim that moral actions are the results of proper habits not just beliefs. Human rationality is weak and temptations many, hence moral training in the early years is crucial for proper moral behavior as adults. Second, knowing human weaknesses implies that we should avoid situations where we might encounter strong temptations. Finally, it suggests we should strive for fuller self knowledge by regularly taking honest and full inventory of our true not pretended values and make decisions to strengthen our genuine commitments. Kant was well aware of human weakness and emotionalism which is why he stressed the role of reason. Mill likewise saw the need for moral training.[28]

8.) Ends/Means Error- assuming that a valid end justifies any means; to hold a view about consequences without sufficient evidence.

Moral debates often concern the proper ends and means. What are our ends or goals and what are the appropriate means to achieving them? This requires, among other things, that we consider the short and long term consequences of actions. Will mercy killing of the terminally ill who request it lead to the killing of the mentally ill and insane? Will it result in the corruption of the medical profession? If the medical profession is corrupted then the cure is worse than the disease since trust in the profession is lost. Fanatics, those committed to some overriding value or goal, often ignore the complexities of moral action and hold that their goal justifies any action. Lenin held that any means are appropriate to bringing about the communist revolution.[29]

Aristotle, Kant and Mill knew well the limits of human nature. Mill stressed the importance of the higher pleasures (pleasures of the mind, art, friendship) over the lower pleasures (pleasures of the body, i.e., sex, food, drink) but saw the need for education to bring this about. They also agreed that human behavior can change but that it is a slow process. Aristotle and Mill were especially aware of the importance and impact of the social environment on human development and viewed as naive any approach that stressed preaching alone to change human tendencies.

Aristotle was also well aware that ethics is an imprecise discipline. It lacks precision because the future is uncertain especially as it concerns matters of human behavior and the evolution of social institutions. He would also remind us not to think of morality as consisting of discreet acts but as a product of habits he called virtues. We cannot temporarily take a moral vacation, as it were, and expect it to have no long term consequences.

The Kantian response here is probably the least equivocal. His example of whether it is right to lie to save an innocent life explains his view.[30] His answer is "no" because, he argues, we in fact cannot know with certainty the full consequences of any act and thus must not consider consequences at all. His view may be extreme but it reminds us of the seriousness of violating moral norms even when it seems necessary.

Mill's utilitarianism, as we have seen, is based on consequences. His concern that utility not violate justice shows he did not hold the view that maximizing happiness for the greatest number justifies any means. Mill was aware that means and ends are intimately connected and that the wrong means can, in fact, in the long term at least, undermine our ends as well.[31] Perhaps the failure of Russian communism is due, in part, to this tunnel vision thinking that ignores the inextricable union of ends and means. To ignore these dimensions and complexities is to commit the classic fallacy of oversimplification.

9.) Confusing morality/legality - assuming that just because something is immoral it should be illegal or vice versa.

The distinction between morality and legality was not always made by primitive or tradition based societies which usually viewed all norms as divinely based. The Code of Hammurabi, for example, is said to have been given to King Hammurabi by the god Shamash in 1700 BC and consists of over 300 legal and moral norms without any distinction made between them. Modern societies tend to be less tradition and more rationally based and differentiate between the various norms that exist in all communities by assigning different levels of authority to them. Specifically, it became apparent as early as the ancient Greeks as exemplified by Sophocles' *Antigone* and the teachings of Plato that moral law is of a higher authority than government made norms. Positive law, a construct of morally and intellectually limited men, may, and often is, unjust and immoral.

Legal moralism is a philosophical position which gives government a large role in enforcing morality. The American prohibition laws in the early part of this century which attempted to outlaw alcohol would be an example of extending the moral policing by the state. Some legal moralists overlook other possible means of altering human behavior, such as education, taxation, licensing and other regulatory but not prohibitory, policies. They may also exaggerate human weakness and capacity to make wise choices on their own.

The libertarian position argues for a minimal government and a large role for freedom of choice. They seek the legalization (not necessarily the moral acceptance) of prostitution, homosexuality and some drugs. Though these proposals are of course, controversial, they exemplify the attempt to limit the moral scope of government. Libertarians may commit the opposite mistake of legal moralists by holding an exaggerated view of human rationality.

The proper extent of governmental power is a function of the overall political theory one adopts. All three ethical philosophers considered here saw the moral law as the foundation of positive law and thus a standard that must be used to judge the government made law. They also agreed that the state must, of course, enforce some moral laws such as the moral prohibition against murder, but warned that the power and scope of government must be limited. Aristotle believed the state should promote the good and ethical life but he never approved a totalitarian state, favoring a modified democracy of the middle class landowners as the most realistic political arrangement.[31] Mill's defense of the Harm Principle would argue that to hold such a view gives too much power to the state and reduces individual expression and happiness.[32] Kant would see it as a violation of moral autonomy.

10.) Is/ought confused - mistaking factual (descriptive) claims with moral (normative) claims.

When a belief is widely shared in a group for some time without any challenge or scrutiny it takes on the authority of fact in the minds of the believers. The enculturation process in a close knit traditional community can be so thorough and profound that it seems as obvious as direct empirical experience and becomes part of 'common sense'. Enculturation does not only mean the assimilation of beliefs, customs and values of the group but also the subconscious adoption of a frame of reference or way of looking at the world and interpreting experience. The frame of reference acts like blinders or filters which block out novel, anomalous or potentially unpleasant information. The distinction between fact, something directly observed by the senses, and opinion, an interpretation or conclusion from the facts, is obliterated. Obviously, this limits the acquisition of knowledge. Examples of this sort of thinking would be the belief in the geocentric universe, the flat earth, the inferiority of women, the legitimacy of slavery and the like.

A persistent and widespread practice or norm within a social group can be mistaken for a fact of nature and a universal necessity. Custom can indeed become second nature and indistinguishable from nature itself; a widespread belief becomes viewed as a moral necessity. As such, this error is similar to the fallacy of appeal to the masses, i.e., holding something as true or right because many believe it. In any case, this fallacy usually involves the hidden assumption of facts and value judgement which is not reasoned for but taken for granted. G. E. Moore called this the "naturalistic fallacy," i.e., confusing a natural fact for a moral reality.[32]

Aristotle would condemn this as simply a lack of wisdom and self-knowledge, the foundation of his ethical theory. Although he did believe in slavery and the inferiority of women, once again he seems to have made a factual error about the properties of these classes of persons. Some interpreters of Aristotle believe by slaves Aristotle was speaking of severely mentally retarded persons, which lessens to a degree his error. In general though, he seems to have made these judgments on the basis of the status quo overlooking the issue of the potential of these persons.

Kant explicitly states that facts and circumstances do not determine obligation but the good will as defined by the categorical imperative. He stressed that ethics must be a priori exactly to avoid this contamination of the theory with contingent empirical, social and cultural debris. Mill was well aware of the stultifying influence of custom on belief. He saw himself as a reformer who used utilitarian reasoning to argue for reform in prisons, the treatment of women and other social institutions.

All experience must be interpreted in some way for there is no immaculate perception. Though we must give up the 'myth of the given' this does not mean we should hold a conceptual framework so rigidly and unconsciously that it is not open to adaptation and revision in response to new experience. To do so would be to become prisoners of an outdated paradigm or way of looking at the world.

11.) False Appeal to Tradition- to claim that some practice is right just because it has a long history.

Tradition refers to the set of customs and beliefs that have been an accepted part of a community for a very long time. For many primitive peoples myths and tradition are sacred and any deviation from them may be punishable by death. Tradition in some Eastern and African communities is often supported through the worship of ancestors who are believed to look over their society after death and keep it on the straight and narrow of the past.

Aristotle, Kant and Mill would remind us that the problem with relying blindly on traditions is that sometimes they are just wrong or evil. Some traditions may be based on false beliefs and mistaken interpretations of experience. Slavery, racism and sexism are all traditions common to almost all societies at one time, yet today we would all probably agree they are wrong. Aristotle would see reliance on tradition as lack of wisdom. Kant would remind us that reason not tradition is the basis of ethics. Mill knew that happiness requires knowledge not to worship the past which consists mostly of superstition and prejudice.

12.) False Appeal to Authority- to hold a moral view simply because some authority holds the same view.

To rely on an authority is to rely on a person or persons for your beliefs. For many people it is the main way of justifying beliefs. They appeal to religious experts and the politically powerful to make sense of the world around them. And because of the explosion of knowledge there is increased specialization which requires that we all rely on authorities at times. Children must rely on the authority of others but should we also rely on others for our moral views?

Aristotle would ask us to consider whether the authority in question has wisdom or merely power. He would remind us that authorities can and do disagree. Kant argued that rationality allows persons the right to autonomy or control over their own lives. For Kant, the more we rely on authority for our decisions, the less power and autonomy we have over our own lives. Mill knew that a rational adult after due reflection must make his or her own decisions about their life if they are to have a chance at happiness. Clearly, the chain of appeal to authority must end with the facts not some other authority.

13.) Intuitionism- assuming that one has an immediate and correct insight into the morality of the situation without reliance on supporting facts.

To assume one has infallible insight is to assume one is infallible and this is surely unwarranted. Our intuition or conscience is shaped by our society and upbringing and thus no more infallible than any society. It is also clear that a person's conscience can change over time as shown by common experience and Kohlberg's research. Sometimes, however, an appeal to conscience means that one has carefully considered the situation and reasons for and against and decided to do what one believes is right. This is not a faulty appeal to conscience for it is a conscience that has been subjected to rational moral analysis.

Appeals to intuition or what appears to one to be self evident assumes that the mind is not greatly influenced by socialization and social environment. Psychology and the social sciences have established how social custom, language and experience shapes and influences our thinking and our conceptual frameworks and beliefs. The mind may be a tabula rasa at birth, but it is not so for long thereafter.

Aristotle, Kant and Mill agreed that persons are not infallible but rational. Firmly believing something is so does not make it so. Truth is established by reasons and evidence, not by how 'obvious' it seems to us.

14.) Rationalization - refusing to consider additional evidence or other points of view because of possible harm to self-concept, self-esteem, worldview; explaining away evidence that challenges one's deeply held beliefs.

Rationalization is the conscious or unconscious process of excluding from awareness by re-interpreting or re-conceptualizing some experience that is seen as somehow threatening. Psychologists have long noted how needs, wants, past experience and training can influence our perception.[33] Philosophers such as Thomas Kuhn have shown how the history of empirical science, probably our most rationally rigorous discipline, is at times retarded by outdated "paradigms" or frameworks for interpreting the world.[34] Rationalization is a form of self-deception wherein we attempt to maintain the security of our belief system and our self concept in the face of challenges. The ad hominem fallacy, attacking the character of the person as a way of disproving his statement, may sometimes be an instance of this rationalization for it is prematurely rejecting a belief that may be upsetting, by inappropriately attacking the one who proposes it; a form of blaming the messenger. A threat to one's world view of conception of one self produces anxiety at the possibility of change. New ideas and change in general is often perceived as a threat to our way of life, our reputation or sense of importance and produce what Festinger called "cognitive dissonance."[35] Freud's psychoanalytic theory of defense mechanisms which repress or block painful ideas by pushing them into the subconscious is instructive here.[36]

Rationalization and self-deception implies a closed mind, a mind not receptive to new ideas. A closed mind implies infallibility. i.e., no new data or insight is needed. Again, this contradicts human nature and is an example of irrationality. The pragmatist philosopher C.S. Peirce and others have shown how uncomfortable persons can become with uncertainty and thus seek the peace of mind that certainty brings.[37] Yet, Socrates was surely right that knowledge of our own ignorance is the beginning of wisdom for without this awareness, the search for wisdom would not even begin.

Realizing that knowledge is potentially infinite and our grasp finite, Aristotle, Kant and Mill all stressed the importance of education as a lifelong process. It is true that we cannot live without holding some beliefs (an impossibility) but an open mind does not necessarily imply indecision; it simply means a willingness to consider evidence as it becomes available.

Rationalization is associated with emotionalism since a threat to image or self esteem is a subjectively painful emotion. It suggests lack of self-knowledge, intellectual honesty and authenticity, the foundations or moral rationality.

15.) Scapegoating- falsely blaming a person or a group (minority) for problems that have other causes.

The Bible describes a custom the Jews had of ridding the community of their sins and shortcomings by symbolically projecting them onto a goat and then ejecting it from their midst. There have been several non-symbolic historical example of this practice. The Romans accused the early Christians of many crimes to justify their persecution, the racist discrimination against African Americans often alleges they are fully responsible for such social problems as crime and drug use and the Nazi treatment of the Jews to name just a few. Attributing the cause of social problems to despised minorities protects the self-esteem and esprit de corps of the dominant group and preserves the power of the elite who often instigate the hatred. Freud's concept of projection, the attributing to another person or group the traits and characteristics one finds unacceptable in oneself is present in scapegoating. It is a rejection of personal responsibility for one's moral failures. Scapegoating may also involve stereotypical thinking about the minority in question.

Aristotle would judge scapegoating an instance of the lack of courage to face our own shortcomings. Mill's concern over the "tyranny of the majority" is a dramatic statement of his concern for the rights of minorities.[38] Kant would consider scapegoating a failure to universalize one's maxim.

16.) Judgmentalism- judging others too quickly usually in a negative manner and in a way that makes one appear superior.

Human beings jump to conclusions. Coming to a quick conclusion by labeling precludes the necessity of additional thinking and avoids the unpleasant state of uncertainty. A quick conclusion often assumes a double standard, using one norm to judge ourselves and a more demanding one for others. If someone intentionally deceives us we call them a "liar;" if someone steals from us we call them a "thief." This identification of the agent and the act is fallacious for reflection shows that even basically good persons commit mistakes and can act immorally at times. To identify agent and act assumes the person cannot change or learn. It precludes rehabilitation and is usually an emotional act.

Quick judgements are judgements based on insufficient evidence, a sign or irrationality. To accurately judge another person would entail that one has all the information at one's disposal concerning every significant fact about the person's life and personality and secondly that we are perfect and impartial moral judges-clearly an impossible task. Having *some* evidence about a person's character does not constitute *proof* , (overwhelming evidence beyond a reasonable doubt) nor even *reasonable* belief (belief based on substantial evidence). There is some evidence for even the most ridiculous views such as the flat earth hypothesis; rationality demands more than some support for beliefs. Emotions again play a role here for in judging others we usually seek to indirectly establish our own superiority.

A judgmental attitude also often assumes a simplistic understanding of free will. The belief in free will holds that persons are masters of their own destiny; that they can, at times, overcome the influences of environment and heredity in their behavior by will power and effort alone. Philosophical reflection reveals the ambiguity and complexity of the free will hypothesis; often the belief is simply a reflection of our ignorance of the sometimes subconscious causes of our acts. Scientific findings do not disprove all versions of the free will theory but they do strongly suggest that the impact of environment and heredity is far greater than common sense assumes.[39]

For Aristotle, a person is not any specific act but the sum total of his acts throughout his whole life. Recall his famous saying: "One swallow does not a Spring make.."[40] Kant would see this attitude as a denial of man's autonomy and rationality for both imply the possibility of change in behavior. Mill stressed the importance of education and the influence of the environment on human behavior; he realized that education can make a difference in human moral behavior.

17.) Appeal to the Masses- to attempt to justify a moral position by claiming everybody or almost everybody is doing the same.

The fallacy of appeal to the masses claims something is right or true because many believe it is right or true. Logically, of course, the fact that many persons believe something does not make it so. Historically, most, if not all, believed that the earth is flat and that the sun moves around the earth. Implicitly, however, this fallacy points to the fact that morality must be a matter of universal rules. It is, nevertheless, a fallacy, since it is usually not true that everyone is in fact doing 'it' and 'it' would not be right if they were. For example, belief in slavery and in the inferiority of women were also universally held but that does not make these beliefs correct.

Aristotle, Kant and Mill would agree that this is indeed a fallacy. Aristotle, as we have seen, required that the correct moral theory be based on accurate beliefs about human nature and society. Aristotle would further ask whether the proposed act is consistent with the four main virtues, wisdom, courage, justice and moderation. As mentioned above, Aristotle did believe in slavery and the inferiority of women, but, once again, he simply made factual errors; these views are not necessarily implied by his theoretical framework.

Kant's concept of the categorical imperative does indeed require that moral beliefs be consistently universalizable but he attempted to explicate this criterion, as indicated above, in a manner so as to exclude immoral universal principles. He required, as specified by the second form of the categorical imperative, that no universal principle use persons as a means only. He further stated that one must ask whether such a principle is logically consistent and whether we would be willing to be on the receiving end of such a principle.

Mill's theory would require that any moral rule be such as to maximize pleasure (especially the higher pleasures) and/or minimize pain. Clearly, the alleged fact that everyone is doing something makes it right would not pass the rational criteria put forth by Aristotle, Kant and Mill.

Common Errors

These fallacies are fallacies because they violate some element of rationality. Rationality is a complex and controversial concept but most would agree that rational beliefs to be rational must be well defined, logical (consistent), not based on mere emotion and supported by sufficient evidence.

The above moral fallacies violate one or more criteria of rationality:

-some make errors about the scope or extent of moral principles: egocentrism, ethnocentrism, specieism, scapegoating.

-some hold beliefs on insufficient evidence or make wrong conclusions from the evidence: egocentrism, specieism, scapegoating, prejudice, judgmentalism, ends/means error, is/ought confused.

-some are based on emotion: prejudice, emotionalism, weakness of will, rationalization.

-some assume certain facts about human nature: stereotypical thinking, authority, judgmentalism, intuitionism.

Some make false assumptions about one's society: ethnocentrism, tradition, scapegoating, ends/means error, morality/legality confused.

Given the above discussion of fallacies and the definition of rational moral judgment, the steps in correct moral reasoning would include the following elements:

1.) Defining the moral problem precisely:
>-have we defined the basic concepts clearly?
>-what are the moral values involved?

2.) Gathering facts:
>-do we have all the relevant facts?
>-how trustworthy or reliable are these alleged facts?

3.) Has this problem occurred before?
>-what caused it?
>-what solutions were used?
>-what were the consequences?

4.) What are our goals, priorities?

5.) What are our possible solutions?
>-strengths of solutions
>-weaknesses of solutions

6.) What resources do we have?
>-time
>-money
>-personnel
>-knowledge

7.) What are the long and short term consequences of our options for:
>-ourselves
>-our group
>-society
>-world

8.) Have all the affected parties been consulted and involved in the decision?

9.) What do the main philosophical theories (e.g. Aristotle, Kant, Mill) recommend?

10.) What does our religious tradition recommend?

11.) What does the law demand?

12.) What does our professional or corporate code of ethics, if any, suggest?

13.) What does our conscience suggest?

14.) Do the recommendations of the above agree?

        -To what degree?

        -Do they agree on principles, consequences or both? Why?

15.) What principle are we proposing to solve the problem?

16.) Would publicity about our solution and reasoning about it be embarrassing? Why?

17.) What is the morally best solution?

18.) How can we best implement the solution?

19.) What lessons can we learn form this?

20.) How can we prevent this problem from happening in the future?

        -change education, training?

        -change the law?

        -implement the law better?

        -restructure organization, society?

        -better communication?

        -develop a code of ethics?

Students often come to an ethics class thinking that ethics is just a matter of opinion, feelings or religion. After being exposed to the various theories of the great philosophers they may be bewildered at their disagreements and despair that they can be of any help in solving moral problems in real life. Disagreements, of course, can be at various levels and for various reasons.

A moral theory, like any theory, is a set of systematically related statements that explain, justify or organize some aspect of our experience. The statements that constitute a theory are of different types and of varying degrees of generality. Disagreements between theories may be at the level of some abstract foundational theoretical claim of a metaphysical or epistemological nature. Disputes about whether ethics is deontological or teleological, naturalistic or non-naturalistic are of this type. The dispute may also be at the lower level of principles where principles are general moral claims from which can be derived many specific moral rules. For example, Kant's categorical imperative is a principle but his belief that ethics must be a priori is a foundational epistemological claim. The point is that conflicting views on the foundational theoretical level do not necessarily mean conflicting advice on the practical level of specific judgments and actions. We have seen that Aristotle, Kant and Mill agree on the main fallacies of moral reasoning and agree that certain actions such as murder, stealing, rape, and ignorance are wrong.

Students should also be reminded of Aristotle's remark that not all human endeavors and disciplines provide the same level of certainty or knowledge. Mathematics may have the greatest certainty because of its abstract nature but ethics, Aristotle claims, has a lower degree of precision and clarity because it is involved in practical affairs.

Ethics can outline parameters of reasonable moral action but may not necessarily provide exact and specific guidelines in all cases for at least four reasons. First, disagreements exist about worldviews. Some with a religious worldview argue from religious premises others from non-religious premises. Second, it is at times difficult to agree on definitions of key concepts such as what exactly is a 'person'. Thirdly, we are often lacking all the relevant information or knowledge of possible consequences. Fourth, persons are morally and rationally limited. Fifth, we cannot control fully the actions of others.

To conclude from the lack of certainty that ethics is simply a matter of opinion or unreasoned custom would be fallacious. This would be tantamount to arguing that just because the social sciences do not allow the certainty of the natural sciences that they are no better than common sense in the information they offer us. This would be an instance of the fallacy of bifurcation or black/white thinking, i.e., to assume that there are only two possibilities when there are in fact more. The above list of fallacies will hopefully go some distance in persuading some that there is a great deal of agreement on the practical level and that ethics is a far more rational discipline than they give it credit for.

Finally, we must keep in mind that mistakes in moral reasoning are not only intellectual errors but may lead to crimes and cruelties which fill the pages of history and our own times.

NOTES

A version of this essay appeared in *The International Journal of Applied Philosophy, Summer, 1996.*

1. Useful sources of classic fallacies is: Michalos, Alex. 1970. *Improving Your Reasoning*, Englewood Cliffs, NJ: Prentice-Hall; For a useful source of moral dilemmas for classroom discussion see *Moral Choices*, Joseph Grcic, ed., St. Paul, MN: West Publ. Co., 1989.

2. Aristotle, *Nicomachean Ethics*, Bk.1,6.

3. Mill, John Stuart, *Utilitarianism.*

4. Kant, Immanuel, *Foundations of the Metaphysics of Morals.*

5. Ibid., Sect. 2.

6. Ibid.

7. Bedau, Hugo Adam, ed. 1982. *The Death Penalty in America*, 3ed., New York: Oxford.

8. This is to be distinguished from emotivism which is a metaethical theory about the meaning of moral concepts. One must also distinguish emotionalism from empathy which is a general concern for a person and provides a motive to do the moral action on the basis of facts other than the emotion itself.

9. Napoli, Vince, et al. 1982. *Adjustment and Growth in a Changing World,* St. Paul, MN: West Publ. Co. pp. 189-191.

10. Aristotle, op. cit., Bk. 2.

11. Op. cit, Bk. 1.

12. Kant, op. cit, Sect.1.

13. Piaget, Jean discussed in Howard Gardner. 1978. *Developmental Psychology,* Boston: Little, Brown, pp. 63-7.

14. Freud, Sigmund, in Gardner, op. cit., p. 201.

15. Aristotle, op. cit., Bks. 8,9.

16. Kohlberg, Lawrence. 1970. *Moral Education: Five Lectures* , Cambridge: Harvard.

17. Descartes, Rene, *Discourse on Method,* in *Animal Rights, and Human Obligations,*, ed. by Tom Regan & Peter Singer, Englewood Cliffs, NJ: Prentice-Hall, 1976, p. 62.

18. Spinoza, Benedict de, *The Ethics,* R.H.M. Elwes, trans., New York: Dover, 1955, Proposition 37, note 1.

19. Kant, Immanuel, "Duties Towards Animals and Spirits," in *Lectures on Ethics,* Louis Infield, trans., New York: Harper & Row, 1963, pp. 239-240.

20. Bentham, Jeremy, *Introduction to the Principles of Morals and Legislation*, New York: Hafner, 1948, p. 311n.

21. Mill, John Stuart, *On Liberty.*

22. Kant, *Foundations,* op. cit.

23. St. Paul, Letter to the Romans, 7:15.

24. Martin, Mike W. 1989. *Everyday Morality,* Belmont, CA.: Wadsworth, 1989, p. 108.

25. Aristotle, op. cit., Bk.7.

26. Plato, *Apology,* in *The Trial and Death of Socrates,* G.M.A. Grube, trans., Indianapolis, IN.: Hackett, 1975.

27. Hare, R.M.. 1970. *Freedom and Reason,* New York: Oxford Univ. Press, pp. 67-85.

28. Mill, J.S., *Utilitarianism.*

29. Lenin, Vladimir Ilyich, 1932. *State and Revolution,* New York: International Publishers, pp. 71-75.

30. Kant, I., *Lectures,* op. cit, pp. 224-234.

31. Mill, J.S., *On Liberty,* and Dewey, John, *Human Nature and Conduct,* New York: Random House, pp. 25-35.

32. Moore, G.E., *Principia Ethica.*

33. Gardner, op. cit. p.45.

34. Kuhn, Thomas. 1962. *The Structure of Scientific Revolutions,* Chicago: Chicago Univ. Press., pp.43-66.

35. Festinger, Leon, discussed in Leonard Berkowitz. 1987. *A Survey of Social Psychology,* Hinsdale, Il: The Dryden Press, pp. 72-74.

36. Freud, Sigmund, in Gardner, op. cit., pp. 197-8.

37. Peirce, C.S. "The Fixation of Belief."

38. Mill, J.S., *On Liberty* .

39. In Gardner, op. cit., pp.293-7.

40. Aristotle, op. cit., Bk.1.

CHAPTER 6

KANT AND RAWLS
ON MORAL THEORY

In his *A Theory of Justice*[1] (henceforth: **TJ**) John Rawls claims his two principles of justice are an interpretation of Kant's second formulation of the categorical imperative and that the Original Position is a procedural interpretation of Kantian autonomy. The thesis of this essay is that Rawls' theory is Kantian only in its articulation or formulation, not in its foundation or justification. It will be argued that Rawls' two principles are a plausible construal of Kant's categorical imperative, but that Rawls' foundation is really a synthesis of Kantian and utilitarian principles. Let us briefly consider Kant's theory.

In the opening section of his *Foundations of the Metaphysics of Morals* (henceforth: FM), Kant states that the ground of morality 'must not be sought in the nature of man or in the circumstances in which he is placed, but sought *a priori* solely in the concepts of pure reason'(FM, 5).[2] This must be so, Kant goes on to argue, because for a law to be a moral law, it must hold with 'absolute necessity' and for 'all rational beings' (FM, 5), not just men. By claiming that the foundation of morality must be *'a priori,'* Kant means that it must be entirely free of empirical foundations and flow from 'pure reason' alone.

In the opening sentence of the first section of the *Foundations,* Kant asserts, "Nothing in the world - indeed nothing even beyond the world - can possibly be conceived which could be called good without qualification except a good will" (FM, 9). A good will is present, according to Kant, if the motive or reason for an action is entirely unaffected by the agent's inclinations and *self-interest,* and acts only *for the sake* of duty, not merely in *accordance with* moral duty. Secondly, a good will exists if the person acts with an abiding sense of respect for the moral law. Thirdly, the moral worth or value of the will is not contingent on the realization of *any end or purposes,* for then the good will would be only a means and hence its value would be based upon the achievement of the intended goal. But, for Kant, the goodness of the will must be unconditionally intrinsic, i.e., based only on the principle which it exemplifies.

Clearly, then, Kant rejects utility as irrelevant in the moral assessment of an action. If moral worth were based on pleasure or happiness, then the ground of duty would be empirical, and hence, for Kant, not universal, and therefore not moral since moral laws must be universally applicable. The value of actions is based on the good will which is good if it is grounded on the 'categorical imperative' which states 'I should never act in such a way that I could not also will that my maxim should be a universal law' (FM, 18). (A 'maxim' is the "subjective principle of volition" (FM, 17), i.e., the particular principle which is implicit in the volition.) A moral rule, Kant contends, must prescribe to us categorically, not hypothetically, for a moral rule must obligate without reference to any purpose or consequence. A 'hypothetical imperative,' on the other hand, obligates us to do something only if we wish to bring about certain ends, and if we do not, it loses its prescriptive force, whereas a moral imperative must be absolutely relevant.

To clarify the meaning of the categorical imperative, Kant offers an additional formulation of it. In this alternative form, it reads: 'Act so that you treat humanity, whether in your person or in that of another, always as an end and never as a means only' (FM, 47). This version is based on the understanding of a moral rule as binding only rational beings, and to be consistent, a rational being must always treat every other rational being the same way he treats himself. It is Kant's conviction that each rational being recognizes himself as having absolute worth or 'dignity' (FM, 53) as an end, not merely a means for which he can be used. Hence, no principle of conduct can be universally prescriptive on all persons as rational beings which treats others merely as means.

With this sketch of Kant's moral theory as background, let us consider Rawls'.[3] In the concluding chapter of his *Theory of Justice,* Rawls presents his general views on the nature of justification in moral theory. He suggests that thus far only two basic methods of justifying moral principles have been developed: (1) the 'Cartesian' method of discovering self-evident principles from which one deduces specific moral judgments, and (2) 'Naturalism' where one defines moral concepts in terms of nonmoral ones and shows by science and common sense that these judgments are true. Our discussion will focus on the first model since this is the model that most closely resembles Kant's method.

Rawls rejects the first model because "there are no ... first principles that can be plausibly claimed to be necessary" (TJ, 578). He rejects this foundational approach and argues that a moral theory is to be justified like any other theory; "justification is a matter of the mutual support of many considerations, of everything fitting together into one coherent view" (TJ, 579). The coherentist approach is even more evident in the following remark on the purpose of moral theory: "what is required is a formulation of a set of principles which, when conjoined to our beliefs and knowledge of the circumstances, would lead us to make these judgments with their supporting reasons were we to apply these principles conscientiously and intelligently" (TJ, 46). In other words, a moral theory is 'true' if it "matches" (TJ, 579) our "considered judgments," or "judgments in which our moral capacities are most likely to be displayed without distortion"(TJ, 47).

If such a match does exist, then we have what Rawls calls "reflective equilibrium." This is the state "one reached after a person has weighed various proposed conceptions [theories] and he has either revised his judgments to accord with one of them or held fast to his initial convictions" (TJ, 48). That is, reflective equilibrium is an "equilibrium" since "our principles and judgments coincide" (TJ, 20) and "reflective" because "we know to what principles our judgments conform and the premises of their derivation" (TJ, 20). Reflective equilibrium exemplifies what Rawls calls the "Socratic" (TJ, 49) nature of moral theory, i.e., "we may want to change our present considered judgments once their regulative principles are brought to light. And we may want to do this even though these principles are a perfect fit. A knowledge of these principles may suggest further reflections that lead us to revise our judgments" (TJ, 49). Hence, both poles of reflective equilibrium— judgments and principles are revisable.[4]

Rawls' idea of the Original Position is an instance of this method of reflective equilibrium. Recall, the Original Position (0P) is a hypothetical choice situation consisting of "individuals" who are under a "veil of ignorance," i.e., they do not know their place in society, their natural talents, conception of the good, psychological properties or to which generation they belong. They do know that they are under the "circumstances of justice" which means they know there exist many individuals in a world of moderate scarcity. Furthermore, they are aware that they are rational, free, self-interested, and equal, at least in the 0P.

Finally, they are also cognizant that outside the OP individuals have some similar and differing interests and that they are in some way morally and intellectually limited. Under these circumstances, Rawls argues, these individuals would agree to two principles of justice, namely: (1) "each person is to have an equal right to the most extensive basic liberty compatible with a similar liberty for others," and (2) "Social and economic inequalities are to be arranged so that they are both (a) reasonably expected to be to everyone's advantage, and (b) attached to positions open to all" (TJ, 60). These principles would be chosen because they would ensure the "primary goods" which are necessary means to whatever ends one has. Specifically, these goods are: rights, liberties, opportunities, income and wealth, and self-respect.

The definition of the OP is based on judgments about which Rawls believes "there is a broad measure of agreement" (TJ, 18). These judgments consist in intuitions about fairness, equality and what constitutes morally relevant information. The two principles of justice are the principles chosen by the hypothetical individuals in the OP which, Rawls claims, match our considered judgments about justice in reflective equilibrium.

This conception of moral theory departs significantly from that of Kant in several respects.

Rawls himself concedes that he has departed from Kant when he states, "it is a mistake to...emphasize the place of generality and universality in Kant's ethics...the real force of his views lies elsewhere" (TJ, 251). Rawls suggests that the notion of morality as based in rational choice among free and equal persons is the real contribution of Kant. According to Rawls, a person is acting autonomously "when the principles of his action are chosen by him as the most adequate possible expression of his nature as free and equal rational being" (TJ, 252). To support this contention, he observes that the OP may be construed "as a procedural interpretation of Kant's conception of autonomy and the categorical imperative" (TJ, 256). That is, the categorical imperative results from a procedure of "choice" of the hypothetical individuals in the OP, not by a priori deduction as in Kant. Further, by "autonomy" Kant meant a moral rule, if it is to be *moral,* must be self-imposed, i.e., to be *morally* bound, a person must understand that one is so bound by reason, and not by an external authority. Rawls believes his Veil of Ignorance provides the conditions which preclude the choice of nonautonomous principles. These principles are, according to Rawls, his two principles of justice, principles of conduct that apply to an individual simply by virtue of his nature as a rational, free and equal being. He adds that, unlike hypothetical imperatives, his principles do not "presuppose that one has a particular desire or aim" (TJ, 253), only that one has a desire for "primary goods" i.e., "things that it is rational to want whatever else one wants" (TJ, 253). Rawls contends this interpretation is superior to Kant's version in that the categorical imperative is no longer "purely transcendental and lacking explicable connections with human conduct" (TJ, 256). Nevertheless, Rawls concedes he has "departed from Kant's views" in that the choice of his principles is "collective because the principles chosen must be acceptable to other selves" (TJ, 257), whereas Kant's theory is a choice of the individual noumenal self. But he immediately adds that his theory can also be rendered as the choice of a single self.

Rawls' theory of justice does offer a plausible interpretation of Kant's second formulation of the categorical imperative, "Act so that you treat humanity, whether in your person or in that of another, always as an end and never as a means only" (FM, 47). As we have seen, Rawls' first principle of justice guarantees equal right to the most extensive liberty for all persons which clearly precludes using persons as a means only. Thus, Rawls has provided a helpful construal of an imperative which has often been criticized for being hopelessly vague.

Though Rawls is justified in calling attention to the Kantian elements of his theory, he has in fact glossed over at least three significant additional differences. First, it is true that members of the OP do not choose principles based on their *particular* ends, but they do choose them (primary goods) as *general* ends because they know they have some specific goals, though they do not know what there are. Primary goods then, are *both* means and ends; they are necessary general *means to* specific but yet unknown personal goals and they are *ends* in that they are chosen in the OP as desirable social structures. This teleological element in Rawls is not incidental but essential to his theory. It is essential because a procedural account of the categorical imperative, as that given by Rawls, must import motivational or teleological elements to bring about the result, in this case, the two principles. But, as we saw, individuals in the OP are amoral creatures and hence the motivation cannot be devotion to duty, as it was in Kant, but rather self-interest, which is a prudential, not a moral, reason. This is the whole point of Rawls "thin theory of the good" whose "purpose is to secure the premises about primary goods required to arrive at the principles of justice" (TJ, 396). Rawls notes that he needs a thin rather than a rich theory of the good because he doesn't want to "jeopardize the prior place of the concept of right" (TJ, 396). In justice as fairness, however, this priority does not exist on the level of justification, i.e., in the OP, but only on what may be called the level of *articulation* or definition, the two principles of justice. However, in Kant, right is prior in *both* domains; whereas in Rawls, right is justified *as means* to other ends, the primary goods, not as an end in itself.

This fact also sheds light on the degree to which Rawls' individuals in the OP approximate Kant's idea of autonomy. Kant defined autonomy of the will as "that property of it by which it is a law to itself *independently of any property of objects of volition*" (FM, 59, emphasis added). Autonomy, then, has two dimensions for Kant, the dimension of individual as rationally and freely prescribing rules for him*self and* this independently of any goal or purpose, i.e., *a priori,* since a goal or object would contaminate the volition or rule with empirical elements, thus making it nonuniversal and contingent on the particularities of human nature and its circumstances. Individuals in the OP do prescribe rules for themselves freely and rationally, but only to ensure the 'primary goods', thus departing from Kant's idea of autonomy.

Secondly, as we have seen, for principles to be Kantian moral principles, they must have absolute and unconditionally universal scope for all rational creatures for all time. Whereas Rawls, as has been shown above, viewed moral theory as Socratic (TJ, 49) or dialectical, the two poles of the dialectic being considered judgments and principles. The justification of a moral theory is, as any other theory, "a matter of the mutual support of many considerations of everything fitting together into one coherent view" (TJ, 479). As noted above, Rawls explicitly rejects what he calls the "cartesian" (TJ, 577) view of ethical theory which finds self-evident principles from which to justify moral actions, saying "There are no first principles that can be plausibly claimed to be necessary [truths]" (TJ, 578). If this is so, why did Kant argue that moral principles must be *a priori* (FM, 5) and be "absolutely necessary" (FM, 5)? It should be clear that Kant is in fact using what Rawls termed the Cartesian model as his paradigm of moral theory construction, not reflective equilibrium. Indeed, the equilibrium technique is impossible on Kant's foundational or Cartesian model for the foundational propositions are incorrigible and beyond revision, whereas in Rawls, intuitions or considered judgments are revisable and may even be discarded, and similarly, the theories which are derived from them.

Finally, Rawls mentions that his theory takes into account the conditions of human life such as the scarcity of goods and the circumstances of justice. However, most interpreters of Kant take him to be developing a doctrine to apply to all rational creatures, including angels, and so ignore man's social conditions as irrelevant. Rawls confesses, "I do not believe that Kant held this view" (TJ, 257). But Kant *did* hold exactly this view as we saw in the passage quoted above from the *Foundations,* namely, "the grounds of obligation must *not* be sought in the nature of man or in the circumstances in which he is placed" (FM, 5, emphasis added).

These aforementioned differences between Kant and Rawls indicate that unlike Kant, who sought *necessary* moral rules, Rawls' principles are *contingent* in at least three different respects: First, they are relative to our present understanding of human nature and the circumstances of justice as they exist today. Second, they are relative to the finite set of available alternative theories of justice that the people in the original position (POPs) have to choose from (utilitarianism, intuitionism, perfectionism, etc.). Finally, they are contingent on the initial consensus among the participants; different groups of POPs at different times will, presumably, decide on other possible principles. (This may explain the inconclusive nature of the debate between Rawls and his critics, especially Nozick.) Rawls has said as much in a recent article:

. . . we are not trying to find a conception of justice suitable for all societies regardless of their particular social or historical circumstances. We want to settle a fundamental disagreement over the first form of basic institutions within a democratic society under modern conditions . . . . Our hope is that there is a common desire for agreement as well as a sufficient sharing of certain underlying notions and implicitly held principles . . . the aim of political philosophy. . . is to articulate and to make explicit those shared notions and principles...[6]

Our intention here has been to clarify the differences and similarities between Rawls and Kant. Rawls clearly had the same goal as Kant, to emphasize the priority of right over the good, but because Rawls has a different theory of rationality of moral beliefs, a different kind of justification was required. The OP is a response to this need, and as has been indicated, it does incorporate teleological elements, such as wants and needs, and a theory of means-end rationality.[7] Accordingly, one may consider Rawls' theory as a synthesis of the deontological and teleological ethics, with a teleology (limited by the constraints of the OP) as the foundational substructure supporting a fully deontological superstructure, the two principles of justice. The validity of this synthesis, has, of course, been subjected to innumerable critiques; the point of this essay has been to shed some additional light on this ongoing controversy.

NOTES

A version of this essay appeared in *The Journal of Value Inquiry*, 17, 3, 1983.

1. Rawls, John. 1971. *A Theory of Justice,* Cambridge: Harvard University Press.

2. Kant, Immanuel. 1959. *Foundations of the Metaphysics of Morals.* New York: Bobbs-Merrill.

3. For Rawls' earlier conception of moral theory, see his 'Outline of a Decision Procedure in Ethics, *Philosophical Review*, 60 (1951):177-97; for a comparative study of Rawls' changing methodology see C.F. Delaney, 'Rawls on Method,' in *New Essays on Contract Theory*, ed. K. Nielson and R. Shiner (Guelph: Canadian Association for Publishing in Philosophy, 1977).

4. Additional studies on the questions of Rawls' method can be found in Norman Daniels, *ed., Reading Rawls* (New York: Basic Books, 1975), especially by David Lyons and Ronald Dworkin; and Ronald Dworkin, *Taking Rights Seriously,* (Cambridge: Harvard University Press, 1977).

5. For a discussion of the nature of these social structures, see Joseph Grcic 'Rawls and Socialism,' *Philosophy and Social Criticism,* (Winter 1980).

6. John Rawls, Kantian Constructivism in Moral Theory, *Journal of Philosophy,* (September 1980):518.

7. For an illuminating analysis of Rawls' use of 'rationality', see Edward Walter, 'Personal Consent and Moral Obligation, *Journal of Value Inquiry, V15* (1981):19-33.

CHAPTER 7

TYPES OF POLITICAL THEORY

Human beings live in diverse communities that continue to evolve in innumerable ways. At first, understanding the nature and purpose of change and community was achieved by appeal to myth, tradition and religious belief systems. These perspectives on human social existence were generally not critical, rational or comprehensive. This traditional thinking on society was usually undertaken as ideology to justify the status quo and perpetuate belief in the superiority of the existing social system. A fully systematic and rational understanding of the human community did not begin until the development of the discipline of philosophy.

Political philosophy seeks to understand our social existence through the use of reason, logic and experience. It is a systematic, critical and rational reflection on the nature of political power. Questions that philosophers have pondered over the years include: Is the justification for political authority based on religion, power, tradition, moral virtue, knowledge or consent? What is the purpose of government? Is it to preserve peace and order, glorify God, safeguard a culture, transform and develop human nature, bring about a utopia, promote religious faith, protect human liberty or equality?

What are the limits of governmental power? Is there a higher law than that of the government made law? Should all laws be obeyed? What is the defining line between private and public? These questions have been answered differently by different political philosophies.

Before we can begin to consider the answers to these questions, we must define some key terms. Government is usually defined as an institution that has a monopoly of supreme power in an area. It has the power to make and enforce laws for the entire community and collect taxes to pay for its services. Government is a decision making structure used to resolve conflicts, control crime and protect the society from external attack. Modern governments may also provide services such as education, old age pensions and other forms of social welfare programs.

Politics defines the human community and our relations with each other. The power of making and enforcing laws is the power to shape society and the future of the world. A historical perspective on the varying forms of political power will shed light on current problems and future prospects.

Our earliest ancestors were hunters and gatherers. They lived in small groups or clans and moved around looking for fruits, berries and any animal they could catch and kill. They, like any group, had to make decisions and organize themselves to be successful in killing game, overcoming enemies and surviving. There was no separate government as we know it today, but the elder men probably gathered together as need dictated and discussed their problems and how to solve them. There was no written law, no police force and no jails. Customs and traditions were 'law' and any violations meant punishment of different kinds. There were no clear lines drawn between law and morality or the private and public the focus being usually on mere survival.

The discovery of agriculture about 8,000 years ago changed everything. Agriculture, the ability to make food, allowed humans to live in one place and thus grow in numbers and develop civilization. When you have to move around to follow the hunt, you can only keep what you can carry, but if you can live in one place, you can build homes, cities, furniture, pottery, temples and palaces. As the food supply increased so did the population. With agriculture we also see the development of division of labor. Some people became warriors to protect the city, others priests to serve the gods, and still other became kings to make decisions for the community as a whole. With the development of agriculture, we see the first real divisions of society into economic classes of different wealth and power. This is the real beginning of government as we know it.

The first governments were usually a monarchy. The king typically claimed his the right to rule came from a god or gods. In fact, most kings, like the Egyptian pharaohs and Roman emperors, claimed not only to rule by god's will but insisted they were themselves divine. The basis of political power in this type of society was religion, tradition, and military might, with no limit to the power of government. There was no constitution or individual rights, or elections or political parties. Power was usually inherited so when the king died, the eldest son took over. It was maintained through religious ritual, terror and military might. This pattern of brutal, inherited military based power continued throughout the world for thousands of years.

The justification for political power was initially based on myth, tradition and religion. Slowly there emerged a group of writers which developed a justification of political power on the basis of reason rather than tradition. One of the first thinkers on political matters was the Indian, Kautilya.[1] Living in the fourth century BC, he advised the king to keep in touch with his people and promote their welfare and happiness, not his own. However, Kautilya did not develop a comprehensive political philosophy nor did he challenge the role of the Hindu caste system which divided people into rigid social classes based on birth.

It was Buddha (563-483 BC) who rejected many of the ideas of Hinduism including the caste system.[2] Buddha was a radical in his belief in the power of knowledge over tradition, his defense of greater human equality and abandonment of the caste system. Buddha, with his stress of the central importance of the value of compassion for all living things, is also credited with developing some democratic ideas but he did not develop a complete political philosophy. The Indian king Asoka in the third century BC converted to Buddhism and tried to rule by its principles of peace and compassion.

The Chinese philosopher Confucius (551-479 BC) articulated a more complete political philosophy based mostly on traditional teachings.[3] He argued that a moral ruler is not above the law but one who obeys the "mandate of heaven." The mandate of heaven idea is that the ruler rules through the permission of the gods in heaven. To keep his right to rule, the ruler must promote the welfare of the people and teach them virtue by his own example. One way he is to do this is by selecting not relatives and friends for advisors, as was the custom all over the world and still is today in many parts, but competent and knowledgeable ministers to help him rule. In this way Confucius is credited with originating the idea of a meritocracy or rule by the most virtuous and wise. If the ruler disobeys the mandate of heaven and rules only for his own pleasure and benefit, the people then have the duty to overthrow and replace him with a true ruler.

The ideas of Confucius were not to rule without any challenge. The ancient Chinese school known as Legalism including philosophers Shang Yang (390-338BC) and Han Fei Zi (280-233 BC) disagreed with Confucius on many ideas. Whereas Confucius saw social order as based on ethics, ritual and moral government, the Legalists saw it as based on law enforced by a totalitarian dictator who was above the law and free to do anything to keep and expand power. They saw political rulers as always seeking to increase their power in any way possible. To keep this power, the Legalists persuaded the emperor Qin Shi Huang Di, (the first unifier of China) publicly killed over 400 Confucian philosophers by burying them alive and had their books burned.

Although political ideologies continued to arise in other parts of the world, the first systematic political philosophy started in ancient Greece. It was there that the revolutionary experiment of democracy began. The word 'democracy' itself is Greek and it means a society where the people rule.

The Greek city-state of Athens had a direct democracy. That is, they themselves voted directly on the issues, not through representatives. To be sure, only men with property could vote, women, the poor and slaves were excluded. In any case, it was a world shaking experiment in the fifth century BC but, unfortunately, it lasted for less than a hundred years. It was quickly forgotten, and throughout the world inherited monarchies ruled and warred as they pleased. The Greek democratic idea was to be rediscovered in the seventeenth century by the British and later by democratic revolutions around the world.

Plato

Although democracy began in Athens, one of its greatest philosophers, Plato (427-347BC), was its bitter foe. No doubt his ideas about democracy were colored by what happened to Socrates (469-399bc). Socrates was a philosopher who saw himself as having a divine vocation to increase knowledge and wisdom of his fellow Athenians. He went around asking questions and raising issues about the meaning of 'justice', 'piety' and the like. By pointing out the stupidity and ignorance of many powerful people, he made many enemies and was sentenced to die in 399 BC. To Plato, a student of Socrates for many years, this proved that the ordinary people were not wise and virtuous enough to rule. In place of democracy, Plato proposed the idea of the Philosopher-Kings.[4]

The Philosopher-Kings were individuals of the highest knowledge and virtue. They should rule, Plato argued, just as the captain of a ship should run the ship because he is the most knowledgeable person, not the most popular. The Philosopher-Kings are the most knowledgeable because, according to Plato, they, after a long period of training and education, alone come to know the Forms or eternal Ideas. Plato's eternal and unchanging Ideas exist independently of this world, are the blueprints of this world and the foundation of the cosmos.

Plato's great classic work, *The Republic*, explains his theory of Ideas more fully. In a story called the Allegory of the Cave, Plato sees ordinary and unenlightened people as prisoners in a dark cave where they mistake shadows for reality, opinion for knowledge. Ordinary people, according to Plato, lacked not only knowledge but they also lacked discipline, and virtue. To solve this problem, he outlined a rigorous educational system which would educate everyone as far as they were able to progress. In this limited sense he was democratic, for anyone with ability could become a Philosopher-King. The best and the brightest would become rulers and to prevent selfishness, would own no property and have wives and children in common. Those who were less intellectually inclined but had strength and courage would become the soldiers. The third class would be the merchants and ordinary workers. For Plato, justice existed if each class performed their proper function.

Many have criticized Plato's ideal society, even his famous pupil Aristotle (384-322BC). Aristotle believed that no society could guarantee that such perfectly wise rulers as the Philosopher-Kings could actually be found or developed. Later in life Plato himself abandoned the idealism of *The Republic* and proposed a more practical but still controversial system in his dialogues *The Laws* and *The Statesman*. Aristotle also questioned Plato's communal nature of wives, children and property of the rulers. According to Aristotle, that which is held in common is not cared for properly and will not develop fully or be used to best advantage.

Others took Plato to task for other reasons. Many pointed out that Plato could not prove that eternal Forms really existed or how they related to the material world. Some questioned his belief that any educational system could prevent the Philosopher-Kings from ruling in their own interest. If he could nor ensure this, his political system could turn into a corrupt dictatorship.

Plato's contributions to political knowledge are, nevertheless, immense. Immense, not because it could work as he proposed, but because, for Plato, political power is justified or made morally legitimate by wisdom and virtue, not by tradition, myth or mere military might. Plato's other main contribution was his belief in equality of opportunity. He argued that for the best to rule and for society to be organized on the basis of ability, all children must have an education regardless of sex or class, to develop their potential to the fullest.

Though he was critical of some of Plato's ideas, Aristotle's theory of government was greatly influenced by his teacher. He agreed with Plato that the purpose of government was to promote human happiness.[5] Happiness, for Aristotle, required the development of moral and intellectual virtue in all to the degree each was capable. But unlike Plato, Aristotle developed his theory not just through philosophical reflection but with the help of his empirical studies of actual states. He also agreed with Plato that rule by an aristocracy of the wise and virtuous was best in theory but in practice, it was difficult to find.

Aristotle called the best workable state "polity." This was a state which avoided the extremes of oligarchy and democracy. In an oligarchy, the rich rule, in a democracy the poor rule. He believed the rich were too preoccupied with wealth and the poor were too ignorant and preoccupied by greed. Aristotle argued for a kind of limited democracy where political rule was by a landowning middle class of men. He defined a stable society as one with a large middle class and where the gap between the rich and poor was not great.

Aristotle's polity would be a stable state where revolutions were unlikely. Based on his studies of history, Aristotle believed that the main cause of political revolutions was the desire for equality on the part of the poor and powerless. In addition to preventing a great gap between the rich and the poor, Aristotle saw the need for treating citizens fairly and according to the law. This means that bribery of politicians and judges must be prevented. He also saw the usefulness of reminding the citizenry that there were external enemy states who would exploit any sign of social conflict.

Aristotle's theory has continued to be highly influential. His critics point out that he accepted slavery and believed women were intellectually inferior. Others note his rejection of democracy by denying the poor a role in running the state.

Aristotle's contributions, however, were significant according to most scholars. He is credited with understanding the importance of an educated and virtuous citizenry and the rule of law. The rule of law and a written constitution is better than the rule of men who tend to judge with emotion when they lack the guidance of law which is based on reason. Aristotle is also praised for developing the idea of the separation of powers. That is, he argued that the efficient government would be divided into three branches, the legislature which makes the laws, the executive which enforces the laws and the judiciary which determines if the laws have been violated.

The Athenian experiment in democracy did not last long. Tyrannical monarchies were the general reality and ruled Europe and the world. In Europe, Christianity, once persecuted by the Roman Empire, was legalized in the fourth century by Emperor Constantine. As the Roman Empire declined in power, the church grew in number and strength. Some church leaders argued that since salvation was the most important goal and one which the church provided, the church was therefore superior to any king. Others argued for the theory of the Divine Right of Kings. This theory held that kings ruled by God's will directly not by the permission of the church. This debate was resolved for a time by the great medieval thinker Thomas Aquinas (1225-1274).

One of Aquinas' major contributions was his conception of law.[6] He defined law as "An ordinance of reason for the common good, promulgated by him who has care of a community." He went on to explain that there were four kinds of law, eternal, divine, natural and human. Eternal law is the law of God's mind and unknown to us directly. Divine law is God's law as revealed in the Bible and Church teachings. Natural law is the moral law which is knowable by human reason. An human law is man-made law derived from the natural law and designed to govern the daily life of persons in society.

Aquinas, following Aristotle, sees government as natural and necessary. It exists to promote the common good, human virtue and preserve peace and order in society. Aquinas rejects democracy because, to him, it means rule by the ignorant and morally mediocre masses. He prefers a good monarchy because it allows for greater social unity. The state has authority within its realm and over those who are not Christian. But the Church has final authority as concerns matter of salvation and the natural law over the faithful. For Aquinas, no king has the right to violate the natural law or block the road to salvation, which is the ultimate goal for all persons. The Church has supremacy only over those matters that pertain to salvation.

The power of the Church declined after its height at the time of Aquinas. The Renaissance, Protestant Reformation, the growth of nationalism and the scientific revolution tended to separate church and state and strengthen the political state.

Machiavelli

The Renaissance Italian political theorist Niccolo Machiavelli (1469-1527) is considered by many to be the first political theorist to separate politics from religion and ethics. He studied the way politics is actually carried out in the real world, not the way morality or religion said it should be carried out. Machiavelli wrote about how rulers actually keep their power and manipulate the masses to keep it.

At one point in his famous work, *The Prince*, Machiavelli asks a crucial question: 'Is it better for a ruler to be loved or feared?'[7] His answer is, both, if possible, but since this is difficult, it is better to be feared. Fear is preferable for Machiavelli because, when others fear us, we control them, when they love us, we must act as they wish to continue to be loved. Though love is not necessary, hatred must also be avoided because it could cause a revolution.

To prevent hatred, the ruler should rather kill a loved one than confiscate property. Machiavelli believed that people get over the loss of a loved one sooner than the loss of property. The prince must also appear virtuous, mild, and religious, but in secret he should be as immoral and deceitful as necessary to keep power. He himself should give honors and favors, but let others do the dirty work of criticism and punishment. He should always appear in a positive light and engage in projects that amaze the public but not tax them more than they can bear. To control the people, he should practice 'divide and conquer' and sow discord among various groups when necessary to keep the attention on himself.

The prince should be like a fox and a lion. He must be cunning and strong and make alliances and promises when necessary but break them when needed. What Machiavelli describes, now referred to as Realpolitik, is, of course, an accurate description of much of past and present politics. It is a sober warning about the corruptibility of power and the consequences of human weakness.

Machiavelli's prince describes how a king must behave to keep and expand power. In his book *The Discourses*, Machiavelli presents his ideas for a better political system modeled in part on the ancient republic of Rome. Here he defends the idea that a republic not an inherited monarchy is the best form of government. This republic would be a blend of democracy, monarchy, and aristocracy. It is a form of government which protects the general welfare through good laws, a good leader and by developing the proper virtues in the people. Though he was critical of Christian morality because of its emphasis on humility and other-worldliness, Machiavelli believes in the social power of religion to unify society and limit selfishness. Like Aristotle, he also warns about the dangers of a large gap between the rich and poor as destabilizing society.

Many scholars believe *The Discourses* of Machiavelli is superior in that it does not separate ethics and politics as he did in *The Prince*. He did, however, argue that the leader can violate ordinary morality for reasons of state or the common welfare. Other criticisms of *The Prince* include the characterization of human nature as purely egoistic and selfish ignoring the role of social conditions in shaping human behavior.

Hobbes

One philosopher who shared Machiavelli's view of human nature was the British thinker Thomas Hobbes (1588-1679). His great work, *The Leviathan* (1651) was written during a time of social and political upheaval. His approach to political philosophy was shaped by the emerging scientific and naturalistic worldview. Hobbes saw human nature as motivated by two basic drives, desire and fear. What we desire we call 'good' and what we fear we call 'evil'. Happiness consists in simply fulfilling as many desires as possible. The more power we have the more of our desires we can fulfill. Therefore, according to Hobbes, self-interest and the desire for power are the underlying motives for all that human beings do.

Given Hobbes' view of mankind as basically egotistical and power hungry, the state of war is the natural condition. The "state of nature" is what Hobbes calls the condition of humanity without the common authority of political institutions. In such a state, there is no morality or justice but a war of every man against every man. Security and civilization was impossible and the life of man was "solitary, poor, nasty, brutish and short"[8]

The state of nature and war is not conducive to survival or happiness. It is a condition ruled by what Hobbes calls the "law of nature." The law of nature is not a set of divine rules but simply a set of rules discovered by human reason that promotes self-preservation. This law gives all persons the right to do whatever benefits their survival. It is this law of nature which moves humanity to escape the state of nature and form political authority as the only means for security.

For Hobbes, the only way out of the state of nature is to create a common political power through a social contract. A contract is an act consisting of a mutual transfer of rights.

This social contract occurs when all persons "confer all their power and strength upon one man or assembly of men."[9] This transfer of power creates the leviathan, the government. This political power is according to Hobbes, without limit.

Hobbes gives an interesting defense of why his leviathan is without limit in power. The only way to limit power is, according to Hobbes, by a social contract. But he argues that the state cannot make a contract with the people for the following reasons. He claims that before the social contract, the people are not unified therefore cannot make a contract with anyone. After the contract is made and political power exists, no contract can exist between the people and the leviathan for there is no one to decide when the contract has been violated or to compel the leviathan to keep his contract. As such, for Hobbes, the sovereign cannot be accused of injustice since only the contract defines justice and the sovereign is not party to any contract. Hobbes has thus outlined a totalitarian state, a state that has total or absolute power. This power was to dominate over all churches and questions of religion as well.

Hobbes' theory of politics is admired more for his method than his conclusions. He is credited with being one of the first political scientists in following a systematic methodology of definitions and conclusions from basic premises. Hobbes defined a model of the totalitarian and absolutist state and the implications of such a model. However, most political theorists consider his model instructive for what must be avoided.

Many criticisms of Hobbes have been suggested throughout history. Many point out that his theory of human nature is one-sided stressing selfish and power hungry elements but ignoring other dimensions. He stressed egoism and the need for security but neglected the power of compassion, love and the desire for freedom.

Other critics have noted an apparently contradictory aspect of Hobbes' theory. His defense of the absolute power of state without contract with the people recreates in a more stark manner the state of nature and the state of war between the people and the state. Hobbes, in attempting to escape the state of nature created a more unequal and harsher state of nature.

Hobbes' idea of a social contract as transferring all rights to the state (except the right to self-preservation) is seen as no contract at all. What the contract really is according to critics is a defense of the idea that might makes right. Might makes right is another name for a state of war.

Hobbes' theory seems to assume that social order comes only from political power. On the contrary, it seems clear to many social scientists that social order also comes from the pre-existing morality and other social institutions. Perhaps the environment of social, religious and political chaos in which Hobbes lived helps explain much of his political theory.

Locke

The British philosopher John Locke (1632-1704) was one of the first modern thinkers to resurrect the democratic idea.[10] Locke's democracy was in some ways also the culmination of many political developments in England. The Magna Carta in 1215 in England limited the rights of the king and provided for the right of trial by a jury of one's peers. Later developments in England further limited the power of the king by strengthening the power of Parliament.

In order to defend democracy, Locke first had to discredit the prevailing theory, the "divine right of kings." This theory maintained that kings rule by the right bestowed on them by God. Locke claimed in his *First Treatise of Government* that no such a right could be proved. Even if such a right were originally given to Adam, there is no way to prove, according to Locke, that the current king was the result of an unbroken and continual succession from the time of Adam. Having refuted this theory to his satisfaction, Locke goes on to defend a democratic theory of government in his *Second Treatise of Government*. In place of an inherited monarchy he proposed the social contract theory as the proper basis of political power. Though the term reminds one of Hobbes, Locke's theory is dramatically different.

Locke, like Hobbes, also starts from the idea of a "state of nature." The state of nature is a state without government and one of equality and freedom. It is also a state with a Natural Law or a moral law which holds that each person has certain moral rights, namely life, liberty and property. Though persons have these rights, their enjoyment of these rights is uncertain. It is uncertain because the state of nature lacks the three essential powers of government. These powers are a specific written law, an impartial judge to decide cases of conflict and a power to enforce the decisions of the courts and promote social order and peace. The only way people in the state of nature can protect their rights is to form a government.

People in the state of nature form a government to protect their rights through the social contract. The contract requires that all persons agree to form a system of political authority to defend their rights. They also agree that once government is formed, majority rule will decide matters of law. According to Locke, this consent to form a government was explicit and unanimous. Those who come after this original contract, are obligated to obey by what Locke calls "implicit" consent. Consent is implicit if one resides in a state and receives benefits from it.

The government Locke defends is one where there is a separation of powers. Separation of powers exists to prevent the likelihood of concentrating power in too few hands where the possibility of abuse is greater. Locke outlines three distinct branches of government. The first and supreme power lies in the legislature which makes the laws. The courts judge whether a law has been violated and what punishment is appropriate. The executive carries out the decisions of the legislature and the courts. The federative power deals with foreign nations and matters of foreign policy and is usually in the hands of the executive. Locke also specifies that there must be separation of church and state with each having its own sphere of power.

Since, according to Locke, the political system exists to protect the rights of the people, the people have the right to revolution. The people exercise this right when the government no longer protects their rights and rules in its own interest, not the general interest of the people.

Though Locke's theory has been greatly influential, it also has its critics. Some point out that his list of rights as consisting in life, liberty and property problematic in some respects. Locke saw these rights, which are now called negative rights, as rights which require that persons not be interfered with. Positive rights, such as the right to welfare or an education, are rights which require the community to provide resources that meet some need of individuals. Can democracy exist without an educated populace? In a post-industrial society where knowledge plays such a pivotal role, what would the absence of a free education mean?

Other theorists are troubled by some aspects of Locke's contract. There seems to be no historical record of an actual social contract. Furthermore, Locke's idea of implicit consent as a kind of a contract is troubling to many. Does simply receiving benefits obligate one to the state? How can one fail to receive some benefits from even the most corrupt state?

Many critics have also found fault with Locke's defense of property. Locke argued that private property is a moral right based on labor. Land which is previously unowned becomes one's own by working on it and improving its value. However, there are limits to this acquisition. One must not take more than one needs and there must be enough and as good left for others.

This initial limit on private property, however, Locke believes is nullified with the invention of money. Money allows great accumulation of wealth and property. Locke argues that the use of money implies consent to this great inequality of property. Many have found this part of Locke's theory morally and logically suspect. Does using money imply consent to the inequality of property as Locke claimed? Do we have a real choice about using money in a money economy?

Nevertheless, Locke's contributions to the idea of democracy are many. His revolutionary idea that human beings are equal in having the rights to life, liberty and property established the moral basis of democratic government. This equality is not one of intelligence or strength or beauty, but a moral equality which holds that all persons have a right to live their life as they see fit as long as others are given the same right. Locke opposed the idea that might makes right and maintained that right is defined by the free and informed agreement among equal citizens. His ideas of the rule of law and majority rule have become basic to any democratic government. He realized that rulers are human and morally limited and so must be kept from ruling in their own interest. Democracy is a result of a realistic look upon the moral and intellectual limitations of persons and how we can best organize our society without falling victim to the corrupting temptations of power. These ideas have become the core of the democratic ideal. It is an idea which continues to revolutionize societies in our own time.

Mill
Although democracy is widely considered to be a superior form of government, it also has its critics. One problem addressed by the British thinker John Stuart Mill (1806-1873) is what he called the "tyranny of the majority."[11] Since democracy means majority rule, there is the possibility that the rights of the minority may be violated. Mill proposed that the rights of the individual and minorities must be protected if social welfare, progress and happiness is to be protected.

There are three basic rights, according to Mill, which promote happiness and social progress. These rights are the rights of conscience or free speech, the right of individuality or lifestyle and the right of assembly or association.

The basis of Mill's rights and political philosophy in general is his moral theory called utilitarianism. This theory is based on the idea that the desire for happiness is the foundation for everything we do and are. The theory is based on the principle of utility which holds that all persons must act so as to maximize happiness for all involved in that action. The question then is, how do we organize our political system to maximize happiness and minimize suffering?

The answer, for Mill, is expressed by the three basic liberties. The first right, the right to free speech, Mill defends with several reasons. First, Mill takes it is a fact that people have a need and desire to express their ideas and communicate with others. We are social creatures and communication is the glue of any social unit. Free speech also promotes the growth of knowledge; how can knowledge grow if people are afraid to propose new ideas and discuss them freely? At one time every idea we accept as true and good was opposed including the abolition of slavery, the equality of women and that the earth is round. If Galileo who proposed the heliocentric view of the universe, (sun as the center, not the earth) was completely suppressed, how would our understanding of the world grow? Knowledge, in turn, promotes human happiness by reducing disease, curing illness, promoting time-saving technology and generally expanding human opportunities for a better life.

Mill understood that not all new ideas will be right or valid. But it is only through open discussion that the truth can be discovered. Finally, free speech is also necessary to preserve democratic government for it allows us to criticize our political leaders and make them more accountable to the citizens. Mill's second basic liberty, the freedom of individuality or life style, is grounded on several generally accepted facts. First, we are all different in our personalities and needs; human beings are the most diverse species on earth. Diversity is good because it allows us to adapt to more kinds of environments, see things from different points of view and come up with more varied ideas. We need to express our selves if we are to be happy. By expressing ourself, we offer different possibilities for living which increases individual choices and ways to live. Of course, not all of these ways of living will turn out good, but life for Mill is a series of experiments, some which make and some don't. For him, there is no other way progress can occur in the science of life.

The third liberty, the liberty to associate with whomever we wish, is implied, Mill claimed, by the freedom of individuality. The freedom to associate and organize with whomever we wish is an expression of our personality, goals, interest, beliefs and values. Developing clubs, corporations, political parties and the like are ways of achieving our plans and expressing our way of life. Without this right all changes would have to be made by individuals alone, a very tall order.

However, these three freedoms are not absolute. Mill argues that the Harm Principle must be our guide in determining the extent of our freedoms and what laws we make. That is, we should outlaw only those acts which harm others, no those that harm the self. If some action harms only the well informed rational adult who is doing it, then it must be allowed. To restrict the liberty of a rational adult who may harm himself is according to Mill to assume we know more about his or her life than they do and to impose our value system on that person. Your life is more important to you than to anyone else, you have a right to live it as you see fit as long as you do not harm others.

Mills' theory of individual liberty is a development and defense of ideas articulated by Locke and others. Though Mill is credited by many for defending individualism, some questions still persist.   Some critics question whether the utilitarian theory can securely defend individual rights. Some claim that utilitarianism allows in principle the violation of individual rights for social benefits. Conservative theorists believe Mill overestimated the rationality of individuals. They claim most people are not sufficiently rational and if given freedom will abuse it. There are also some problems with the definition of 'harm'.

Marxism

At the time when Mill was developing his defense of democracy, another defense of a different kind of society was being formulated by Karl Marx. Marx, (1818-1883) developed radial philosophical critique of society and democracy that revolutionized history. His analysis of society starts with his understanding of reality and history.[12]

Marx's metaphysics or theory of reality is a form of materialism. That is, he believed reality was basically material and rejected all belief in religion and God. Borrowing some ideas from Ludwig Feuerbach (1804-1872), Marx claimed religion was the "opium of the masses."[13] For Marx, religion was a kind of drug used to pacify the suffering masses by promising them a better after life. Religion was simply an illusory projection of human needs and wishful thinking. 'God' is simply an expression of what humans want to be themselves. Saying 'God is love' is a way of saying we need to be loved, saying 'God is immortal' is a way os saying we want to be immortal. In essence, according to Marx, religion exists because of human limitations and human suffering. The belief in an after life is simply a way of promising humanity things they cannot get in this life. In this way religion is used by the ruling class, the rich, to control the masses by telling them that this life is not important and that God will make everything right in the next life.

What is history? What difference is there between the society Socrates lived in and our life? The difference is not in biology since Socrates and we have the same biological nature. History is the record of change in how we live, work and organize our social existence. But what causes this change? Marx's answer is that human beings seek to satisfy their needs by increasing their knowledge, developing technology and changing their economic system. However, although we all seek to improve our lives, there seems to be a scarcity of the goods we all want. This leads to what Marx called the "class struggle."

The class struggle is the conflict between the few powerful rich and the many poor. The rich own the resources such as land and technology, and the vast majority who own little or nothing. Government, he went on to argue, has throughout history served the interest of the rich although pretending to be concerned for the general welfare. It is this class struggle and technology that makes history according to Marx.

Marx focused his attention on the economic system he knew best, capitalism. Capitalism is an economic system that, depending on one's definition, has ancient roots. It was defended by Adam Smith (1723-1790) and others who defined it as a system based on the private ownership of the means of production (factories, corporations, land and natural resources) and the free market.[14] The free market means that production of goods and services is not determined by the government but are produced to meet the needs of the consumer and provide profit for the owners with prices set by the law of supply and demand. (High demand and low supply raises prices, high supply and low demand, lowers prices.) Prices are kept down by competition among different companies seeking more customers.

The Industrial Revolution, like the agricultural revolution before it, transformed society, capitalism and history. Starting in the later part of the 1700's in England, the Industrial Revolution, with its new technology, new sources of energy led to the development of factories for the first time in history. Factories were privately owned and worked by ever larger army of workers or wage laborers who had nothing to sell except their labor. Marx saw that industrial capitalism, although extremely dynamic and productive in terms of the quantity and variety of goods produced, was inhumane and unfair to the workers or the proletariat as he called them. The capitalists, or bourgeoisie, in fact, Marx argued, control the government and society of even apparently democratic systems which ruled and passed laws in favor of the rich.

Although Marx granted that capitalism was a productive system, it also had certain serious flaws, weaknesses or contradictions. Adam Smith, for example, defended factory production on the basis of the division of labor- where a complex task such as making a pin is broken down into thousand of simple tasks each done by a different person. Smith saw this as efficient because it allowed quick training and replacement of workers and reduced mistakes. This was one of the flaws of the system which Marx called "alienation."

The repetitive and mindless work of the assembly line is alienating for Marx because it does not promote the development of the mind and spirit of the workers. Alienation was the condition of workers (including children) who worked long hours in conditions which were unhealthy, unsafe and monotonous denying them the opportunity to develop their full human potential or their "species being."

Secondly, capitalism was an unstable system which suffered from various recessions and depressions putting vast numbers out of work. Thirdly, capitalism lead to the 'polarization' of society or ever greater class divisions with the rich getting richer and the poor, poorer.

Finally low wages and constant fear of unemployment resulted in what Marx called 'exploitation' the systematic cheating of workers of a fair wage. Marx believed that profit really belongs to the workers but is taken by the capitalists.

Marx believed that capitalism would eventually destroy itself due to these built in conflicts or contradictions. He foresaw economic depressions becoming so severe that workers would revolt under the guidance of the Communist Party and establish the "dictatorship of the proletariat" or a socialism run by the workers.

Socialism was Marx's answer as the next stage of what he believed was a true democracy. It was a true and full democracy because he saw it as expanding the democratic idea into the economic realm where workers would participate in the running of their factories and set policy and conditions. Private ownership of the means of production (factories, corporation, land) would no longer be possible although personal property would still exist. Workers would have a greater opportunity to express themselves at work and develop new ways of organizing labor that would allow them to overcome alienation. Although wages would not be exactly equal at this first phase of the revolution because different income would still be necessary to motivate people to accept responsibility and additional training, they would be far more equal than they were under capitalism.

Eventually, Marx envisioned a future society beyond socialism. This society called communism, would be more equal and alienation would no longer exist. Unfortunately, Marx did not say much about this future utopian society.

A form of Marx's theory was tried in the Soviet Union and elsewhere to some degree. Lenin headed the Communist Party which finally overthrew the Russian czar in 1917 and established a kind of socialism. We know that this version was not economically productive and generally did not work well. In practice Marx's theory became not a democracy of the workers as he wanted but a dictatorship of the Communist Party.

Critics point out that the Soviet experience indicates the dangers of the concentration of power in government. The old saying that 'power corrupts and absolute power corrupts absolutely' has been proven correct many times and the Soviet experiment is no exception. Without an independent press or communication media and competition for political power, it is impossible to keep people in power honest and responsible. Critics also point to the need for competition in economic efficiency, monopolies or single producers have no incentive to produce quality products at a reasonable price. Others have claimed that Marx did not establish that atheism is in fact true nor that history moves in predictable laws. He is also accused of underestimating the adaptability of capitalism to meet new challenges. Contemporary capitalism is far different and, most agree, far more humane, than the capitalism he knew.

Though Marx's theory has been criticized by many, others today like Jurgen Habermas, William McBride, Carol Gould and Milton Fisk still defend some version of it. Marx's basic insight that the essence of power is the control of the means of production makes sense to many. To control the economy is to control the survival and happiness of the people. This is why Marxists believe that there can be no true democracy as long as a minority control the means of production.

Many supporters of Marx accept his idea of species being a proper ideal for which to strive. His denunciation of political corruption and control of the political system by the wealthy is echoed by many today who seek reform of campaign financing. Marx's outspoken criticism of the harsh working conditions of the poor and his demand for the abolition of child labor is praised by many. His demanded that all have access to a free and equally good education regardless of social class is supported by many today.

Marx saw history as dominating and oppressing humanity with two tyrannies, that of nature and of men. The tyranny of nature is the tyranny of poverty and disease. The tyranny of men is the control and oppression of one small class or group of the great majority of the ignorant and powerless. Many find his goal for the elimination of all types of tyranny appealing, the question is how best to overcome these tyrannies.

Fascism

Although Marx's ideas captured the imagination of many, his ideas were opposed vehemently by others. One of the main obstacles to communism was Marx's rejection of nationalism.

To Marx, nationalism was a primitive tribal and ethnocentric way of thinking and living that denied the equality of humanity. It promoted war, racism and even genocide for it taught the superiority of one's own nation and the inferiority of other cultures. Marx believed that nationalism was used by the powerful to 'divide and conquer' the masses and so better use and control them. However, according to fascism, he overlooked man's need for identity and the need to belong to a group. This need was used by men like Hitler and Mussolini to gain power.

This need to uphold traditional national beliefs and values found expression in the political theory of fascism. It is not a monolithic ideology but one which borrows ideas from may sources, including Machiavelli, Hobbes, Nietzsche (1844-1900), Johann Fichte, and Giovanni Gentile among others.[15] Fascist theory combines nationalism, totalitarianism, and the belief the individual as less important than the traditional cultural ideas which give the individual identity and meaning. In place of the equality and individualism of democratic theory, it uses the organic metaphor of each person playing different roles in the nation as a living being. Fascism glorifies the leader and war as necessary to keep a country strong and for the spreading of its cultural values.

Though fascism has few defenders today, the power of nationalism is still a reality. It was, of course, this ideology which eventually resulted in aggression and the start of World War II. The brutality which comes from the glorification of war, genocide and destruction resulting from fascism was sufficient for most to reject this view of political authority.

Libertarianism

Contemporary political philosophy continues to debate the issues raised by Plato, Marx and others. Some like the contemporary Harvard philosopher Robert Nozick and other libertarians value human liberty above all. They want a very limited government because they believe history shows that powerful governments will lead to the dictatorships like those of Hitler and Stalin. Libertarianism has its roots in anarchism, the rejection of all government as evil because it restricts human liberty.

Nozick defends what he calls the "entitlement theory of justice."[16] This view holds that persons have the right o accumulate, own and dispose of their wealth as they see fit as long as it was not acquired through violence or fraud but in a free market transaction. They do not see it as unjust that a basketball star earns millions while others earn far less. The sport star earns more because he provides what more people are willing to pay for.

Libertarians reject the welfare state. The welfare state now common in the USA and Europe provides many services such as education, unemployment insurance, welfare payments, medicare, social security and the like through general tax revenue. The libertarians see these taxes as government stealing money from the wealthy and giving it to others. They see this as violating their rights of property and liberty. They believe individual liberty is the supreme value and government should simply protect our liberties against criminals and foreign attack, leaving everything else to the personal free decisions of individuals and private organizations.

Libertarians also reject the government's enforcement of moral beliefs beyond that of the right to liberty. They favor legalizing many drugs now illegal, homosexuality, prostitution, gambling, pornography and other now generally forbidden activities. To some, this is enough to discredit the theory. Others believe that a society without even free elementary education, social security or unemployment insurance, will divide into two extreme camps of wealth and poverty. Philosophers like James Sterba believe the libertarian philosophy is inconsistent. He claims that although the libertarian philosophy is based on the ideal of liberty, it restricts the liberty of the poor to take from the luxury goods of the rich what the poor need for survival. Aristotle believed a society divided into the rich and poor would lead to crime and revolution.

The entitlement theory has also been questioned on many levels.[17] Some find the political superstructure of libertarianism lacks an adequate moral theory. The idea of natural rights defended by most libertarians is rejected by utilitarians and others. Some question whether liberty alone is a sufficient moral basis for a society. Most human beings also desire security and some form of equality.

Other critics see the theory of liberty of the libertarians as negative liberty. Negative liberty is the liberty of being free from the interference of others including government. However, the critics point out that this overlooks the necessary conditions for the development and use of negative liberty. Without the positive liberty to an education, what sort of liberty can one exercise? Can a community that shares only the idea of liberty function as a community?

Libertarianism is also taken to task for ignoring the role of great injustices of the past. History shows that slavery, racism, sexism and outright criminality contributed to the present distribution of wealth. If so much wealth and property has been accumulated with force, fraud and threats, then, the critics urge, we must abandon the theory which is oblivious to these glaring facts of history and contemporary life.

What kind of society would libertarianism produce? Can a society that denies even a free minimum education avoid the radical inequality of power and wealth that would corrupt even the minimal government of the libertarians? If this happens, and given the moral weaknesses of human beings in and out of power, what is to stop the government to rule in their own interest and the interest of the rich? Liberty without some level of equality of opportunity and power will, the critics claim, lead only to the greater violation of liberty.

Finally, many social scientists and historians see changes in the size and nature of government as a responses to different problems. For example, the great expansion of governmental services and role in the economy under President F.D. Roosevelt, was a response to the great depression and the social problems it evoked. In addition, changes in the institution of the family have necessitated that government take up many of the traditional roles of the family. Here, support of the aged through social security which, in agrarian times of the extended family, was done within the family comes readily to mind. Add to this the apparent fact that the movement of history is towards ever greater complexity and interdependence, both nationally and globally. As the complexity of society from new technology and a global economy increase and create greater problems such as environmental pollution, a larger government, and finally a world government, will be necessary according to many theorists.

Welfare Liberalism

Many of the above criticisms of libertarianism come from theorists who defend what is known as welfare liberalism. Philosophers like the contemporary John Rawls believe that government should provide for greater equality. Traditional democratic liberalism of John Locke sought to protect individuals from an all-powerful government by arguing for a limited government and individual rights such as the right to life, liberty, property, speech, religion and the like.

Contemporary liberals like Rawls accept the need for a democratic government but seek to expand individual freedom by eliminating or reducing social conditions such as poverty that restrict the liberties and opportunities of many. To nullify the effects of unequal social conditions, welfare liberals feel the government should provide services such as a free education and payments such as unemployment benefits to lessen the harsh effects of poverty on the struggling middle and lower classes. To eliminate a sexist society and give women equal opportunity for education and professional development, welfare liberals want to provide government financed day care for children of the disadvantaged. How does Rawls justify this theory?

For Rawls, the first question for political theory is to specify what conditions are right for deciding this question about the role and nature of government. That is, making this decision with a gun pointed at our heads would not be the right way to make such a decision. What would? His answer is what he calls "the Original Position."[18] This is an imaginary situation which includes the "Veil of Ignorance." This imaginary veil is necessary, Rawls argues, because, following his interpretation of the ethics of Immanuel Kant, it excludes information which is not morally relevant or is a product of factors that are unjust. For example, the fact that one may be rich is excluded, for how we became rich may not be moral; we exclude knowledge of our sex because sex is not relevant for determining rights. This information must be disregarded because knowing these facts would bias us selfishly in our decision about the basic structure or form of government. Information excluded involves our sex, social class, race, religion, intelligence, jobs, education, personality and all things that distinguish us from each other. All that is left is the Kantian idea of the "noumenal self" the self as it is in its pure form without the influences of the society one is born into. This is the self which includes our awareness and our rationality. Rawls adds to this his understanding of human nature with our general needs for what he calls "primary goods," life, survival, liberty, self esteem, material goods provided by income of some kind. If this is all we knew about ourselves, what kind of government would we choose?

Rawls' answer is welfare liberalism, an attempt to blend the central values of democracy, liberty and equality. Rawls believes we would agree to two principles of justice. The first principle states: "Each person is to have an equal right to the most extensive basic liberty compatible with a similar liberty for others." The second principle requires: "social and economic inequalities are to be arranged so that they are both a) reasonably expected to be to everyone's advantage, and b) attached to positions and offices open to all."[19] The first part of the second principle is called the "Difference Principle" and it requires that all inequality in economic matters benefit all members of society especially the least-advantaged or the poorest class. That is, Rawls allows for different incomes and social positions as long as the inequality benefits society in general. For example, Rawls would allow that brain surgeons make more money than bus drivers because we need monetary incentives for people to enter professions that require a high degree of education and skill.

The second part of the second principle requires what Rawls calls "fair equality of opportunity."[20] Fair equality of opportunity requires not only that there are no legal obstacles for any position in society but it would provide for equal staring social conditions for all. Rawls believes that we should all have equal chance to achieve any position in society regardless of who are parents were, what our social class, sex, religion and ethnic background happens to be. No matter whether we were born into a family of millionaire Ph.Ds or alcoholic, single high school drop out mother, we should have an equal shot to become brain surgeons, physicists or whatever our heart desired and effort and ability allowed.

Rawls is here addressing an issue that concerned Marx, the fact that people born into different socioeconomic classes have greatly different opportunities in life. Those born into rich families go the best private schools, meet the most powerful people and have the best medical care; the rest do not. Government would have to make sure that people have such equal opportunity by combating racism and sexism, providing equally good education, health care, unemployment insurance, social security and other services intended to prevent great social inequality in income, opportunity and wealth. This means a large role for government and extensive taxation but within a free market economy.

Critics of Rawls come from the political right and left.[21] Those on the right feel he overemphasizes equality and puts too much power in the hands of government. Libertarians believe he has reduced liberty too greatly and allowed for the violation of the right to property by allowing taxes of the rich to help the poor. His supporters argue that any other system will increase social divisions and conflicts caused by the growing gap between the rich and poor.

Critics of Rawls from the left believe he has allowed too much inequality. Socialists believe that capitalism allows too much power in the hands of the capitalists. They believe that a capitalists society would allow capitalists to continue to control government for their interests. Others point out that the increased complexity and interdependence of the economy, technology and life itself with its greater impact on the environment, seems to call for a greater role in government to coordinate, monitor events and plan for the future.

Still other critics called communitarians offer additional challenges to Rawls. Communitarianism is by no means a unified theory but rather offers criticisms where it feels liberalism and libertarianism fail. Communitarians like Michael Sandel and Alasdair MacIntyre believe that liberal philosophers like Rawls place too much emphasis on individual rights and not enough on the role of the community and individual responsibility.[22] They object to what they see as Rawls' attempt to step outside of history and culture in formulating his model of the 'self' in the Original Position as misleading and, in the end, an impossibility. Without a sense of belonging to a community with a common good, individuals will not have the desire to participate in political processes. Rawls' new work, *Political Liberalism* attempts to address some of these issues.[23]

Feminism raises some additional concerns for theories like that of Rawls and Nozick. Feminist philosophers like Carol Gilligan claim traditional liberal theorists place too much emphasis on abstract principles and not enough on the value of caring.[24] An approach from the perspective of care is more typical of women than men according to Gilligan. Without a value of caring and compassion, persons will lack the motivation to be moved to action on matters of justice. Feminists believe a theoretical model which encompasses the perspectives of care as well as abstract principle will be a more complete approach to matters of political philosophy.

The history of political philosophy presents a complex and diverse set of theories. All theories of political systems see the need for government to control a geographic area through a monopoly of power, to formulate and enforce laws necessary for social order, to resolve conflicts and provide other services. These common social needs and goals can be accomplished by different governmental structures depending on other variables, belief systems and circumstances.

The diversity of political theory is in part explained by the fact that no theory develops in a vacuum. All theory formation take place and is embedded in various kinds of conceptual frameworks and historical circumstances. One central element of a conceptual framework is the epistemology or theory of knowledge it assumes. A theory of knowledge will determine what is knowable in the area of political theory and what is not. The epistemology of Plato was very different from the epistemology of Rawls and it surely, in part, explains the very different theories they developed.

Ones epistemology will also greatly influence the nature of the belief system which serves as an overall theory of reality or metaphysics. Metaphysics deals with determining what is ultimately real. For example, Plato had his Forms or Ideas, Aquinas his God, Marx his materialism and others had other worldviews. These worldviews influenced and informed their respective political theories in many ways.

In addition to metaphysics, conceptions of human nature play a central role in political theory. Is human nature rational or emotional, good or evil, social or egocentric? If emotional and evil, then perhaps as Hobbes argued, a more authoritarian government would be justified. Are we creations of a divine being or a blind evolution? Are persons defined by biology or shaped by the environment? Are human beings plastic and greatly influenced by environment or not? Do we have free will or is determinism true? Are we material beings or made up of a body and a soul? Are men and women different due to nature or nurture?

In all theory formation which deal with practical normative dimensions of society, moral theory will play a defining role. If one's moral ideal is liberty, certain political consequences will follow. If the ideal is equality, other implications will flow. The degree and scope of moral and religious pluralism and diversity will also contribute to the structure and functions of political systems.

All these conceptual elements are created and take shape within certain social and historical circumstances.   To various degrees these circumstances impinge and influence theory formation. In times of social instability, for example, as Hobbes experienced, a totalitarian government may be seen as necessary. In agrarian societies, land will play a pivotal role, in industrial and post-industrial societies, knowledge becomes paramount.

The nature and social role of other social institutions will also impact political theory. The major social institutions, in addition to government, are usually said to include the family, the economy, religion and the educational system.   In times where the institution of the family has evolved from extended to nuclear form, some functions of the family, such as economic security, may shift to the state or other institutions. In a complex knowledge based economy, education can no longer take place solely in the home but require advanced and extensive educational institutions.

Political philosophers continue to debate many of the issues that concern the nature of power in the evolving social system. However, one thing that seems fairly clear is that we increasingly live in a post-industrial age or the information age where knowledge is central. Scientific and other types of knowledge is said to double every five years. He who controls the educational system and the flow of information controls the minds of the population.

We also live in a dynamic and pluralistic multi-cultural society embedded in an even larger pluralistic world. Global issues such as the escalating conflicts between the wealthy developed countries and the poverty of the third world will undoubtedly increase. Pollution of the environment, global warming, rampant growth in population, proliferation of nuclear weapons and the continued demands for greater democracy in nondemocratic countries will persist into the future. Growing economic interdependence of the global economy will increase, locking each country's fate to that of others. An expanding and complex economy requires greater coordination and planning. When one adds to this the rise of nationalistic and religious conflicts such as in the former Yugoslavia and Soviet Union, the need for a true world government more effective than the present United Nations to solve our problems seems clear to many.

The world is becoming one global community tied through instantaneous communication. Greater awareness and consciousness of unequal wealth and standard of living give rise to greater expectations that must be addressed. History shows as Aristotle saw over 2,000 years ago and Machiavelli 400 years ago, that great inequality of wealth, power and respect does not lead to harmony or peace but conflict and the oppression of the majority by the minority.

One thing is clear, we are social creatures and cannot escape politics. Whether we like it or not, we live in a society with a certain form of government and certain political institutions. The kind of government we have locally, nationally and globally will determine the kind of life, opportunities, success and happiness we will have.   Our increasing technological society is more complex and requires greater knowledge to make intelligent decisions and keep democracy alive. In the final analysis, Plato was partly right, we must all become wiser, more active and more compassionate if the community of mankind is to live in a flourishing democracy rather than live under a Machiavellian rule that only serves the interests of some.

NOTES

1. See *A Source Book in Indian Philosophy*, edited by S. Radhakrishnan and C. A. Moore, Princeton Univ. Press: Princeton, NJ., 1957.

2. Ibid., pp. 272-300.

3. See Yu-Lan, Fung, *A Short History of Chinese Philosophy*, The Free Press: New York, 1966, pp.38-48.

4. See Plato, *The Republic, The Laws* and *The Statesman*.

5. See Aristotle, *The Politics*.

6. See Aquinas, *Summa Theologica*.

7. See Machiavelli, *The Prince*.

8. See Thomas Hobbes, *The Leviathan*.

9. Hobbes, p. 108, in *Great Traditions in Ethics*, ninth edition edited by T. Denise, et al., Wadsworth: Belmont, CA., 1999.

10. See Locke's *Second Treatise*.

11. See Mill's *On Liberty*.

12. See Marx and Engels' *Communist Manifesto,* and Marx's *Paris Manuscripts*.

13. Marx, Karl, *On The Jewish Question*.

14. See Adam Smith's, *On the Wealth of Nations*.

15. For primary sources on fascism see J. Somerville's

16. See Robert Nozick's *Anarchy, State and Utopia*.

17. For criticisms of Nozick and libertarianism, see *Reading Nozick*, edited by J. Paul, Rowman & Littlefield: Totowa, NJ. 1981.

18. See John Rawls' *A Theory of Justice*, Harvard Univ. Press: Cambridge, MA., 1971.

19. Ibid., p. 60.

20. Ibid., pp. 83-89.

21. For criticisms of Rawls see *Reading Rawls,* edited by Norman Daniels, Basic Books: New York, 1975.

22. See Michael Sandel's *Liberalism and the Limits of Justice* and *Democracy's Discontent;* see Alasdair MacIntyre's *After Virtue*, Univ. of Notre Dame Press: Notre Dame, 1981.

23. See Rawls' *Political Liberalism*, Columbia Univ. Press: New York, 1993.

24. See Carol Gilligan's *In a Different Voice*, Harvard Univ. Press: Cambridge, 1982.

CHAPTER 8

ROUSSEAU AND RAWLS ON THE SOCIAL CONTRACT

John Rawls claims his social contract theory as presented in his *A Theory of Justice* can be considered part of the social contract tradition which includes Locke, Rousseau and Kant.[1] The purpose of this essay is to determine what defines a tradition such as that of the social contract and to evaluate Rawls' claim that he is in the same tradition as Rousseau. At the same time, I analyze the general nature of the contract model and so clarify some of the controversial points in Rawls' and Rousseau's political theories.

In *The Social Contract,*[2] Rousseau characterizes the contract in these terms: "although they (the clauses of the contract) have perhaps never been formally set forth, they are everywhere the same and everywhere tacitly admitted." (14) Rousseau believes these clauses can be reduced to one: "the total alienation of each associate, together with all his rights, to the whole community."(14) Each must alienate all rights since if any right were left to individuals, without a "common superior" to decide between conflicts of individuals and public, the state of nature would ensue and the association dissolve. Each participant, "...in giving himself to all, gives himself to nobody; and as there is no associate over which he does not acquire the same right as he yields others over himself, he gains an equivalent for everything he loses, and an increase of force for the preservation of what he has."(14)

In another definition of the social contract, Rousseau introduces the key concept of the "general will" (volonté generale) (henceforth abbreviated GW). Rousseau states: "Each of us puts his person and all his power in common under the supreme direction of the general will and in our corporate capacity, we receive each member as an indivisible part of the whole."(15)

In his work *The Emile* Rousseau is even more insistent on the radical nature of the alienation demanded by the contract: "As an individual everyone of us contributes his goods, his person, his life, to the common stock under the supreme direction of the general will."[3] The body politic of the sovereign, then, derives its existence only from the contract. The sovereign, being only the aggregate of the individuals, is the supreme power in the society.

Few concepts in the history of political theory have been as controversial as Rousseau's notion of the GW. There is no question, however, that it is the key to understanding Rousseau. According to Rousseau, each individual has a particular will which aims at his particular interests. In the state of nature only the particular will and private interest exist. The GW, which exists only in the political state, aims at the common or general interest. For Rousseau, then, the 'will' is distinguished by its object; the private will tending towards the private interest, the general will at the general object of interest. Sovereignty is nothing else but "the exercise of the GW."(23) Moreover, Rousseau contends that the GW "is always right,"(26) but he does not take this to mean that the majority is always right. Rousseau wants to draw a distinction between the GW and the "will of all," the latter being simply the sum of particular wills.(26) How then is the GW ascertained if not by a majority vote?

Rousseau's answer is as complex as it is elusive. At first he suggests that the GW remains as "sum of the differences" between the particular wills.(26) More specifically, the GW emerges from the deliberation of all the citizens when they have the "adequate information" and if the "citizens had no communication with one another,"(27) i.e., when there are no factions or parties within the state which seeks their own ends rather than the common end. Though Rousseau rejects the view that the GW is simply the aggregate of particular wills, he does believe it can be expressed by a majority will under certain conditions. The majority will is the GW if when the issue is before the national assembly, "the people is asked not exactly whether it approves or rejects the proposal, but whether it is in conformity with the GW, which is their will . . . and the GW is found by counting votes."(106)

If one finds oneself in the minority, then Rousseau believes one must conclude "I was mistaken" about the GW *and* one's own will. In the above quotation Rousseau states the GW "is their will," i.e., the will of the individual; does then each person have two wills, the general and the particular? No, what Rousseau must mean is that the GW is the will of the individual *as citizen,* not as a private individual. Hence if one is in the minority on a given vote, one is in error as to one's interest *as citizen,* though not necessarily as a private person.

Once the contract is completed, the individual parties to it have renounced all rights and possessions to the body politic. For Rousseau, there are in principle no limits to the GW; "the social compact gives the body politic *absolute power* over all its members."(28) If an individual finds oneself in disagreement with the GW, he will be "compelled to do so by the whole body. This means nothing less than that he will be forced to be free."(18) If 'freedom' is construed as the absence of external coercion, then "forcing" someone to be free is a contradiction in terms. But another interpretation of this Rousseauan definition of freedom can make this notorious passage consistent. In the state of nature man enjoyed what Rousseau calls "natural liberty,"(19) i.e., the unlimited right to do anything and have anything instinct suggested without coercion from others. In civil society one loses natural liberty but gains civil or "moral liberty."(19) This is freedom to do what is morally permissible as defined by the GW. Moral liberty "alone makes (man) truly master of himself."(19) Doing what one wants, or natural liberty, is to follow "the mere impulse of appetite (which) is slavery."(19) Moral liberty is desiring to do what one ought to do, not merely want to do, which only "obedience to the law" can reveal as the expression of the GW. Hence Rousseau saw freedom as doing what one ought to do, or being unrestrained from doing what one ought to do; if one erred as to what one's true moral duty was, one could be forced to be free, i.e., forced to do what is really in one's interest, as opposed to doing what is only apparently one's interest.

Rawls believes his principles of justice would be chosen by free, rational, equal and self-interested individuals within a well-defined context which he calls the "Original Position" (henceforth, OP).[4] As in Rousseau, this agreement is not an historical event but a hypothetical construct; it consists in the claim that 'individuals' or persons of the OP (henceforth, POPs) would choose certain principles of justice under properly defined circumstances. These circumstances which define the OP consist of what Rawls takes to be certain rules of rationality, general empirical facts and relevant moral institutions.

The "Veil of Ignorance" expresses some of the conditions that members of the OP are subject to. This fictional veil means POPs are ignorant of: a) their place in society, status or position; b) fortune, natural talents such as intellectual ability or physical strength; c) their particular conception of the good; d) their psychological propensities; e) to which generation they belong. These conditions allow for the principles of justice to be chosen without the influence of prejudice that knowledge of one's natural and social circumstances would lead to. To allow information about such matters of social happenstance would be to select principles which would be shaped, at least in part, by this 'prior' society and its social contingencies which may be an unjust society.

This way of regarding justice Rawls calls "justice as fairness" for these principles would result from free agreement among individuals under the above described circumstances. For Rawls, a practice is fair when none of those participating in it feel he is being taken advantage of or being compelled to give in to what he considers illegitimate claims.

Having described the limits on the knowledge of these hypothetical persons, Rawls must next give these individuals some content to explain their decision in favor of some principles of justice rather than others. By stipulating that these decision-makers are "free" Rawls means they have no authority over one another. By "rational" he means they are interested in furthering and taking the most effective means to their given ends.[14] By "equal" is meant POPs are capable of having a conception of the good and a sense of justice and, in addition, they have the same degree of decision-making powers in the OP.(19) Finally, by adding that POPs are "self-interested" Rawls does not intend to convey that POPs are egoists, but merely that they are concerned in advancing their goals and desires.

Given these conditions, Rawls believes the principles of justice chosen would be:

    I) "Each person has an equal right to the most extensive total system of equal basic liberties compatible with a similar system of liberty for all.

    II) Social and economic inequalities are to be arranged so that they are both:

        a) to the greatest benefit of the least advantaged consistent with the just savings principle and

        b) attached to offices and positions open to all under conditions of fair equality of opportunity."(302)

By "basic liberties" is meant the right to vote, hold public office, free speech, assembly, thought and property.(61) Rawls believes these two principles are a special case of a more "general conception" of justice, namely: "...all social values, liberty and opportunity, income and wealth and the bases of self-respect distribution of any or all these values is to everyone's advantage."(62)

The reason POPs would choose these principles is that they provide for what Rawls calls "primary goods" or "what a rational man wants whatever else he wants."(92) That is, they are necessary means to fulfilling one's plan or goal of life, whatever these happen to be. These goods include rights and liberties, opportunities and powers, income and wealth and self-respect. The two principles would be chosen by rational self-interested persons as the best way for each to secure his ends. Though POPs do not know their particular conception of the good they do know they have a rational life-plan and to achieve this end they prefer more primary social goods which the two principles of justice guarantee.

III.) The Logic of the Contract:

The theories of Rousseau and Rawls, and that of Locke and Hobbes as well, are complex structures made up of what may be termed formal and material components. Contract theory is distinguished from other models of political obligation in that agreement or consent is the foundation of any legitimate political authority. This is the formal dimension which all contract theories share. In Rawls, the agreement is hypothetical, i.e., what properly defined individuals would agree to in the OP. The hypothetical contract obligates, Rawls believes, just as a real contract does because it is a result of moral beliefs we in fact possess or can be persuaded to hold after proper consideration. Rousseau's contract also has the non-historical or hypothetical form for, as has been pointed out above, Rousseau concedes the contract as he describes it may "have perhaps never been formally set forth."(14) (Indeed, considerations to follow will show that the contract **cannot** be other than a hypothetical one.) However, this similarity of the formal component is only partial, for the hypothetical aspect of Rousseau's contract has an actual element which is essential for its completeness.

Recall, in the Social Contract, Rousseau first stipulates that for the GW to emerge from an assembly of citizens three conditions must be met: 1) relevant information must be available;(27) 2) citizens must not form parties or communicate with one another;(27) and 3) the question must be put to the assembly in this form: "Is it in the common interest?" and the decision makers must ignore their own private interests. Now, this closely approximates Rawls' Original Position; the last two conditions correspond to the Veil of Ignorance and the formal constraints of universality and generality on principles of justice and the first to the general knowledge people in the Original Position are said to have at their disposal. The crucial difference, however, is that Rawls' OP is a conceptual device constructed so as to lead to the desired conclusion, the two principles, whereas Rousseau's recommendations are for a real assembly of people who know who and what they are and what they want. This difference is not without significance.

The problematic character of the idea of the GW is revealed when the presuppositions of the three conditions that the General Assembly must meet to derive the GW are made explicit. First, to disregard one's own particular interests assumes a kind of altruistic moral perfection, which Rousseau cannot explain or guarantee. But even if they were to disregard their interests, this would presuppose that some sort of cognitive perfection has been attained, for they must know infallibly what their interests are if they are to effectively disregard them. Even granted that such a state were attainable, it would still be a private psychological state for which there seem to be no public criteria and therefore no way to determine whether the condition is in fact present. The second condition states that the Assembly must have all the "relevant information"(27) but Rousseau gives no criteria for this relevance. The third and final pre-condition for the Assembly requires that there be no factions or parties formed. Clearly, this condition, too, is unattainable for it would necessitate an omnipresent and omniscient state to monitor all communications between individuals at all times. In sum, to assert, as Rousseau does, that the GW is infallible,(26) is to make the implausible claim that human society composed of fallible and finite creatures can reach political infallibility in history.

The above difficulties with the GW are compounded by the fact that the GW has only a procedural interpretation. That is, the GW is the outcome of a procedure followed by the General Assembly. There are no independent substantive criteria for judging whether the Assembly's decisions are in fact the GW. Using Rawls' terminology, Rousseau's method is an instance of "pure procedural justice,"(86) which obtains when there is an appropriate procedure which, if followed properly, will yield the correct or just result, but there is no independent criteria with which to evaluate the outcome. As in games of chance, so too in the case of the GW, the procedure must actually be carried out before the solution can be known. In Rawls, however, there is a relatively independent set of criteria by which to adjudicate the outcome of his procedure, our considered moral judgments. Thus, Rawls' approach may be termed what Rawls calls "imperfect procedural justice" because criteria of the correct outcome do exist. In imposing conditions that can only be applied in a hypothetical situation on an actual collection of persons, Rousseau has outlined a decision procedure which cannot be actualized in the real world. But without the General Assembly to complete and define the nature of the political community which the General Will demands, Rousseau's contract remains an empty abstraction.

This limited concurrence in the definition of the formal component of the contract in Rawls and Rousseau is further diminished when the variables that constitute the material components of contract theory are defined. Agreement never occurs in a vacuum nor is the contract some eternal unchanging form; agreement always results in a specific contract whose specificity is determined by who agrees to what and for what purpose The manner in which these material components are characterized will reveal the sources of the incommensurability between Rousseau and Rawls.

What contractees agree to, the clauses that constitute the contract, is a function of some goal or purpose they wish to actualize. These goals may be values, institutions, relationships, conditions or, more generally, a certain kind of socio-political structure or community. What these goals are is a function of three factors: 1) what the contractees perceive as actual i.e., their circumstances and condition; 2) what they believe is possible for them to achieve given man and his condition; 3) what the contractees see as desirable, the values or rights they wish to promote or preserve.

In Rousseau, the purpose of the contract was not the protection of rights, but the more nebulous one of establishing a society where the values of liberty and equality would be realized and promoted through the General Will and the total alienation of rights. But, more importantly, Rousseau's ultimate goal, as will be shown below, was the creation of a new kind of human nature, a nature more noble, compassionate and wise.

In the case of Rawls, the goal of his theory, from our own point of view, is to clarify our moral intuitions, but from the point of view of the POPs, it is to define principles of justice to ensure themselves the basic goods, namely, rights, liberties, opportunities, power, income, wealth, and self-respect. And to achieve this, they agree to the two principles.

The material category of Agreement 'by whom' is concerned with the definition, essence or nature of the contractees, those party to the contract. This is a crucial component of any political theory, including that of the contract, for the contract consists in the definition of the relations that must exist between those party to it and the nature of the relations must be at least partly based on the nature of the relata, the contractees. In establishing the nature of man three components are especially relevant here: 1) the character and extent of his innate capacities, motivations and weaknesses; 2) the relation and influence of the physical and social environment on his condition and achievements; 3) the nature of his relation to other persons. These elements are relevant in determining the degree and nature of the obligations, functions and responsibilities of the contractees.

Though we cannot here embark on a comprehensive and fully detailed discussion of Rousseau's concept of man, still a brief discussion is inevitable for an understanding of his contract.

It is clear from the *First Discourse,*(FD) and *Second Discourse,* (SD) that Rousseau believes contemporary man has degenerated and become decadent, immoral, in short, alienated from his essential nature.[5] Rousseau's theory of ideal human nature has at least five essential elements. First, Rousseau tells us that the two basic principles of man's essence are those which concern our well-being, namely, "self-preservation" (SD, 95) or "Amour de soi," and the principle which "Inspires in us a natural repugnance to see any sensitive being perish or suffer, principally our fellowmen,"(SD, 95, 130-1) namely sympathy, pity or compassion. The third essential component of man is his freedom, as Rousseau says in his famous lines of the *Social Contract,* "Man is born free and is everywhere in chains."(3, 19) And in the SD, it is man's freedom more than his "understanding" or reason which constitutes man's distinction from other animals.(114) This freedom means man, unlike other animals is not a slave to his instincts but "is free to acquiesce or resist" (SD, 114) his instincts. In addition to this ontological sense of freedom, according to Rousseau, man in the state of nature has what may be called "economic" and "psychological" freedom. By the former, Rousseau means for a man to be fully free, and hence fully human, he must have enough to satisfy his needs so that the does not become a slave to the rich. Psychological freedom expresses Rousseau's belief in the need for the absence of dependence on others for one's sense of worth or respect; recall how in the SD Rousseau laments man's alienated state where he comes to "live in the opinion of others."

The fourth dimension of man's nature is his ability and need to labor to satisfy his wants. Rousseau does not state explicitly that this is part of man's essence, but it is implicit in his writings. We saw that one of his basic critiques of the then contemporary French society in the *First Discourse,* is its luxury and idleness.(46, 49, 53) In the *Discourse on Political Economy,* Rousseau contends society must avoid extreme wealth so that "Labor is always necessary and never useless for its acquisition."(255)[6] And, finally, Rousseau's objections to commerce and his advocacy of agriculture and the barter system, is based on his understanding that entrepreneurs are idle and only farmers are said to really earn their income.

The fifth element of man's essence Rousseau calls man's "perfectibility,"(SD, 115) or the faculty which "successfully develops all the others."(SD, 114) Unfortunately, Rousseau says little beyond this to clarify the nature of this supposed faculty. In addition, he rejects "reason" as essential to man, which seems the only faculty that "perfectibility" may name. Such remarks as "the state of reflection is a state contrary to nature and the man who meditates is a depraved animal"(SD, 110) and "reason engenders vanity and reflection fortifies it"(SD, 132) supports the reading that reason is not part of perfectibility. However, in the *First Discourse,* which is often interpreted as the apotheosis of ignorance and barbarity, Rousseau does in fact allow for the exercise of the intellect and the development of science and the arts as long as their influence consists in increasing the "happiness of the people."(63) This can occur only when governmental power and hman wisdom work together, not separately and at odds with one another. Hence, it seems reason, correctly used, may indeed have a proper role in the ideal human society.

In sum, a person, properly understood, is a creature which preserves itself, has compassion for others, is free, labors and is perfectible (rational). Rousseau objects to the present condition of humanity because it frustrates its nature in that many individuals are rich and idle, and many unfree due to their poverty. And perhaps most significantly, most have lost the virtue of compassion which has hurled society into a veritable state of war. In a corrupt and alienated society "amour de soi" or self-preservation degenerates into "amour-propre" or conceit and vanity. Rousseau believes his social contract reestablishes freedom and compassion by totally alienating all rights, rediscovers the virtue of labor by recreating an agrarian city-state, and baptizes the arts or sciences which now work for humanity, not against it.[7]

Rawls' own views on human nature are not easy to ascertain for he nowhere explicitly states them. Yet his descriptions of the POPs do give some indication of how he sees persons. He sees humanity as morally and intellectually limited, free, self-interested, i.e., concerned to promote its own good, rational and non-envious, since envy tends to make everyone worse off and is therefore irrational. Of all these traits, self-interestedness is the most crucial component of Rawlsian man. It is on that basis that POPs choose to maximize the "primary goods" or "what a rational person wants, whatever else he wants."(92) On this view, rationality logically entails self-interestedness, and without it, the principles of justice POPs would choose would be substantially different. This self-centered view of human nature is further revealed by humanity's existence under what Rawls calls "circumstances of justice"(126) including scarcity of basic goods, which, in turn, adds to the potential for conflict.

Of course, Rawls is quick to note that the motivation of POP is not necessarily that of real people outside the OP.(147-8) Yet if there is no structural isomorphism between the relevant motives within and without OP, then the two principles of justice would be irrelevant to man as he is. In this regard, it is important to mention the Aristotelian Principle, which Rawls doesn't discuss until the end of his treatise. It is, according to Rawls, an important element of human nature which, apparently, POPs do not know about and hence is not a contributing factor in their deliberation.

The most fundamental reason for the difference between Rousseau's and Rawls' political theories lies in their definition of what human nature is. As we noted above, Rawls assumes that human nature as it is, with the tendency to self-interest, was acceptable and a rational starting point from which to build a theory. Rousseau, on the other hand, sought to destroy the roots of self-interest in man for he saw it as a source of decadence, disunity and ultimately war itself. This is quite apparent especially in Rousseau's *Second Discourse*. There Rousseau observes that man's essential trait of sympathy and compassion was overcome and suppressed by the development of private property and the ensuing competition for superiority which brought forth envy and vanity among men. As Rousseau saw it "in a word, competition and rivalry on one hand, opposition of interest on the other and always the hidden desire for profit at the expense of others. All these evils are the first effect of property and the inseparable consequence of nascent inequality."(SD, 96)[8] This eventually resulted in a state of war.

We see then, that the similarity between Rawls' and Rousseau's respective theories of the social contract rests simply in the formal dimension of agreement as the necessary condition for the establishment of political authority; they diverge on *who* (human nature) makes the agreement, and *for what purpose* (their visions of the "good" society). The society which Rousseau envisioned resulting from and constituted by the social contract was radically distinct from the society in which he saw contemporary man. It would be a society populated by a new type of man, a type which had overcome vanity, competition, pride and self-interest. At the heart of Rousseau's theory, then, is a revolutionary interest to transform mankind and society. This approach is diametrically opposed to that of Rawls.

Rawls assumes that our present considered moral judgments and given human nature are an acceptable starting point for political theory. To be sure, the OP does make more precise these moral intuitions, but the changes required by the two principles can be carried out in an evolutionary manner within the existing institutions of western liberal democracy. This is made even more perspicuous by Rawls in a recent article where he states:

> ...we are not trying to find a conception of justice suitable for all societies regardless of their particular social or historical circumstances. We want to settle a fundamental disagreement over the first form of basic institutions within a democratic society under modern conditions...Our hope is that there is a common desire for agreement as well as a sufficient sharing of certain underlying notions and implicitly held principles...the aim of political philosophy...is to articulate and to make explicit those shared notions and principles...[9]

Ultimately, then, what lies at the heart of the disagreement between Rousseau and Rawls is radically opposed visions of what human nature and human society should be. Unfortunately, it is not clear that these respective visions are ultimately persuasive.

NOTES

A version of this paper was previously published in *Auslegung,* 12,1, 1985.

1. Rawls, John, *A Theory of Justice,* Cambridge: Harvard University Press, 1971.

2. All quotations from *The Social Contract* are from G. D. H. Cole's translation, New York: Dutton, 1950. Numbers in parentheses refer to pages of this work unless otherwise indicated.

3. J.J. Rousseau, *Emile,* B. Foxley, trans., New York: Dutton, 1938, p. 424.

4. In this section, numbers in parentheses refer to John Rawls' *A Theory of Justice,* op. cit.

5. Rousseau, *First and Second Discourses,* R.D. Masters, ed., New York: St. Martin's Press, 1964.

6. Rousseau, *Discourse on Political Economy,* in *The Social Contract,* New York: Carlton House, p. 251.

7. Cf. Rousseau, *Considerations on the Government of Poland,* pp. 226-8, and *Project for the Constitution of Corsica,* p. 291, in *Rousseau: Political Writings,* F. Watkins, ed., New York: Nelson, 1953.

8. R.D. Masters, op. cit., p. 156.

9. Rawls, John, "Kantian Constructivism In Moral Theory," *Journal of Philosophy,* September 1980, p. 518.

CHAPTER 9

REVOLUTION AND INEQUALITY IN KANT

The publication of John Rawls' *A Theory of Justice* has stirred renewed interest in the historical roots of the theory of liberalism. Rawls contends his social contract theory of justice is a development within the liberal tradition which includes Kant, Locke and Rousseau. In this essay I analyze Kant's political theory and show that his discussion of revolution is inconsistent with his own moral theory. I also contrast Kant's politics with that of Rawls and suggest that Rawls' perspective on economic inequality is more characteristic of contemporary liberalism than is Kant's.

Kant did not devote as much time to political theory as he did to other areas of philosophy, nevertheless, the extant writings do provide us with sufficient materials to establish Kant's political philosophy. The major primary sources are: *On the Common Saying: This May be True in Theory, but it Does not Apply In Practice (1792)* (henceforth, *Theory and Practice*), *Metaphysics of Morals*, Part 1: *Metaphysical Elements of the Theory of Right* (1797), and *Perpetual Peace* (1795). The minor relevant essays are two in number, *What is Enlightenment?* and *Idea for a Universal History With a Cosmopolitan Purpose*, both written in 1784.

As all contractarians, Kant builds his theory on a conception of the apolitical state, the state of nature. For Kant, the state of nature exists whenever individuals do what they desire or seems right to them. It is not necessarily a state which existed only in the past, but, on the contrary, is an ever-present possibility. As in Locke, Kant's state of nature is not necessarily a state of injustice, but a state devoid of justice where disputes cannot be settled peacefully. Kant concludes, "If he [person in state of nature] does not wish to renounce all concepts of right, he will be [obligated] to adopt the principle that one must abandon the state of nature in which everyone follows his own desires and unite with everyone else (with whom he cannot avoid having intercourse) in order to submit to external public and lawful coercion." Unlawful and arbitrary coercion and violation of liberty characterizes the state of nature, and only the rule of law can overcome such anarchy.

Kant holds that the social contract is not a historical event that took place at some remote time, but a model for a rational decision. It is an "idea of reason" and the only foundation for a "completely lawful constitution." It is a criterion which every law must pass:

... it can oblige every legislator to frame his laws in such a way that they could have been produced by the united will of a whole nation ... This is the test of the rightfulness of every public law. For if the law is such that a whole people could not *possibly* agree to it, it is unjust; but if it is at least *possible* that a people could agree to it, it is our duty to consider the law as just.[3]

For Kant, then, the contract is a "rational principle for judging any lawful public constitution whatsoever."[4]

The contract is a formal principle for the evaluation of the justice and lawfulness of the public constitution which has specific material components. Kant states, "In all social contracts we find a union of many individuals for some common end which they all share."[5] This end Kant expresses in three principles of the lawful civil state. The first is the "freedom of every member of society as a human being."[6] This means that no one can coerce another to be happy or lead a life contrary to one's own beliefs; rather "each may seek his happiness in whatever way he sees fit, so long as he does not infringe on the freedom of others."[7] Consequently, a paternalistic government which treats its subjects as immature children, destroys the freedom and becomes "the greatest conceivable despotism."[8]

The second principle of the just state is the "equality of each with all the others as a subject."[9] This equality is not one of wealth; Kant believes political equality is consistent with economic inequality, the equality is that of "before the law"[10] or of rights. Equality, as Kant construes it, also excludes hereditary privileges; "everybody must be entitled to reach any degree of rank which a subject can earn through his talent, his industry and his good fortune."[11]

The third and final principle of the legitimate constitution is that of the "Independence of each member of a commonwealth as a citizen."[12] A 'citizen' is defined by Kant as one who has the right to vote on legislation, which includes only adult male who is "his own master,"[13] and has some property. 'Property' is defined as "any skill, trade, fine art or science."[14] He goes on to make an important distinction between what he terms "active" and "passive" citizen. "The category of passive citizen includes minors, Apprentices to merchants or tradesmen, servants not employed by the state, women, and all those who are obliged to depend on their living, i.e., food and protection, on the offices of others (excluding the state) - all of these people have no civil personality, and their existence is, so to speak, purely inherent."[16] These individuals Kant calls "mere auxiliaries to the commonwealth, for they have to receive orders or protection from other individuals, so that they do not possess civil independence."[17] Though these individuals are free and equal as human beings, they are not so as citizens.

A society which instantiates the above three principles is a just society, a society based on the "universal law of right".[18] The law of right, according to Kant, is instantiated when three conditions are fulfilled: First, it must apply only to external relations between persons or to actions which influence each other directly or indirectly. Secondly, it is concerned with the wills of the individuals, not their desires. Thirdly, it pertains not to the goals individuals seek, the Wills, "material aspect," but only in the "form of the relationship between two wills ... whether the action of the two parties can be reconciled with the freedom of the other in accordance with a universal law."[19] "Right" is then defined as the "sum total of those conditions within which the will of one person can be reconciled with the will of another in accordance with a universal law of freedom."[20] And, correspondingly, the Universal Law of Right stated in the imperative form reads "let your external actions be such that the free application of your will can coexist with the freedom of everyone in accordance with a universal law".[21]

The state, as defined by Kant, must have three distinct powers, the legislative, executive and judicial.[22] The legislative power belongs ultimately to the "united will of the people"[21] who are obligated to obey the law simply because they have "consented" to it, either directly or through representatives, factually or hypothetically. The "true republic" is a "representative system of the people whereby the people's rights are looked after on their behalf by deputies who represent the united will of the citizens".[24] In addition, the republican government is one where the executive and the legislature are separate.[25] If these two powers are not separate, then despotism may result.

We have seen that Kant believed the legitimate government to be based on the consent, actual or hypothetical, of the citizens. Accordingly, the legislative power is sovereign and belongs to the will of the people. Given this, it is surprising that Kant holds that the moral obligation to obey the law is not *prima facie,* but absolute and overriding in all circumstances. Consequently, revolution or resistance is never justified. In Kant's words,

The reason why it is the duty of the people to tolerate even what is apparently the most intolerable misuse of supreme power is that it is impossible ever to conceive of their resistance to the supreme legislation as being anything other than unlawful and liable to nullify the entire legal constitution.[26]

The citizen has rights of coercion over other citizens, but not over the head of state. Finally, even if a revolution should occur, the ruler cannot be punished or made to account for past acts.[27]

Unlike some political conservatives, Kant does not invoke the wisdom of tradition or appeal to the state as an entity having a value that transcends the value of the individual members to defend his rejection of the permissibility of revolution. Rather, his position is based on moral, legal, practical and logical considerations. In the *Metaphysics of Morals* he states:

For before such resistance could be authorized, there would have to be a public law which permitted the people to offer resistance: in other words, the supreme legislation would have to contain a provision to the effect that it **is** not supreme, so that in one and the same judgment, the people as subjects would be made sovereign over the individual to whom they are subject. This is self-contradictory, and the contradiction is at once obvious if we ask who would act as judge **in** this dispute between the people and the sovereign (for in terms of right they are still two distinct moral persons). It then becomes clear that the people would set themselves up as judge of their own case.[21]

In *Theory and Practice,* Kant is more emphatic:

> ... and even if the power of the state or its agent, the head of state, has violated the original contract by authorizing the government to act tyrannically and has thereby, in the eyes of the subject, forfeited the right to legislate, the subject is still not entitled to offer counter-resistance. The reason for this is that people, under an existing civil constitution, *has no longer any right to judge bow the constitution should be administered.*[29]

Here, as in the above quoted passage, is Kant's claim that the right to revolution is inconsistent because to revolt is to make the subject the superior, which is contradictory. But, on the contrary, it is more likely that it is Kant who is inconsistent. Earlier he had argued that individual consent is the basis of *de jure* government, as he states in *the Metaphysics of Morals* "the supreme power originally rests with the people."[31] Hence, there really is only one supreme power for Kant, and that is the will of the people and the power of the state is contingent on the will of the people.

Besides this logical objection, there is Kant's legal objection, i.e., that there could be no *legal* right to revolution is uncontroversial, but the real question is whether there is a moral right to revolution. Kant's reply to this move would be to claim that the "preservation of the state from evil is an absolute duty"[31] and the duty to preserve oneself is only a relative one. This, however, is clearly inconsistent with his moral theory!

In the opening sentence of the first section of the *Foundations of the Metaphysics of Morals* Kant asserts, "Nothing in the world - indeed nothing even beyond the world - can possibly be conceived which could be called good without qualification except a good will."[32] A good will is present, according to Kant, if the motive or reason for an action is entirely unaffected by the agent's inclinations and self-interest, and acts for *the sake* of duty, not merely in *accordance with* moral duty. Secondly, a good will exists if the person acts with an abiding sense of respect for the moral law. Thirdly, the moral worth or value of the will is not contingent on the realization of any end or purposes, for then the good will would be only a means and hence its value would be based upon the achievement of the intended goal. But, for Kant, the goodness of the will must be unconditional and intrinsic, i.e., based only on the principle which it exemplified.

It is clear that Kant rejects utility as irrelevant in the moral assessment of an action. If moral worth were based on pleasure or happiness, then the ground of duty would be empirical, and hence, for Kant, not universal, and therefore not moral, since moral laws must be universally applicable. The value of actions is based on the good will which is good if it is grounded on the "categorical imperative" which states "I should never act in such a way that I could not also will that my maxim should be a universal law."[33] A maxim is the "subjective principle of volition,"[34] i.e., the particular principle which is implicit in the volition. A moral rule, Kant contends, must prescribe to us categorically, not hypothetically, for a moral rule must obligate without reference to any purpose or consequence. A "hypothetical imperative" on the other hand, obligates us to do something only if we wish to bring about certain ends, and if we do not, it loses its prescriptive force, whereas a moral imperative must be absolutely relevant.

The concept of will is central in Kant's metaethics; it is the legislator and the source of the moral rules that bind all persons. However, for a rule to be moral, it must be self-imposed by the individual's will alone. If a rule of conduct were imposed on one by someone else, such as the state, or God, or one's parents, then it would not be a moral rule. To act from coercion is not to act from devotion to duty, hence to act from a non-moral basis. To be bound by a moral rule means that the law is prescribed for oneself as a rational being, and as such, implicitly prescribed for all rational beings universally. This Kant calls "autonomy of will" and its absence, "heteronomy of the *will.*"[35]

If all individuals were to be morally autonomous, they would form a basis of the moral community of mankind. This kingdom of "realm of ends" would be "the systematic union of different rational beings through common laws." [36] In such a society each person would be the originator of the rules as well as subject to the same. All would act according to rules they formulate and accept, not rules imposed on them. Naturally, Kant is speaking of an ideal society and his political theory is a further articulation of this ideal.

If, as is clear from the above discussion, Kant holds that the morality of an action is not based on the empirical consequences for ourselves or others, but the logical structure of the maxim on which the action is based, how then can the preservation of the state be an *absolute* duty, since the only absolute imperative is the categorical imperative, which makes no mention of the state? A revolution is a coercive action to be sure, but Kant has previously allowed for coercion to safeguard one's freedom.[37] If a tyrannical government is one which violates freedoms, which it seems to be, then the logic of Kant's morality would seem to allow, if not obligate, the overthrow of the government.

In the final analysis, Kant's argument against revolution is in essence an argument for *the impractability* of a revolution. Kant believes a state of nature and a state of anarchy will occur following a revolution which will prove to be "far more oppressive than the one they abandoned."[38] The reason for this is that there would be no authoritative judge to decide between the various factions. In effect, then, Kant is using a *utilitarian* argument for his position which is inconsistent with his general ethical position.[39]

Though Kant does not countenance revolution, he does allow that citizens may "lodge complaints"[40] against the state. To express these objections they have the "freedom of the pen ... the only safeguard of the rights of the people."[41] They may also use the "negative form of resistance"[42] by refusing to meet the demands of the executive. Indeed, Kant adds "if the people were to comply with all occasions, it would be a sure indication that they were decadent." However, what Kant overlooks is the possibility that a state may be so despotic that it denies freedom of speech, press and passive and peaceful resistance; Kant simply fails to face the realities of such a situation. If he had, he would have realized as Rawls has that revolution may be the only moral exit from such a state of affairs.[43]

Before considering Rawls' position, a brief outline of his theory will be helpful.[44] What has traditionally been referred to as the 'state of nature', Rawls calls the 'Original Position' (OP), a hypothetical choice situation consisting of 'individuals' who are "under a veil of ignorance," i.e., they do not know their place in society, their natural talents, conception of the good, psychological properties or to which generation they belong. They do know that they are under the "circumstances of justice" which means they know there exist many individuals in a world of moderate scarcity. Furthermore, they are aware that they are rational, free, self-interested, and equal, at least in the OP. Finally, they are also cognizant that outside the OP individuals have some similar and differing interests and that they are in some way morally and intellectually limited. Under these circumstances Rawls argues these individuals would agree to two principles of justice, namely: (1) "Each person is to have an equal right to the most extensive basic liberty compatible with a similar liberty for others;" and (2) "Social and economic inequalities are to be arranged so that they are both (a) reasonably expected to be to everyone's advantage, and (b) attached to positions open to all."[45] These principles would be chosen because they would ensure the "primary goods" which are necessary means to whatever ends one has. Specifically, these goods are: rights, liberties, opportunities, income and wealth, and self-respect.

Though Rawls does not consider revolution per se in his discussion of civil disobedience, Rawls clearly presents a view contrary to that of Kant. He defines civil disobedience as "a public, nonviolent, conscientious yet political act contrary to law usually done with the aim of bringing about a change in the law or policies of the government."[46] The Justification is clearly that based on the moral principles which define and provide a framework for the political institutions. As Rawls puts It, "In justifying civil disobedience ... one invokes the commonly shared conception of justice that underlies the political order."[47] Specifically, civil disobedience is morally allowable, indeed, obligatory, if the two principles of justice are violated. As for revolution, it too is justified on the same grounds; "in certain circumstances militant action and other kinds of resistance are surely justified."

Inequality

We have seen in our discussion of Kant's metaethics that morality binds all rational creatures. It binds them internally and in an autonomous manner such that the obligation is self-imposed; to impose a moral imperative on anyone constitutes coercion which is a violation of the autonomy of the individual. Kant's theory of the ideal society consists in a community of persons whose sovereign being is both the source and subject of all the rules obligating him, thus creating the "kingdom of ends." In this realm of ends, "all rational beings stand under the law that each of them should treat himself and all others never merely as a means but in every case also as an end in himself."[49]

It seems, however, that once Kant's ideal moral theory is applied to the political reality, not all rational beings have equal autonomy. The issue, here, of course, is the status of what Kant calls "passive citizen"[50] which includes all individuals "who are obliged to depend on their living (i.e. for food and protection) on the offices of others."[51] This, in effect, would deny the right to vote to most people within any given state, especially since Kant excludes all women from the class of active citizens, regardless of their economic status. In the *Foundations,* full autonomy seemed to be based on rationality, but in the *Metaphysics of Morals,* it has an additional stipulation, namely, economic independence.

Unfortunately, Kant hardly gives a clue as to why this restriction should exist except implicitly, in that those who are economically independent have more stake or interest in the state, therefore, should also have more say. But how does economic interest override the demands of duty and autonomy? An argument can be made to show, on the contrary, if economic dependence is an obstacle to full autonomy, Kant, on the basis of his ethics, should have argued that these dependent individuals are in fact being used as means to others' gain and hence violate the categorical imperative. To safeguard autonomy, Kant should have argued that it is the duty of each state to ensure economic independence, and not comprise autonomy with economic circumstances. As Kant himself asserts in the early pages of *Foundations:*

The ground of obligation here must not be sought in the nature of man or in the *circumstances* in which he is placed, but sought a priori solely in the concepts of pure reason.[52]

Kant rejects the view that the purpose of the state is to promote happiness. He states, "No generally valid principle of legislation can be based on happiness ... [because] the highly conflicting and variable illusions as to what happiness is."[53] The primary purpose of the state is to safeguard its citizens from external enemies and internal violence and instability.[54] Yet, in his essay *Idea for a Universal History With a Cosmopolitan Purpose* Kant contends that "the highest purpose of nature - i.e., the development of all natural capacities - can be fulfilled for mankind only in society."[55] But Kant does not say the state should do anything more than provide freedom from coercion as a background condition for this development. Yet in the *Foundations* Kant concedes that "one's own happiness is at least indirectly a duty"[56] because in a state of many wants and dissatisfaction a "great temptation to transgress duties would occur."[57] But one may also conclude from this that it is a duty of the state to ensure the minimum conditions for individual happiness to prevent the violations of freedom that would be more likely to occur in a society of squalor. In fact Kant does say in the *Metaphysics of Morals* that the state should provide the poor with the "rudimentary necessities of nature,"[58] but gives no substantial reason for it at that time, but the above mentioned reason would have been sufficient.

The germs of a more extensive notion of the state can also be perceived in his short composition *What is Enlightenment?* Here Kant defines 'enlightenment' as "man's emergence from his self-incurred immaturity."[59] Immaturity he goes on to say, is the inability to use one's own understanding due to a lack of courage. Therefore, to achieve enlightenment one needs courage, plus freedom: "freedom to make public use of one's reason in all matters."[60] But surely Kant would agree that reason and understanding are potentialities which cannot be actualized spontaneously but require the proper social conditions. Accordingly, besides providing the poor with the minimum, the state must also ensure proper education, health and living conditions for the full development of man's faculties as a moral and rational creature. As for happiness, perhaps there is enough serious disagreement about its nature that a state should not attempt to maximize it in their citizens, but is unhappiness or pain equally controversial? What makes people happy may differ by time, place, and individual, but are the causes of hunger, disease, poverty, ignorance so relative? From these conditions man almost universally flees and seeks to avoid. Moreover, their causes and remedies are obvious and beyond dispute. Happiness, as Kant suggests may indeed be too elusive and vague to define and actualize, but suffering and pain are more concrete and within the scope of government in power to alleviate. These remarks indicate that implicit in Kant's political theory are the makings of a kind of welfare-state which approximates more closely the view of Rawls that would at first seem.

Conclusion

Kant saw the transformation of the state of nature to the political state as the alienation of the right of coercion and judgment in criminal cases, not the total abdication of rights. The contract represents the present moral structure of all *de jure* societies, and is not an ideal to be realized in the distant future.

As universalizability and autonomy are presuppositions of moral obligation, so the social contract is a presupposition of political obligation. If some law is proposed which all the citizens as moral agents would not agree or give their consent, then the law violates the contract, the criterion of the justice and moral worth of any law. As we saw, the contract is not a historical presupposition, but a logical or a hypothetical one; and idea of reason relevant to all moral creatures.

There can be no question that Kant's theory is a foreshadowing of Rawls' own views. Recall Rawls' first principle states "Each person has an equal right to the most extensive total system of equal basic liberties compatible with a similar system of liberty for all"[61] is essentially identical to Kant's Universal Law of Right "let your external actions be such that the free application of your will can coexist with the freedom of everyone in accordance with a universal law."[62] Despite this initial agreement, the concurrence diminishes beyond this point.

Rawls' second principle brings out a salient contrast with Kant. The second principle reads: "Social and economic inequalities are to be arranged so that they are both: A) to the greatest benefit of the least advantaged consistent with the just savings principle, and B) attached to offices and positions open to all under conditions of fair equality of opportunity."[63] Now, clearly Kant accepted the equal opportunity clause, but has a narrower interpretation of its meaning. In Theory and Practice Kant rejected hereditary privileges upholding the view that all "must be entitled to reach any degree of rank which a subject can earn through his talents, his industry and his good fortune."[64] Rawls called his construal of equal opportunity as "liberal equality"[65] and rejected it because it overlooks the fact that background social and economic and educational conditions can be unequal, and because it assumes that wealth and position should be determined by natural distribution of talents.[66] But, surprisingly enough, Kant has the germ of Rawls' insight, but failed to develop it. He observes in Theory and Practice "birth is not an act on the part of the one who is born, (therefore) it cannot create any inequality in his legal position."[67] If birth is not a morally relevant act to the one born, then neither are the talents one is born with, hence if the former does not entail inequality, neither should the latter.

As has been noted above, Kant did believe the state has an obligation to provide to the poor the necessities of life. Rawls too, of course, believed his theory would provide a social minimum as well, but he went beyond this. He claimed all social and economic inequalities must be to "everyone's advantage"[68] and especially to those least advantaged. This amounts to an extension of Kant's poorly argued minimum because it reemphasizes the importance of the condition of the poor, and our moral duty to them. To Rawls, a just society is one that is justifiable to those occupying the least favorable position. This degree of moral sensitivity to the least-advantaged is lacking in Kant.[69]

NOTES

An earlier version of this essay appeared in *Kant-Studien*, 77, 4, 1986.

1. Unless otherwise stated all references to Kant are from *Kant's Gesammelte Schriften*, Koniglich Presssusche Akademie der Wissenschaften, Berlin: Druck und Verlag von Georg Reimer, 1910 (henceforth: Ak). Translations used are from Hans Reiss, ed., *Kant's Political Writings*, Cambridge University Press, 1970, and L. W. Beck, trans., *Foundations of the Metaphysics of Morals*, Bobbs-Merrill Co., New York, 1959.

2. *Metaphysics of Morals*, Ak VI, 312. Reiss, 137.

3. *Theory and Practice*, Ak VIII, 297. Reiss, 79.

4. Ibid., 302. Reiss, 83.

5. Ibid., 289. Reiss, 73.

6. Ibid., 290. Reiss, 74.

7. Ibid., 290. Reiss, 74.

8. Ibid., 291. Reiss, 74.

9. Ibid., 290. Reiss, 74.

10. Ibid., 292. Reiss, 75.

11. Ibid., 293. Reiss, 76.

12. Ibid., 290. Reiss, 74.

13. Ibid., 295. Reiss, 78.

14. Ibid., 295. Reiss, 78.

15. *Metaphysics of Morals*, Ak VI, 314. Reiss, 139.

16. Ibid., 314. Reiss, 139.

17. Ibid., 315. Reiss, 140.

18. Ibid., 231. Reiss, 133.

19. Ibid., 230. Reiss, 133.

20. Ibid., 230. Reiss, 133.

21. Ibid., 231. Reiss, 133.

22. Ibid., 313. Reiss, 139.

23. Ibid., 313. Reiss, 139.

24. Ibid., 341. Reiss, 163.

25. *Perpetual Peace*, Ak VIII, 352. Reiss, 14.

26. *Metaphysics of Morals*, Ak VI, 320. Reiss, 145.

27. Ibid., 323. Reiss, 17.

28. Ibid., 320. Reiss, 145.

29. *Theory and Practice*, Ak VIII, 299. Reiss, 81. Emphasis added.

30. *Metaphysics of Morals*, Ak VI, 341. Reiss, 163.

31. *Theory and Practice*, Ak VIII, 300 (footnote). Reiss, 81.

32. *Foundations*, Ak IV, 293. Beck, 9.

33. Ibid., 402. Beck, 18.

34. Ibid., 400. Beck, 17.

35. Ibid., 440. Beck, 59.

36. Ibid., 433. Beck, 51.

37. *Metaphysics of Morals*, Ak VI, 231. Reiss, 134.

38. *Theory and Practice*, Ak VIII, 302. Reiss, 83. Occasionally, it seems, Kant departs from this austere non-utilitarian and purely logical, nonempirical discussion, as in the example of the wealthy man. In that example he asks whether the rich man can consistently will to ignore the needs of the poor. He says: ". . . although it is possible that a universal law of nature according to that maxim could exist, it is nevertheless impossible to will that such a principle should hold everywhere as a law of nature. For a will which resolved this would conflict with itself since instances can often arise in which he would need the love and sympathy of others..." *(Foundations*, Ak IV, 423. Beck, 41). This perhaps suggests that the moral agent must consider empirical consequences for himself and others in formulating his maxim. If this is so, then Kant is *inconsistent* in formulating his ethical theory as is clear from his remarks such as "the ground of obligation must not be sought in the nature of man or the *circumstances* in which it is placed" *(ibid.,* 329. Beck, 5. Emphasis added), and if the basis of the universality (of moral principles) by which they should be valid for all rational beings without distinction ... is derived from a particular tendency of human nature or the accidental *circumstance* in which it is found that universality is lost" *(ibid.,* 422. Beck, 60-61. Emphasis added). This is the basis of Kant's distinction between 'counsels of prudence' which concern human welfare and happiness, (therefore empirical and contingent) and moral principles which are a priori and necessary. Finally, even if one allows that Kant's moral theory does incorporate empirical consequences as relevant to the formulation of the intention, it is still not clear that a total moral prohibition of revolution follows for it is not obvious that the consequences of revolution are necessarily morally worse than refraining from revolution and enduring the status quo.

40. *Metaphysics of Morals,* Ak VI, 319. Reiss, 143.

41. *Theory and Practice*, Ak VIII, 304. Reiss, 85.

42. *Metaphysics of Morals*, Ak VI, 322. Reiss, 146.

43. It should be noted that 'revolution' is here understood as only the overthrow of certain power relations and segments of *positive* law which support these relations; it does not mean the suspension of the moral law in any sense.

44. John Rawls, *A Theory of Justice,* The Belknap Press of Harvard University, Cambridge, MA.:1971.

45.Ibid., 60.

46. Ibid., 364.

47. Ibid., 365.

48. Ibid., 368.

49. *Foundations*, Ak IV, 433. Beck, 52,

50. *Metaphysics of Morals*, Ak VI, 314. Reiss, 139.

51. Ibid., 314. Reiss, 139.

52. *Foundations*, Ak IV, 389. Beck, 5. By 'economic independence' I do not mean economic quality but merely a sufficient economic minimum so that individuals do not become subject to and thus lose their autonomy to their employers or individuals of superior economic wealth.

53. *Theory and Practice*, Ak VIII, 298. Reiss, 80.

54. Ibid., 298. Reiss, 80.

55. *Universal History*, Ak VIII, 22. Reiss, 45.

56. *Foundations*, Ak IV, 399. Beck, 15.

57. Ibid., 399. Beck, 15.

58. *Metaphysics of Morals*, Ak VI, 326. Reiss, 149.

59. *What is Enlightenment?* Ak VIII, 35. Reiss, 54.

60. Ibid., 36. Reiss, 55.

61. Rawls, *Theory, op. cit., p. 302.*

62. *Metaphysics of Morals*, Ak VI, 231. Reiss, 133.

63. Rawls, Ibid., p. 302.

64. *Theory and Practice*, Ak VIII, 293. Reiss, 76.

65. Rawls, Ibid., p. 73.

66. Rawls realizes, of course, that the lottery of natural talents and the resulting economic inequality cannot be eliminated hence he suggests that we consider the wealth produced by talents as, at least partially, *social*, (not individual and personal) in nature and to be used, in part, to benefit the least advantaged individuals as specified by the Difference Principle.

67. *Theory and Practice*, Ak VIII, 293. Reiss, 76.

68. Rawls, 58.

69. For an analysis and comparison of Kant and Rawls' moral theory, see my "Kant and Rawls: *Contrasting Conceptions of Moral Theory,*" Journal of Value Inquiry, V. 17, No. 3, 1983.

CHAPTER 10

THE ETHICS OF
FINANCING ELECTIONS

Liberal and Marxist theorists have often pointed out the tension between economic inequality and political equality. The economic realm in a free enterprise society is the realm of unequal wealth, income, power and self-interest, whereas the political realm is defined to be the sphere of equal rights and opportunity, impartiality and concern for the general welfare. Liberal philosophers who have sought to defend political equality have been concerned with maintaining the political equality without abandoning economic inequality. One way to promote the separation of the economic and political spheres is to regulate and structure the election process. The election process is crucial in this goal of separation for it is through the election process that individuals move from the economic realm of inequality to political equality. If the two spheres are to be kept distinct, this transition must occur in such a way that ensures their separation. The thesis argued here is that rational elections and an impartial government require at least two conditions: 1) certain limitations on monetary contributions to the campaigns of candidates for public office, and 2) government funding to provide a relevant minimum of financial resources to those candidates that need them in order to compete in the election.

Political institutions are distinguished from other institutions by their authority to make and enforce decisions for the community as a whole, and by their monopoly of power within a geographic area.[2] The legitimacy of this supreme monopoly of power derives from the *role* of political institutions, i.e., to maintain the basic structure of the community. Basic structure is used here in the Rawlsian sense as the system of fundamental social institutions that specify basic rights and duties as a framework for determining the correct division of benefits and burdens among individuals in that community.[3] The role of government, then, is crucial in promoting the continued existence of the community by protecting it from external and internal aggressors, and generally promoting its internal welfare (as understood by that community). It also follows that the nature of government, especially the law-makers and judges, the interpreters of the law, is crucial in determining the character of the community as a whole. If this is so, one must then consider what the necessary conditions are for law-makers and judges to perform their function properly, i.e., make and apply laws that will in fact promote the basic structure of values of that society.

The basic structural values of most communities must take into account certain realities of human nature. Among these realities must be included the fact that most persons are not complete altruists or morally perfect, but morally limited. Morally limited here means, that persons may occasionally act contrary to the requirements of the basic structure of values as defined by that association. But if the basic structure is to be maintained, this tendency to act "selfishly" must be controlled. Societies have attempted to do this in various ways. The idea of punishment by divine entities before or after death, removal from the community, torture, even death have been used to promote the basic values and discourage contrary behavior. Yet, the most effective way to insure the integrity of the basic structure is to attempt to identify one's self-interest with the basic structure, or general interest. This attempt manifests itself in the inculcation and enculturation of each new number of the community in the values of that community by developing within each a 'conscience'. Conscience here means a set of beliefs and attitudes, namely the belief that one should not act against the basic structure, and the feelings of guilt and shame when one does.

In some ways, political structures can be seen as the institutional correlative on a societal level of what an individual conscience is on a personal level. The nature of a conscience, as described above, consists in the internalization of group norms or basic structural values as overriding one's self-interest when they do not coincide. Analogously, political institutions as described here have the distinctive role of maintaining the basic structure and containing and resolving conflict between individuals and groups when their goals conflict with the fundamental structure. On this construal of political structures, the importance of selecting and maintaining the right institutions and personnel is central to the existence and welfare of society. Problems arise, of course, because legislators, judges and executives are human and therefore morally limited and imperfect. That is, they may be tempted to act in their own interest, or in the interest of those who finance them, in violation of their role responsibilities as law-makers for the general welfare. Legislators have a double responsibility, for as private citizens they have a responsibility to act morally, i.e., consistently with the basic structure and, in addition, they must perform their function properly, i.e., make laws that are consistent with and promote the basic structure. This means, among other things, appointing the most qualified individuals, awarding contracts fairly, and framing legislation impartially. Because of the power that legislators have, they are understandably the target of groups and individuals who would prefer laws that serve their interest even if to the detriment of the general interest.

A historical survey of past elections in the U.S. and other democracies will show that some individuals and groups who contribute large sums of money to campaigns sometimes expect certain favors from the candidate if and when she is elected. These favors have included appointments to ambassadorships, awarding of contracts, shaping of legislation to suit special interests, etc. If we understand by 'bribery' as the offering of money, or some equivalent (such as a promise of a future job) for opposing or supporting a bill, then the public official who acts in such a manner is in fact being bribed and is acting in violation of his contractual and role obligations to his constituency.[4] But, clearly, if the basic structure is to be protected, this possibility must be minimized. That is, we must insure that the impartiality or fairness of the law makers is maintained. The sense of fairness or impartiality used here is that of Rawls who describes it in these terms: "when a number of persons engage in a mutually advantageous cooperative venture according to rules, and thus restrict their liberty in ways necessary to yield advantages to all, those who have submitted to these restrictions have a right to a similar acquiescence on the part of those who have benefited from their submission."[5] The intuitive idea is that a law is fair if it imposes burdens and benefits consistent with the basic principles of justice as determined by the basic structure.

Though impartiality is a necessary condition for the proper functioning of the legislator, it is not by any means sufficient. As I have suggested above, the legislative is the supreme body in the community and consequently its performance will most vitally affect the welfare of the community. But if this is so, surely the community interested in its welfare would attempt to ensure not only impartial legislators, but that they possess those qualities necessary to perform their function well, what Aristotle called 'virtues.'[6] The virtues will differ among individuals according to their role or function, and will differ among societies according to their different basic structures. That is, a 'virtue' is defined by different societies as those properties that promote and consistent with the basic structure of that society.[7] To ensure that virtuous individuals are legislators, we must remove all unreasonable obstacles to them from becoming legislators as well as remove obstacles that would keep them from fulfilling their functions properly. However, this must be done in such a manner that is consistent with the basic structure which we are trying to protect. In the U.S., for example, one may look at the Constitution as expressing at least partly, the basic structure of the American society. An essential component of that Constitution is the belief in political equality. Here, political equality means that each individual has an equal chance to participate in the decision-making process of the community. That is, each adult person has one vote and no more than one vote. This theory of equality is further grounded in the basic structure which includes principles of equal basic human rights as specified by the Bill of Rights such as the right to life, liberty, free speech, to hold public office, etc. From this theory of political equality it follows that political decisions are made on the basis of majority vote (or plurality, in the event of more than two candidates).

This political equality is expressed through an electoral system. The electoral system is a set of rules through which the members of the community cast votes to determine issues concerning the governance of their community. Election systems may include two types of processes, a referendum where questions of public policy are decided directly, or the election of persons as representatives who in turn will decide policy issues.[8]

If the election process is to achieve its goal, i.e., select virtuous and competent individuals and/or decide referenda, it must be conducted in a rational manner. A rational decision would have to consist of several components. First, a rational act must act towards a goal on the basis of all relevant available information. Secondly, rationality requires we consider available alternative goals and choose the goal or goals that are most consistent and that maximize the overall end we seek to realize. Thirdly, consider all the possible means to the chosen goal(s) and choose the mean(s) that will most effectively achieve the goal(s). "Effectively" here means those steps that are most efficient (least costly) and have the highest likelihood of success to bring about the desired end.[9] In this case, the goal would be the maintenance or adaptation of the basic structure. To attain this purpose, one must elect individuals who will be most willing and able to promote this goal. In other words, the chosen candidate should have a program or policy consistent with the basic structure, and be willing, i.e., have the moral character or proper virtues to act on this program consistently. Without a character of sufficient integrity to withstand the temptation of self-interest (when incompatible with the general interest) or favoritism of special interests (again, when incompatible with the general interest) to those who may offer various inducements (financing of campaign, gifts, jobs, etc.) the representative is not truly representing *all* of his constituents for which he was elected, therefore violating his contractual obligation.

The problem of maintaining the integrity of the electoral system is due to three prevalent circumstances. Firstly, the high costs of federal and state election campaigns. Secondly, the unequal distribution of wealth, income, and educational opportunities, due to different socioeconomic background, (what Rawl's calls the "lottery of birth,")[10] which give some individuals greater access to resources to run a significant campaign. Thirdly, human moral limitations and weakness such as love of power and status will lead some politicians to compromise their impartiality in return for campaign contributions. As long as these conditions exist, there will be present within the structure of the political system the continuing possibility of bias and corruption. Let us consider each of these conditions and possible remedies.

The facts concerning cost are simple enough. To be a legislator, one must be elected, to be elected, one must have a well-financed campaign. How does one finance a campaign? There are essentially five possible sources of funds:

1. the candidates' own resources
2. the political party he belongs to
3. other individuals
4. other organized groups, (such as PAC's)
5. the community as a whole (govt. financing).

How do these sources impinge on the value of impartiality, free speech, democracy, and the other relevant elements of the basic structure? The Federal Election Campaign Act of 1971, (FECA), was a significant attempt to regulate the various sources of funding. Among its main provisions were:

1. limits on media expenditures for candidates for federal positions, including primary and general elections.
2. an upper limit on contributions by the candidate or his immediate family to his own campaign.
3. provision for a federal bureaucracy (Federal Election Commission)

to monitor campaign practices, including reporting and public disclosure of contributions over $100.

4. a requirement that each candidate and political committee report total expenditures.

In 1974, several amendments were added to the bill including:

a. public funding for presidential conventions and elections

b. contribution limit of $1,000 per individual for each election

c. independent expenditures by political committees (PAC's) for a specific candidate are limited to $5,000 per election.[12]

The logic behind the provisions was to provide for the independence and impartiality of elections by controlling the role of money. Limits on total campaign expenditures would serve to make political office more accessible to individuals of limited financial means. Restrictions on individual and group contributions were meant to reduce illegitimate influence on public officials by reducing the source of the influence, money. The disclosure requirements would lift the cloak of secrecy under which money influence thrives. Public funding would further weaken the link with any special interest group or individual. However, subsequently the U.S. Supreme Court substantially altered and eliminated some of these requirements.

In Buckley v. Valeo (424 U.S. 1976) the Supreme Court overturned many provisions of the FECA of 1971 and 1974. Among other points the plaintiffs contended that the legislation violated the First Amendment freedom of speech and association and discriminated against nonincumbent candidates and minor parties in violation of due process of the Fifth Amendment. The court ruled that the limitations on contributions to a political campaign "necessarily reduces the quantity of expression by restricting the number of issues discussed, the depth of exploration and the size of the audience reached."[13]   With respect to overall candidate spending limits, the court decided that candidates who accepted public financing must also accept spending limits. Limits on personal spending by the candidate himself and independent spending by others on behalf of a candidate were unacceptable. The court upheld the limits on individual and group contributions to campaigns agrees that there was indeed a real or apparent corrupting influence of large contributions on candidates positions. Furthermore, the Supreme Court accepted all the disclosure requirements of the law and the public funding provided by federal law.

The court rightly saw the major dilemma as that of free speech and maintaining the integrity and impartiality of government. The question was put by Justice Potter Stewart: Is money speech and speech money?[14] If money is speech, then the above dilemma is unresolvable and consequently the integrity of elected officials will always be in question. But if money is not speech, money is still necessary to communicate with a sufficiently large audience to have a chance of winning an election, and clearly not all candidates are equally financially endowed to accomplish this. How then does one ensure a genuine competitive and rational election which allows for the scrutiny of policy and character?

The concept of free speech suggests four essential components. First, it means that there are no legal restrictions on the *content* of the speech. That is, no point of view or subject matter is forbidden by law. Further, free speech may mean no legal limit on the *scope* of one's speaking, i.e., no restriction to the extent, timing or location of the potential audience. In addition, speech or self-expression can be *direct* or *indirect*. In direct speech, the individual himself expresses his views; while in indirect speech, the individual gives some form of support to someone else's speech. Clearly one can limit speech by restricting any one of these elements of speech. However, whether any such limitations are justified can only be answered by analyzing the role of speech in the basic structure.

The role of free speech, as viewed by Mill, for example, is to provide a necessary condition for a rational society and the growth of knowledge.[15] Since for Mill no society has achieved perfection in its institutions or knowledge, to make progress towards the pursuit of truth, every society must allow the expression of new ideas and theories. It must then test these ideas and theories in public dialogue, and accept or reject them depending on their validity.

If we apply Mill's argument to the problem of elections, it follows that a full public debate is necessary to determine rationally the merits of the various candidates' policy and character. This, as we have seen, requires access to mass media, which is costly. It follows, therefore, that a full rational discussion would not be possible without some minimum funding for each candidate to communicate effectively with the electorate. The minimum must be sufficient to offer the electorate a fair hearing of all candidates. This funding can originate from the individual candidate, other individuals or groups, or the government. A guaranteed minimum funding restricts no one's speech, whereas a net maximum or upper limit could limit the scope of speech as the Supreme Court rightly stated (depending, of course, on how low the maximum is). However, once the necessary funding has been acquired, there is still the other problem of maintaining impartiality and the integrity of character of the candidates who receive funding from other individuals and groups. Should these other individuals and groups be allowed to contribute at all? The answer to this question requires us to look at the concept of 'contribution' more

closely. The general meaning of contribution is to support in some way
someone or something. One can do this in several ways. One can actually
give money to someone's campaign, one can donate one's labor, or one can
labor or spend money on behalf of another without the other's control,
approval or guidance. Clearly one can influence a candidate one is
supporting in any of these ways and hence the possibility of bias exists.
It seems reasonably clear that one cannot legitimately restrict a person who
wishes to contribute his or her labor to another's cause for this would be
to infringe on that person's autonomy and direct speech. However, it is
also true that this form of contribution is the least potential source of bias
since it will have a relatively small impact on the overall effectiveness or
financial success of a campaign especially on a national or state level.
This type of contribution should therefore not be restricted, unless these
individuals are being paid by someone else to work for the candidate,
which brings us to the next type of contribution.

Direct contributions into the campaign fund are the most threatening to
the impartiality of the candidate. We must, therefore, look at a balance
between two distinct values, the value of free speech and the value of an
impartial representative. This balance can be struck by allowing some
levels of contributions (with a maximum low enough that many persons
can meet it). This restriction is justifiable because it is first of all merely
a limit on indirect speech and on the scope of speech, not on the content
of speech. It preserves the impartiality of the candidate while the
minimum governmental funding ensures the proper total necessary scope
to communicate with the electorate. The morally crucial factor is that the
relevant ideas be expressed and debated in the election campaign, not
necessarily that some specific individual actually state those ideas. To
further insure impartiality, those contributing should be anonymous. That
is, there should be a governmental agency to process contributions and
distribute them to the proper candidate in such a way that the candidate
does not know who the contributor is. This would be more effective than
the disclosure requirements required by the FECA.

The third form of contribution is independent spending by others on
behalf of some candidate. Independent spending is a form of direct speech
and thus, *prima facie,* it deserves protection. However, it can corrupt the
political process just as much as unlimited contributions into a campaign
by someone known to the candidate. However, we must distinguish
between direct speech for one's own candidacy and that for another's.
Since the latter creates the preconditions for possible partiality, it should
be restricted, but it should not be banned. It cannot be banned for it would
be a violation of free speech, but it can be limited. It can be limited for
spending limitations are a restriction on the scope of speech not the

content, which is the paradigm case of censorship and therefore must be avoided. Limiting independent spending to some small fraction of the candidate's campaign fund will preserve the impartiality of the candidate while giving the freedom of others to speak in favor of their candidate. It should be clear that this restriction on the scope of the contributor's speech is not pernicious for the ultimate scope of the speech is not restricted (assuming sufficient minimum of governmental and other support) since the candidate will have sufficient funds to communicate the necessary ideas to the electorate. As in the case of direct contributions, the rationality of the election is assured if all the relevant ideas are in fact communicated to the electorate, not whether a specific person communicates those ideas.

It should be clear from the above discussion that the complete elimination of individual funding by private citizens (and thus making all funding of political campaigns rely on governmental funding) is problematic.

Firstly, it would greatly increase the role of government in the political process, meaning a shift of power and initiative from the people to increased concentration of power in federal bureaucracies. Secondly, it would substantially retard the spontaneity of the people's right to organize and express their views. However, if the above argument is correct, these restrictions would not be necessary in order to achieve the goal, the impartiality and integrity of government officials. Once a sufficient minimum of funding is federally guaranteed to a candidate or incumbent, the possibility of corruption or inevitability of bias is substantially reduced, for they are simply not necessary to have a chance at re-election.

It should be evident now how these restrictions on campaign contributions are not necessarily a violation of the right to free speech. Though Mill recognized the sacred role of the speech in open and democratic society, he nevertheless believed speech can be regulated in some cases. These cases all concern the violation of the Harm Principle: "the sole end for which mankind are warranted, individually or collectively, in interfering with the liberty of action of any of their numbers is self-protection [or] . . . to prevent harm to others."[16] Mill's famous example of the corn dealers suggests that time, place, and manner of certain forms of speech can be restricted if it would cause unjustifiable harm to innocent individuals, as in the classic example of falsely yelling 'fire' in a crowded theater. Similar restrictions against libel and slander have been recognized as legitimate limitation on speech.

The harm we are concerned with here is not directly against specific individuals but the basic structure of political institutions. Providing a minimum of financing by government, and restricting the amounts of contributions, can be viewed as restrictions of free speech that are legitimately based on the need to prevent harm and corruption of the central institutions of government by providing for greater impartiality and integrity of legislators, presidents, etc. As we have seen, impartiality is a necessary condition for the proper performance of governmental functions, i.e., to maintain the basic structure. If the basic structure is undermined through bribery and bias, so is every element that structure includes and protects, including the right to free speech.

Whether it is seen as necessary for the pursuit of truth, or the expression of individual autonomy or the maintenance of social stability and welfare, free speech can only achieve these ends when it occurs within a certain structure of rules and conditions that actually maximize total free speech and allow the purpose of speech, rational discussion, to be more fully realized. Just as parliamentary rules of order enable discussion to be meaningful by regulating who can speak when, so regulation of election campaign funding is carrying the rules of ordered discussion to the state and national level. Free speech, therefore can legitimately be restricted in content (e.g. libel) in time and place (falsely yelling 'fire' in a crowded theater) scope (protect minors from 'pornography') manner (following parliamentary rules of order) and in terms of providing the necessary conditions for effective speech, (minimum funding), speech that is rational and capable of serving the basic structure. The right to a minimum of government financing is continuous with the right to an education for both are necessary for a rational and full discussion of the issues and for discerning the character of the candidates and the protection of rational self-rule or democracy.

Minimum funding not only allows for a more impartial election it also provides for a more rational election by expanding the spectrum of heard views on matters of public policy. Funding of minor party and independent candidates provides the electorate with an opportunity to hear opinions they would ordinarily not hear or seriously consider. This is obviously a more rational electoral process for rationality means choosing on the basis of best information or ideas available not just the ideas that happen to have financial backing.

In the interest of clarity it may be helpful to consider some further objections. First the idea of a guaranteed minimum may suggest the possibility of too many candidates or frivolous candidates interested only in publicity. This problem can be handled by requiring proof of some minimum support in terms of signed petitions indicating some existing support among the electorate. What this minimum is will depend on the size of the community and the nature of the election. A further problem suggests itself in determining the actual formula for distributing the funding. Here the solution must be based on the total available funding for the election to be distributed among the total set of legitimate candidates in proportion to their support in the community as evidenced by past elections and/or the number of signatures on petitions. Further specific determinations will depend on the actual conditions and experience as the program is implemented in national, state and local elections.

A final problem concerns the appropriate spending of the minimum once it is distributed. Obviously the funds must be spent on legitimate campaign purposes not on personal matters or matters irrelevant to the campaign. The answer to this question must be based on what the purpose of a political campaign is in a rational electoral system. That purpose is to communicate the candidates' ideas and the nature of his character to the electorate. These are the only relevant factors in a rational election and only money spent to that end is properly spent. In practice a committee to monitor spending will have to be formed.

The tension between economic inequality and democracy has been discussed by John Rawls. Rawls saw that economic inequality is not simply a function of fixed human nature but of unjust and unequal social conditions. The basic problem of justice for Rawls is that the social structure into which one is born "contains various social positions and that men born into different positions have different expectations of life determined in part by the political system as well as by economic and social circumstances. In this way the institutions of society favor certain starting places over others."[17] Justice therefore requires the greater equalizing of these starting positions so as to give every person a fair equality of opportunity. The actual lack of equal opportunity also affects what Rawls calls the "worth of liberty." The worth of liberty he states "is proportional to their (person's) capacity to advance their ends within the framework the system defines."[18] Rawls feels this difference in the worth of liberty is justified by the fact that allowing economic inequality benefits everyone and raises the worth of liberty for all (though for some more than others). One may not wish to dispute that certain degrees and kinds or economic inequality are necessary for economic efficiency and growth; still the adoption of campaign reform as here described would raise the worth of liberty for the least advantaged without jeopardizing the economic structure of incentives necessary for general economic efficiency.

Indeed one can see this as an extension of Rawls' Difference Principle. This principle states: "social and economic inequalities are to be arranged so that both A) reasonably expected to be to everyone's advantage and B) attached to positions and offices open to all."[19] Clearly guaranteeing a minimum of government funding of elections would make political positions and offices more open to the disadvantaged by increasing their chances at successful competition for these offices.

Reform of the election process would also be a significant response to various traditional Marxist critiques of modern liberalism. Marx states in the *Manifesto* "The executive of the modern state is but a committee for managing the common affairs of the whole bourgeoisie."[20] Briefly stated for Marx political institutions are part of the super-structure which is dependent upon and controlled by the sub-structure consisting of the means and relations of production. The ruling or bourgeoisie class in capitalism controls the politics by controlling the media and educational system and by funding only those individuals who are sympathetic to the interests of the bourgeoisie. Public financing would sever this string of influence and possible source of bias.

The actual details of amount of funding will have to be worked out based on the nature of the election the expenses of the opponents and the cost of an effective campaign. In addition arrangements must be made to allow participation and funding of minor party candidates possibly by way of matching funds or based on previous support in elections or by various indications of established support.

The reforms argued for here are meant to be perfectly general and apply to federal and state as well as local primary and general elections. The argument presented here for a federally guaranteed sufficient minimum of funding of election campaigns is based on the need for the rational selection of impartial lawmakers. To be sure requiring minimal funding monitoring contributions and other aspects related to the implementation of these reforms will require taxing the population to cover these costs. However it is reasonable to hold that these costs are merely a fraction of the costs the citizens now bear for biased and unfair federal and state legislators who grant favors to supporters in the awarding of lucrative contracts appointing personnel and drafting of legislation. The costs of an impartial government are far lower than the costs of a corrupt government. Failure to deal with a unfair and biased election system will create distrust and cynicism about democracy itself and perpetuate injustice, political inequality and excessive economic inequality.

NOTES

An earlier version of this essay appeared in *The Southern Journal of Philosophy*, 25,3, 1987.

1. I am grateful to Michael Bayles, R. M. Hare and Jim Sterba for their helpful comments on an earlier draft of this paper.

2. Cf. Nozick, Robert, *Anarchy, State and Utopia,* New York: Basic Books 1974, pp. 23-24.

3. Rawls John, "The Basic Structure as Subject," *American Philosophical Quarterly,* Vol. 14 No. 2 April 1977 pp. 160-1.

4. Cf. Danley, John R. "Toward a Theory of Bribery," *Business and Professional Ethics Journal,* Vol. 2, Vol. 3, 1983.

5. Rawls, John, A *Theory of Justice,* Harvard University Press, 1971, p. 112.

6. Aristotle, *Nicomachean Ethics*, Hackett, 1985 pp. 17-20.

7. MacIntyre, Alasdair, *After Virtue,* Notre Dame Press, 1981 pp. 174-8.

8. Cf. Still, Jonathan "Political Equality and Election *Systems,"* Ethics, April 1981, p. 377.

9. Rawls, *op. cit., pp.* 408-9.

10. Rawls, *op. cit., p.* 156.

11. Alexander, Herbert *A., Financing Politics,* Congressional Quarterly Press: Washington D. C. 1976 p. 138.

12. Ibid., p. 274.

13. Fein, Bruce E., *Significant Decisions of The Supreme Court,* American Enterprise Institute, Washington D. C. 1977, pp. 74-5.

14. Ibid., p.13.

15. Mill J. S., On *Liberty,* Bobbs-Merrill Co. 1956, pp. 20-5.

16. Ibid., p. 13.

17. Rawls, op. cit. p. 7.

18. Ibid., p. 204.

19. Ibid., p. 60.

20. Marx Karl, F. Engels, *Communist Manifesto, in Marx-Engels Reader, W. W.* Norton, 1978, Tucker Robert C. ed., p. 475.

CHAPTER 11

DEMOCRACY IN THE CORPORATION

Any discussion of ethical problems must consists of at least three components. First, a general account of the distinctive nature or role of moral rules as contrasted with other rules, must be provided. Second, one must determine the scope of applicability or relevance of moral concepts. Third, once it has been established that moral categories are relevant, then the conditions or structures necessary for maximal compliance with the appropriate moral principles should be addressed. The first two dimensions are generally considered metaethical whereas the third would be in the realm of applied ethics and moral psychology.

The role of morality is to provide a set of fundamental principles which constitute the deep structure of the human community. This fabric of rules is intended to preserve order, harmony and promote the general group welfare as understood by that group. This is one feature that distinguishes it from rules of etiquette, which, though important, are less crucial and basic. Because they are viewed as basic and essential for the existence of the group, moral rules are action guides that are overriding in character; they have priority over all other rules, such as courtesy or matters of taste. They must also be universalizable for they are rules that apply to every full-fledged member of the community. In addition, ascribing moral rules and moral responsibility determines for that group who the true members of persons of that community are; to attribute duties and responsibilities is to imply that individual has a role in maintaining the basic structure of his community. The nature of moral rules as ultimate reasons for or against an action is understandable once we see that they are intended to articulate the necessary conditions for the survival and well-being of the community (as viewed by that community.) Moral rules override all other considerations because the existence of the group overrides all other interests.

This is why there is often an underlying conflict or tension in the human community between individual self-interest and the general interest or welfare. Since the role of morality is to outline the deep-structure of guideline for continued community existence individuals or groups may be called upon to sacrifice their welfare, as in a war, for the good of all. This tension then is a structural one for human society for it cannot always be the case that self-interest is consistent with the general interest. (Though, of course, they may and do often coincide.) It is the task of moral philosophers to analyze and assess this tension.

It seems reasonably clear that moral categories apply to only certain kinds of entities and only certain action or non-actions of these entities. Attributing moral responsibility must presuppose the identifiability of an agent who has performed an action. That is, the event in question must be of the type not caused by some general force or condition but some entity locatable in space and time. In addition, the agent must have some continuity in time, i.e., if the agent is to be rewarded, punished or informed about the moral character of his or her behavior, the agent must continue to exist for a time into the future. Thirdly, the agent must have performed the action intentionally, i.e., the act must not be the result of ignorance or an uncontrollable spasm, but of a conscious and rational sort. Moral responsibility also requires that the agent was neither externally nor internally coerced. Examples of internal coercion in a person would be those mental states associated with mental illness such as forms of psychoses. External coercion would include threats of bodily ham and possibly severe harm to one's economic and social well-being. Finally, only those actions that substantially affect or impinge on the welfare of others are proper targets of moral evaluation.

Though questions can be raised about these criteria, it seems generally agreed that at least some actions of biological persons can be evaluated with these categories. The question, however, is can the corporation as a separate entity meet these conditions as well. The American legal system recognizes that the corporation is an agent that can be held accountable for its actions independently of the actions of any of its directors, executives or employee. For example, when Mr. Grinshaw filed for damages resulting from burns received when his Pinto exploded, he sued the Ford Motor Company, not any individual of Ford. The following analysis of the unique nature of corporate agency will suggest why this must be so at least in some cases.

Each individual working for a corporation is hired to perform some clearly defined function. Thus, employees of a corporation can be said to work and act for the corporation as agents or instruments of that corporation. Let us define "instrumental actions" as those actions executed by virtue of ones role in an institution; instrumental actions are role-actions. When a corporation acts, it acts by virtue of the results of the combined instrumental actions of its employees. Let us term this action which emerges from the set of instrumental actions a "secondary action." A nation state, for example, may wage war based on the instrumental actions of certain politicians within the decision-making body and a corporation may make a product or contribute to a political campaign. For an instrumental action to be properly attributed as such, the agents constituting the institution must perform the act within the framework and rules determining proper procedure. That is, not every act of a person within a firm is an act of the firm, only those actions which are carried out as instances of ones defined function or rule. Let us call agents performing instrumental actions "instrumental agents" and those performing secondary actions "secondary agents."

It is clear that instrumental agents contribute causally to the performance of secondary agents but the moral characteristics of these actions may be quite distinct. In other words, moral responsibility does not always transfer across from one kind of agency to the other. This occurs because the instrumental and secondary agents can be in quite distinct moral positions in terms of the information they possess and the additional obligations they may have to other individuals or groups. For example, an employee may have moral qualms about some action he is to perform, yet he may decide his obligations to his family override these qualms. The bureaucratic nature of the firm explains how this is possible.

Bureaucratic decision-making is characterized by the use of committees at various levels in the hierarchy. Isolation may exist between these various levels which is exacerbated by the extensive use of professionals in decision-making. Additionally, decisions of one committee may be revised by others and the make-up of these committees may change. Individuals who drew-up the charter and set goals for the firm may no longer be employees or in any way related to the firm.[4] No one individual or even group can act with the awareness of all the information necessary for a corporation to take action, consequently, the organization as a whole is responsible as a distinct agent. The structure of the corporation, including its founding charter, its hierarchy of authority, its definition of functions, its hiring policy, contributes a formal cause to the instrumental causes of the employees which produces the secondary action of the corporation. It is this formal component of instrumental actions that allows the distinguishing of moral culpability between instrumental actions and secondary actions. These considerations suggest some of the obstacles to the application of moral categories to corporate acts.

As has been suggested above, moral responsibility presupposes the identifiability of the agent. Clearly, a corporation as a legal entity can be identified as an agent. The continuity condition can also be met in most cases, unless of course the corporation has ceased to function due to bankruptcy or the like. However, continuity is not met if it refers to any one individual in the firm, for there are large turnovers in an institution which is potentially immortal. On the other hand, some have argued that the intentionality condition cannot be met.[5] It may be true that the corporation acts for goals but the reasons individual in the firm act for them may be quite diverse, e.g., profit, salary, promotion. Hence, the argument continues, corporate acts lack the unity of reason necessary for intentionality. However, one must distinguish between what may be termed "primary intentionality" which resides in conscious rational biological agents, which is the paradigm case of intentionality, and the "secondary intentionality" of the corporation. Secondary intentionality is analogous to secondary action in that it is a decision made by an authorized corporate decision-making body to act for some corporate goal. Corporations can act for reasons or goals as set up by its charter, board of directors, etc., and thus intentionally even though the motivations of the constituting individual may differ.

The application of the non-coercion criterion is a complex one. Let us define "coercion" as the limiting of a persons options for action such that any choice but one will result in physical, psychological or financial harm to a substantial degree. The corporation as a whole may experience coercion if its officers lose control of the corporation as may occur in a takeover by another corporation. In this case, the new corporate entity is the locus of action and responsibility.

The above analysis suggests moral categories are applicable to the corporation but not necessarily to the individuals within it when they act as its agents. The corporation can be considered an agent distinct from the individuals who constitute it and any one time. If this is the case, it follows that measures to ensuring corporate moral behavior are separate from measures taken to ensuring the moral behavior of its employees. Let us consider some of these measures.

American courts have given the corporation the status of a 'person'. In this way they sought to protect the constitutional right of persons to organize with full protection of the laws. But corporations are like persons also in that they behave to promote their interest, e.g., profit, which may or may not be consistent with the general group interest. Recent history has shown that pollution of the environment, monopolization, dangerous products, disregard of the health and safety of workers and consumers, and the depletion of natural resources may well be compatible with, indeed perhaps in some cases ensure, increased profit. To meet these problems, government sought to regulate businesses by passing laws limiting pollution, establishing minimal health and safety for the workers, etc. The problems attending morality by regulation are many and well known.[6]

Morality through positive law is limited in that law as a system of general rules cannot deal perfectly with all specific circumstances. Law is by nature a reaction to a problem that has already occurred, and thus will always allow certain immoral actions to occur until the legislature acts. Thirdly, law is usually negative in formulation, telling what not to do, but moral behavior does not just involve the avoidance of evil, but the promotion of good to some degree. Moreover, the law can never completely express the full content of morality, but only that enforceable component; being moral means more than just being law-binding. Fourth, government officials may be too unfamiliar with concrete business practice to regulate it efficiently. Finally, the extensive lobbying and funding of political campaigns by corporations through political action committees, may undermine the impartiality and independence of governmental agencies and individuals.

Christopher Stone's proposal for improving corporate behavior through outside public directors is also too limited.[7] The role of these public directors is to be an ethical watchdog on the affairs of the firm and be available for consultation with employees. The strength of Stone's idea lies in that the public director has no financial interest in the corporation, but it makes the determination of the public interest an interpretation of one individual, the public director. More importantly, there is the problem of selecting, and maintaining the independence and moral integrity of the director.

Another approach that has been suggested is the formulation of code of ethics for each corporation.[8] This too is helpful, but the question of detection and enforcement of violations is unresolved. Additionally, the pressures to immorality that attend a firm caught in a competitive market can be formidable. If an institution is struggling for its very existence, taking unilateral moral action can be detrimental to success of the firm in the market. Secondly, as we have seen the bureaucratic nature of corporate action may make immoral acts more anonymous and thus more tempting. Moreover, moral considerations often concern long-term consequences of actions, whereas the demands of profit maximization are often short-term. The division of labor and function in the corporation has resulted in division, diffusion and obfuscation of responsibility. The answer is not in codes of ethics alone or regulation, but, as in the case of a biological person, the development of a conscience through internalization of moral norms.

As our discussion of the role of morality above suggested, human society is typified by occasional tension or conflicts between individual self-interest and group-interest. Communities that wish to survive and prosper **as** communities must ensure that this conflict be controlled and resolved without serious detriment to the group. Historically, this has been done by developing an elaborate theological sanction for the moral law, by systems of reward and punishment, by education and training through the family, schools, and churches. But, it seems clear, no community thus far has developed means to ensure moral behavior by overt reward and punishment alone for this would require omniscience of all individual actions on the part of the community leaders. Indeed, this is where the idea of divine omniscience plays such a crucial role in theologically oriented communities. The only alternative is the development of a 'conscience,' or an internal monitor and control on the behavior of individuals.

'Conscience' consists of a cognitive element, in that it presupposes knowledge of concepts of right, wrong, duty, as well as an emotive element, the feelings of guilt or shame for falling short of one's sense of duty.[9]   Conscience involves a responsibility for past actions and an awareness of obligations with respect to anticipated future actions. It consists in the capacity for self-observation, and criticism by comparing our actions with values, ideals and group-norms one accepts as correct. Conscience is the assimilation of the rules which provide for the common 'good'. The advantages of conscience to external monitoring and control are clear: the judgment of a properly formed conscience is ever present and certain, whereas external authority and punishment may be avoided, uncertain, and mistaken. But how can the corporation, a theoretical 'person', which has no single unifying mind develop a conscience? The answer lies in structuring the control of the corporation in such a manner as to provide for the same results that a conscience provides. The role of a conscience is to provide for the general welfare by monitoring and controlling individual actions so that they do not override social needs. We must, then, establish control of the corporation so that social welfare is not compromised by installing in controlling positions individuals who directly and personally represent those social concerns. This would, of course, mean equal participation of consumers, workers and investors in the running of major corporations. This type of representation will be the institutional correlative to a person's conscience for it will protect those groups and interest the corporation is most likely to offend; it will be present to protect their interest and at the same time, the general interest. This is why worker representation alone is not sufficient for the interest of workers is not always compatible with the social interest. Similarly, within the present system of capitalism, investors have a legitimate right to be represented to protect their investment. Managers must be represented to provide information for the democratized corporation as a whole.

The actual institutional arrangement can be only briefly suggested since many details will be determined by experience and discussion of the parties involved. Of utmost importance is that the democratization must take place fully at the level of the board of directors and to a more limited extent at the more immediate level of management. The board of directors should include equal, three part representation of the stockholders, consumers and employees. On the daily running of the firm, employee representation in a workers and managers council which meets regularly may be sufficient, though the meeting may include representatives of the general public as well.

Should these democratic structures apply to every firm? Clearly not. The moral nature of past corporate behavior must be considered. If the corporation has behaved in a morally acceptable way, it may not be necessary to alter its structure. The basic idea here is that control of the corporation reflect the scope of impact of corporate policy and actions. Full-scale democratic representation may not be economically feasible for small firms, where government regulation may be sufficient to ensure satisfactory moral performance. The experience of the West German model where a similar program, though without consumer representation, has been instituted in some organizations may be useful.[10]

We have argued that the argument for democratic capitalism is based on the understanding of morality as a system of basic deep-structured rules that are necessary for community life and prosperity. As such, no individual or group has a right to jeopardize the general welfare in pursuit of its own welfare. Consequently, our suggestion cannot be attacked on the basis that it is a violation of the right to property or the freedom to contract. The right to property is a right which exists within the general context of the basic structural fabric of a group's moral code. Consequently, the interpretation and application of that right must be compatible with other basic rights defining the general welfare. The laws against monopoly formation, for example, are restrictions on appropriation based on an understanding of the general value of a competitive market. In other words, the right to property is not absolute but contingent on its harmony with the other basic rights of life and liberty. Moreover, no right can be claimed in such a manner as to preclude the moral exercise of that right. Hence, if the argument here is correct, that the development of something like a conscience is a necessary presupposition for the moral exercise of property rights in the context of the corporation, then no one can legitimately object that a democratic corporate government is a violation of property rights.

Traditionally, the right to property has been interpreted as a two-termed relation. To say, 'Jones owns a car', means Jones has certain special rights with respect to that car that no one else does. However, this analysis is inadequate for it omits the fact that property rights involve obligations on the parts of others and limits depending on overriding rights and the general communal welfare. For example, my right to my car may be overridden by a policeman who may need it to capture a mass murderer, or saboteur. This three-termed view, as has been suggested by others, is a more accurate reflection of property rights understood in the full context of morality.[11] The model of the corporation here de-fended is a reflection of this view of property. The strength of this model is that it institutionalizes this relationship and sets up a procedure where conflicting claims can be adjudicated in an ongoing manner.

The role of morality is not merely the negative one of preventing wrong-doing, but, also the positive one providing for a general welfare. The weakness of morality through regulation consists in the fact that it is merely negative and minimal in scope. This is why democratized capitalism is superior for individuals who have no direct monetary interest in the corporation, the consumers, have the opportunity to introduce positive moral concerns.

There is reason to believe that this democratic corporation will not only instrumentally enhance positive moral performance of the corporation it will also intrinsically enhance the self-esteem and productivity of workers. A recent study by HEW shows that redesigning the workplace can result in higher productivity and greater job satisfaction. These features of the restructured workplace include worker participation in decision-making, greater control over the workplace, closer peer ties and job security.[12]

Conclusion

Most ethical theorists, including Kohlberg, have focused their attention on individual moral behavior and its justification, not group action. Yet, the reality of contemporary life is one where major decision and actions are made by governmental and corporate bureaucracies. This new mode of action requires a new mode of monitoring and controlling group behavior.

Though the role of morality is to provide for the basic structure in which individuals may more fully satisfy their needs, no moral system is complete or perfect at any one time. As our knowledge and experience increases, so do possibilities, opportunities and needs expand. A rational society, therefore, must allow for the dynamic response to this evolving nature of human moral consciousness.

NOTES

A version of this essay first appeared in the *Journal of Business Ethics*, 4,2, 1985.

1. I am referring only of the role of moral rules and not the correctness of the content of these rules.
2. Cf. Copp, David, "Collective Actions & Secondary Actions," *American Philosophical Quarterly* V. 16, No. 3, July, 1979, pp. 177-186.
3. Ibid, p. 184.
4. Werhane, Patricia, *Employee Rights*, Prentice-Hall.
5. Keeley, Michael, "Organizations as Non-Persons," *Journal of Value Inquiry*, 15, 1981, pp. 149-155.
6. Cf. Copp, David, "Collective Actions & Secondary Actions," *American Philosophical Quarterly* V. 16, No. 3, July, 1979, pp. 177-186.
7. Stone, Christopher, *Where the Law Ends.*Harper & Row, New York, NY, 1975, pp. 122-174.
8. Brenner, S.N., Molander, E.A., "Is the Ethics of Business Changing?" *Harvard Business Review* Jan.-Feb., 1977.
9. Cf. Loevinger, Jane, *Ego Development: Conceptions and Theories*, Jossey-Bass Publishers, London, 1976, pp. 397-8.
10. Neuburger, Hugh, "Codetermination-The West German Experiment at a New State," *Columbia Journal of World Business*, Winter, 1978, pp. 104-11.
11. Chaudhuri, Joyotpaul, "Toward a Democratic Theory of Property and the Modern Corporation," *Ethics*, 81, (July 71). pp. 271-86.
12. *Work in America.* Cambridge, MA: MIT Press, p. 87, 96-99.

CHAPTER 12

RAWLS AND THE RIGHT TO POLITICAL LEAVE

The values of liberty and equality are the essence of liberal democracy. But liberty in a free market economy leads to inequality of wealth, power, prestige, and opportunity, what John Rawls calls inequality of the "fair value" or "worth of liberty."[1] Simply put, the wealthy have the economic resources to expand the power of their rights such as free speech and run for public office or influence those who do to a far greater extent than those with lesser economic means. Rawls attempts to reconcile the problem of economic inequality and political equality in his new work, *Political Liberalism* (PL).

The thesis defended here is that Rawls' proposals for reconciling economic inequality and political equality are inadequate. The reconciliation would require far more radical structural changes in the political and economic system. I argue that, among other reforms, what is needed is the implementation of the right to what I call "political leave." This is the right to be a candidate for public office, the right to have the campaign publicly funded and the right to return to one's place of employment at the end of the campaign or term in office. The need for these more fundamental reforms is even more urgent given Rawls' current focus on what he calls the pluralism of comprehensive doctrines.

Rawls believes his new book, *Political Liberalism*, is not a significant departure from his first work, *A Theory of Justice* (TJ).[2] He still adheres to the two principles articulated in Theory but feels it now needs a somewhat new foundation. The main problem for his new book, *Political Liberalism,* is "How is it possible that there may exist over time a stable and just society of free and equal citizens profoundly divided by reasonable, though incompatible, religious, philosophical and moral doctrines?" (PL xviii) Rawls hopes to solve this problem by establishing the following: 1.) to distinguish more clearly the difference between moral and political philosophy; or to distinguish a comprehensive doctrine from a political one; 2.) to emphasize the importance of stability and a well-ordered society in a society of reasonable pluralism of comprehensive doctrines; 3.) to clarify that justice as fairness is not a comprehensive but a political doctrine. 4.) to show that political liberalism assumes and is compatible with a pluralism of reasonable comprehensive doctrines.

Rawls' theory of justice is summed up in his two principles of justice. These two principles are defined in *Political Liberalism* in almost identical terms as in *Theory* as: 1) "Each person has an equal claim to a fully adequate scheme of equal basic rights and liberties, which scheme is compatible with the same scheme for all; and in this scheme the equal political liberties, and only those liberties, are to be *guaranteed their fair value* (emphasis added). (and) 2.) Social and economic inequalities are to satisfy two conditions: first, they are to be attached to positions and offices open to all under conditions of fair equality of opportunity; and second, they are to be to the greatest benefit of the least advantaged members of society."(PL5-6)

Rawls notes that these two principles are political principles to govern the "basic structure" of political society not all institutions. The basic structure are the political and economic structures which define the basic rights and liberties of citizens. They express the idea of "political liberalism" or liberal ideals as they apply to the political institutions of government, such as the courts not meant to govern such institutions as the family, churches or private organizations. Secondly, as political, he believes his theory of justice is what he calls "freestanding" meaning it is a theory not derived from any "comprehensive doctrine" or ideology but is based on an "overlapping consensus" to be found among the main comprehensive doctrines of the West's public culture.(PL12)

This brings us to the third point of the theory as political, or "implicit in the political culture of a democratic society."(PL 13-4) This means that "justice as fairness *starts* from within a certain political tradition and takes as its fundamental ideas that of a society as a fair system of cooperation" .. (PL 14, emphasis added). This political culture includes the ideas of persons as "free and equal" and as rational. By this Rawls means three things. First, persons have a "conception of the good" or a moral, religious and philosophical worldview. Second, persons as free and equal means "they regard themselves as being entitled to make claims on their institutions as to advance their conceptions of the good...."(PL32) Third, persons are "viewed as capable of taking responsibility for their ends" (PL33) or adjusting their goals to conform to the principles of justice.

This political tradition also includes the idea of a "well-ordered society." (PL 35-40) A well-ordered society is a society where there is a fair system of cooperation meaning cooperation is based on "publicly recognized rules" agreed by all as just. (PL16-9, 35) A well-ordered society must also be one where the conception agreed to must be limited to the political. It must be limited to the political and not range over all of society because of three facts. First, there is what Rawls calls "the diversity of reasonable comprehensive religious, philosophical and moral doctrines found in modern democratic societies...."(PL 36) That is there are fundamental disagreements in society that are reasonable and not just based on ignorance thus not rationally refutable and which are expected to continue well into the future. The second fact is that to maintain one comprehensive doctrine as the correct one would entail "the oppressive use of state power."(PL37) Third, a secure democratic government must be freely supported by at least a majority of its citizens. How can a majority support it if there are irreconcilable pluralism of comprehensive doctrines?

Here is where Rawls' idea of an "overlapping consensus" comes in. That is Rawls believes there is a limited agreement about political justice that can be found among the comprehensive doctrines current now in our political culture. This consensus is not a mere "modus vivendi" according to Rawls.(PL 145) That is it is not merely the result of negotiation of self interested parties but rather it is agreed to on shared moral grounds found in the differing comprehensive doctrines.

Rawls wants to argue that the first principle has priority over the second. The first principle guarantees basic equal rights which are "freedom of thought and liberty of conscience; the political liberties and freedom of association, as well as the freedoms specified by the liberty and integrity of the person."(PL 291) These liberties are necessary for what Rawls calls "the adequate development and full exercise of the two moral powers of citizens as free and equal persons."(PL 297) This means, briefly, for example, that it is not allowed to trade political liberties like the right to vote for greater economic wealth. However, Rawls notes that this priority is not absolute or required in all circumstances but only under what he calls "reasonably favorable conditions."(PL297) These favorable conditions include a certain level of economic development and other conditions he does not specify. However, he does believe that the US today does meet these conditions.

Rawls gives three reasons for this priority. First, each person is assured the freedom to pursue their "conception of the good" or way of life including religious and other personal beliefs. Second, this respect for the pluralistic conceptions of what a good life is promotes the "stability" of the society. By stability Rawls means that it likely to be affirmed and accepted by all as harmonious with and grounded in "affirmation of our person" (PL317) as free and equal beings. That is, the justice as fairness is stable because , the priority of liberty protects our "self respect." Self respect means having a "secure sense of our own value" which freedom promotes. Third, the principles of justice promote "social union." That is, it promotes social cooperation and harmony because each person is respected and has the sense of security necessary for trust.

In short, Rawls believes the two principles of justice and the priority of the first are grounded in deep needs of persons as expressed in his "primary goods."(PL308) These goods are primary in that they are "generally necessary as social conditions and all-purpose means to enable persons to pursue their determinate conceptions of the good."(PL307) These goods are necessary means or what a "rational man wants whatever else he wants."(TJ 92) They are: basic liberties (e.g conscience, thought, speech), freedom of movement and occupation, opportunities and powers, income, wealth and the bases of self respect.

Rawls want to ensure that the priority of equal liberty is not just "purely formal." Equal liberty is not just guaranteed by law but also real in the sense that social and economic obstacles not reduce the value of liberty for the poor. This he intends to do with the two principles that constitute the second principle, namely, fair equality of opportunity and the Difference Principle. Fair equality of opportunity means, as he explains in *Theory*, "The expectations of those with the same abilities and aspirations should not be affected by their social class."(TJ73) Rawls also in his Theory added that natural talents cannot be said to be deserved and so must be viewed as social assets; but in Pl this seems to have been abandoned. (TJ, 101-5; PL 283-4)

The second part of the second principle is called the "difference principle." It is meant to keep economic differences between social classes at the minimum without reducing economic efficiency. Economic efficiency Rawls believes requires economic incentives such as profit and wealth to encourage economic investment and productivity. The principle states that differences in wealth are to be justified only if they help the "least advantaged" the poorest members of society. It is these least advantaged, whether due to ignorance, illness or poverty, who also have a lesser worth of the basic political liberties. They cannot participate in the political process equally with those better educated and wealthier who can bear the costs of running for public office and whose knowledge and free speech is far more effective than those who are poor and not as well connected. How does Rawls suggest we deal with this problem?

His answer has several elements. First, he believes that the worth of liberty of the poor "would be even less were social and economic inequalities . . . different from what they are."(PL326) That is, the poor would be worse off economically if society did not provide differential economic rewards for those who invest and take risks which produce wealth. Here he seems to be rejecting the greater egalitarian option in that he feels forced greater economic equality would lead to economic stagnation thus lower standard of living thus a lower worth of liberty for all, including the poor.

Rawls has two additional reasons. First, he states in *Political Liberalism*, using almost the same words as he does in *Theory*, that political parties must be kept "independent of large concentrations of private economic and social power."(PL328) This is not perfectly clear but would seem to imply a limit of the so called 'soft money' where, in the present system, there are no limits for private contributions to political parties as there are to individual campaigns. Secondly, he adds "society must bear at least a large part of the cost of organizing and carrying out the political process."(PL328) Here he is somewhat vague but he seems to be alluding to public financing of political campaigns. The thesis argued here is that these measures, to the degree they are clear, are inadequate and incomplete in providing for the equal worth of liberty.

As Rawls holds, democracy is defined as a political structure where persons freely decide who has political power and how they are to exercise that power. A democratic theory of political legitimacy assumes a moral framework among which the right to political participation is central. It is central for without the right to elect and remove individuals who control the power of government, not only is our right to development of our moral powers as free and equal denied but, even more importantly, all of our other basic liberties and rights listed in the first principle are in jeopardy. Let us how this follows and what it means.

The right to political participation can be construed negatively or positively. In the negative sense, it has usually been defined as the absence of legal impediments in voting and declaring one's candidacy for some office. This idea has been justified by Rawls and others in the following ways: First, as based on what Rawls calls the moral conception of the person as free and equal; as autonomous in having the right to control his or her own life and personality within the parameters of the equal rights of others to the same. Second, as self-protection; controlling the powerful political structure enables one to more fully protect one's rights and interests. Thirdly, the equal rights of persons to what Rawls calls self respect; to actualize their human potential by participating in various activities and functions including political processes. Fourth, as an efficient means to communication and information about the state of the populace thus enabling more adequate policies to address problems. And finally, the right to political participation is based on the assumption that human beings have sufficient rationality, ability and interest to determine their form of government.

Rawls realizes that the negative sense of political participation is inadequate. It is inadequate because it overlooks the social and economic obstacles to participation; the poor face many obstacles not faced by the rich. This is why Rawls calls for "fair equality of opportunity." This equality of opportunity is again, not merely "formal" or one where the laws do not keep one from pursuing an education or some opportunity, but a real one in terms of equal social and economic conditions. He elaborates on this in Theory as requiring that "The expectations of those with the same abilities and aspirations should not be affected by their social class." (TJ73) This means Rawls adds that "The importance of preventing excessive accumulations of property and wealth and maintaining equal opportunities of education for all."(TJ73) What Rawls calls background institutions are such institutions as the family, economic, educational, and communication institutions, among others which exist within the larger basic framework. The function of these background institutions is to help develop the potential needed to participate and guarantee the values of democracy. This implies, in addition to the right to an education, the right to participate in the political process. Moreover, it means more than this, it will be argued, it implies the right to what is here termed positive political participation, i.e. the right to the necessary means to be a candidate for political office.

It should be apparent that the above argument implies that all citizens must have the right to positive participation in the political process. This means going beyond the mere right to speak and vote; it means the *positive* right to run for office oneself. Of course the right to run for political office is already provided in democratic systems in its *negative* or what Rawls calls formal sense as the absence of legal impediments to run; what is not provided are the necessary means by which to do this. In the past, obstacles to full political participation have included legal impediments which have excluded the propertyless, women, racial and religious minorities. Today, legal and other obstacles have disappeared for the most part but economic impediments remain; although property ownership is not a legal condition for voting, lack of economic means is an overwhelming practical obstacle nevertheless. The facts are simple enough; most persons lack the time, money and an adequate education to run for public office. The demands of earning a living, employment and sufficient funds to run a viable campaign limit full political participation to an elite wealthy few.

By 'elite' is meant those individuals who share certain privileges. They have attended and benefitted from prestigious or highly selective colleges and universities and either control wealth of sufficient magnitude or are members of a lucrative profession which allows them self-employment (e.g. lawyers, entrepreneurs, etc.). These persons have the educational background and/or rhetorical skills, time and money to run a political campaign without any significant decrease in their standard of living.[3] This economic dependency and exclusion of the non-elite is incompatible with the Rawlsian basic moral structure of fair equality of opportunity and the equal worth of liberty of citizens to participate in the political process not just as voters but as candidates.

The right to full or *positive* political participation is based on the same Rawlsian reasons for equal value of political liberties and fair equality of opportunity. He states that the equal value of political liberties is so important and must be protected "by including in the first principle of justice the guarantee that the political liberties, and only these liberties, are secured by what I have called their "fair value."(PL 327) He goes on to explain "this guarantee means that the worth of the political liberties to all citizens, whatever their social or economic position, must be approximately equal, or at least sufficiently equal, in the sense that everyone has a *fair opportunity to hold public office* and to influence the outcome of political decisions."(PL 327) But Rawls does not provide for the implementation of this fair value to hold public office nor does he realize what not having fair value implies for the first principle of political liberties.

The lack of provision for positive political participation is inconsistent with several central Rawlsian ideas. First, it denies what Rawls terms the equal right to "adequate development and full exercise of the two moral powers of citizens as free and equal persons."(PL 297) Political elites are free to set the agenda and parameters of political debate leaving voters only the limited choice of reacting to a predetermined set of options. The current privately financed economic structure of the media is incapable of rectifying this problem fully for it is itself part of the economic nexus of the elite since it is owned by members of the elite and depends on that elite for financing through advertising. Consequently, it is not presently structured to provide complete and impartial information about the political or economic systems.[4] It denies the non-elite the equal right to full self-development in being excluded for economic reasons from full participation in the electoral process.

Lack of the right to positive political participation also undermines

Rawls' idea of social "stability." His conception of stability means two things. First, it means citizens have a "sufficient sense of justice" (PL141) so that they generally comply with and have an "allegiance" to the basic political institutions. Second, stability means citizens "generally endorse" the political system from their own respective comprehensive doctrines albeit for different reasons.(PL39) Rawls specifies that allegiance requires at least two conditions. First, a recognition of the right to pursue our conception of the good; and second, protection of our self respect.

Self respect, Rawls explains, is protected by upholding the priority of the first principle over the second. To Rawls self respect means having "self-confidence as a fully cooperating member of society capable of pursuing a worthwhile conception of the good over a complete life;"(PL 318) it provides a "secure sense of our own value."(PL 318) Without self respect, Rawls states, "nothing may seem worth doing."(PL 318) Can allegiance be maintained if the vast majority are excluded from active political participation? Can one's self respect be maintained without positive political participation? Can one pursue one's conception of the good when one is denied positive access to the machinery of power? No, exactly because what Rawls concedes is a fact of contemporary society, a pluralism of comprehensive doctrines.

The reality of pluralism of reasonable doctrines explains the urgency for positive political participation. That is, if we all shared essentially the same comprehensive doctrine or worldview, lack of equal political participation would not be a substantive political issue for judgments of those who had the power would flow from basically the same moral, religious and other fundamental assumptions. But since there is no shared comprehensive conception of the good, no shared religion, no shared overall philosophy, then a systematic lack of access to political decision-making puts in jeopardy one's own conception of the good and status as a free and equal member of society.

The fact of philosophical pluralism is exacerbated by human moral limitations. When the fact that only the social and economic elite have the resources to run for political office is combined with the given fact of human self interest and moral limitation, then the resulting possibility of the lack of equal consideration of the rights, self respect and conceptions of the good of the non-elite are obvious. It may also be a fact, as many have argued, that the elite generally share a comprehensive worldview that is distinct from the worldview of the less educated and economically disadvantaged. It should also be clear that the elite generally have an interest in maintaining the status quo and thus excluding significant change that may enhance the welfare of the non-elite at the cost of the elite. This, of course, contradicts the Rawlsian idea of equal worth of liberty, fair equality of opportunity and stability and thus undermines the basic structure of the liberal democracy.

This weakens another idea of Rawls, that of "social union." Social union is fostered when citizens see themselves as part of a fair system of cooperation, when "everyone participates in this good" of social cooperation. (PL320) Social union also includes the idea of "reciprocity" (PL321) of everyone contributing to society what they can and benefitting from the contribution of others. Clearly Rawls' idea social union implies participation at every level of the basic structure for to exclude some from contributing at any level is to abandon fairness and cooperation. Lack of participation by the non-elite also denies the political system adequate information feedback to enable the formulation of policies with the complete set of relevant facts in at least three ways. First, direct positive political participation by all socio-economic levels is the best way of ensuring that the circumstances of the non-elite are accurately represented since it would eliminate intermediaries from the elite class who may distort or simply be oblivious of the true interests of those whom they claim to represent. Second, if rationality is defined as choosing the best means to achieve some goal, then full considerations of all possible means is necessary. Positive political involvement enables greater access to the political debate by all strata of society thus expanding the pool of ideas, professions, approaches and policies thereby enhancing the rationality of the electoral process. Third, by expanding the pool of candidates, the likelihood of the most qualified emerging from the contest for power is increased.

Finally, inability to participate fully in the electoral process increases the alienation of vast numbers who sense the de facto system is designed to exclude full consideration of their rights by favoring the interests of the ruling elite. This sense of exclusion is made even more acute when combined with an ideological socialization which promises equality. As Rawls himself states, "for without the public recognition that background justice is maintained, citizens tend to become resentful, cynical and apathetic."(PL 363) The awareness of inconsistency between ideology and reality exacerbates alienation and reduces general loyalty for the system thereby increasing the possibility of social conflict and instability thus endangering the rights of all.

It follows, that the present structures of democracy must change in the following manner. First, all political campaigns must be publicly funded to the degree of allowing an adequate campaign. Second, private contributions to campaigns are allowed as long as they are anonymous. Third, contributions of one's own resources are allowed as long as matching funds are then contributed to opponents from the public funds.

(This will effectively limit contributions from one's own resources to a manageable limit.)[5] To this must be added the crucial component that employees must have the right to what one may call political leave: the right to paid leave from place of employment and the right to return to the same or equivalent at the former employer or similar job after the campaign or after one's term of office is over.[6] This could be implemented as a kind of affirmative action for former public servants.

Political leave is necessary for the implementation and realization of the equal values of liberty. How can an ordinary worker launch campaign with all the uncertainty this entails without the guarantee of re-employment if he or she loses or after the term of office is over? Without this provision, only the wealthy or self employed could have the luxury of taking the risk of running for office. Just as family leave reflects the value of the family, so political leave reflects the value of political participation.

Property rights cannot override this right to political leave and the right to an equivalent job after public office. Rawls himself believes only in the right to what he calls "personal property" (PL 298) not the right to own the means of production of natural resources. The right to private property cannot be used to deny this expansion of the value of political rights and employee rights. As argued above, the right to property cannot be absolute because to maintain that is to contradict what Rawls calls the basic structure of liberal democracy providing for equal or fair value of rights. To hold that the right to private property is absolute to the degree of denying the right to political leave and the necessary resources to do so would indefinitely exclude most members from full political participation thereby jeopardizing their basic rights which democracy promises. That is, rights that cannot be defended through participation in the process that defines and enforces them are obviously not real but merely formal or paper rights. This would be analogous to arguing that the right to property precludes taxation of any sort; but without taxes government and all rights would not exist or be in the insecurity of state of nature. This means that the right to private property is not basic or absolute but instrumental in that it is a form of social ordering of resources which, thus far, has been found to be, when properly limited, the best means to enhance the welfare and protect the basic rights of persons as defined in the democratic framework. If the above argument is persuasive, there is no alternative means to safeguard the basic rights of persons except through full access to the political process. This must mean the right to political leave as defined.

Rawls' concept of fair equality of opportunity also implies more than the equal right to participate in the political process. Money and time are not all that is needed to compete, other social institutions must also be equalized. This means equality of educational facilities. Schools must be equally good regardless of the social class one happens to fall into due to what Rawls calls the "lottery of birth."(TJ102) This would actually necessitate greater funds be allotted to the least advantaged to compensate for the advantages of the well to do have on the basis of the family they were born into. This also means programs for re-training later in life to meet new economic conditions in a dynamic economy.

These measures can also be seen as specifying the meaning of Rawls difference principle more fully. The difference principle, you recall, states that social and economic inequalities must benefit the least advantaged. Rawls never fully explains what this means. Part of its meaning surely involves social welfare programs such as unemployment insurance and the like. But the measures Rawls has in mind here are more distributive rather than political. To benefit the least advantaged in a more lasting way is to provide for the social and economic conditions for them to rise above their conditions and avoid these conditions. As the old saying goes, one can help the poor by giving them a fish or teaching them to fish; teaching them to fish is more in harmony with the Rawlsian conception of persons as free and equal.

There are some objections to this expansion of equality that should be mentioned. Rawls might argue that greater economic equality reduces incentives for investment, production and thus harms all. What Rawls does not seem to be aware is that one must distinguish between temporary and permanent lesser value of liberties. The least advantaged might well agree to a temporary lesser value of liberties with reasonable assurance for long term gains. There may be some reduction in economic production but at the long term gain to the least advantaged of equal citizenship. The kind of equality argued for here is not that of results but of opportunity. Indeed, the proposal here defended would increase the pool of talent from which greater excellence and economic efficiency could flow.

John Rawls' theory is based on the central value of the right of persons as free and equal. Rawls views his principles of justice as an attempt to rectify what he calls in *Theory* the "lottery of birth," the undeserved social circumstances of birth that restrict autonomy and equal opportunity of the lowest socio-economic strata of society.[7] Positive political participation is a step in the direction Rawls envisioned and one that is implied in the full realization of the democratic ideal of equal autonomy and right to self-development. When Rawls speaks of the priority of liberty, he means the moral priority of liberty over economic conditions. What Rawls seems to have overlooked is what Marx saw more clearly, at least in this instance, the economic forces have a practical priority in history and society over political structures.   To mitigate this practical and political priority, Rawls' ideas of fair equality of liberty and fair equality of opportunity necessitate greater political and economic reforms than he seems to be aware. Without direct access to the decision-making loci of power, the basic structure becomes the structure that serves the interests of those that do have that access. The connection between economic power and political participation must be severed if political equality is to be preserved. Without the equal fair value of liberty, liberty becomes just words on paper.

NOTES

A version of this essay appeared in the *Journal For Peace and Justice Studies*. 9,2.1998.

1. Rawls, John. 1993. *Political Liberalism*. New York: Columbia University Press.

2. Rawls, John. 1971. *A Theory of Justice*. Cambridge: Harvard University Press.

3. It does not weaken my argument to claim that the elite class is open to new members. As long as a society is stratified by socio-economic classes, and as long as predominantly one class has the means and connections to attain power, then the values of democracy lack full implementation.

4. See my "Freedom of Speech and Access to Mass Media" in *The International Journal of Applied Philosophy*, V4, N1, Spring 1988, pp. 51-58.

5. This must include the right to a salary equal to what one would be earning if employed (paid as part of public financing) if the campaigning is full time as may be the case in federal elections. I have argued for something similar in my "The Ethics of Financing Elections," *The Southern Journal of Philosophy*. V25, N3, 1987, pp.331-342.

6. The implementation of this right may require the exemption for some small businesses which may not be able to economically sustain the burden of re-hiring employees who, having won an election requiring full time service, were long absent. To ensure no serious economic hardships ensue former public servants, alternatives such as preferential treatment for former public officials would have to be given serious consideration. To be sure, there will have to be a procedure to eliminate frivolous candidates.

7. Rawls, John. *A Theory of Justice. Op. cit.*, pp. 60, 102-7; see also my, "Rawls and Socialism," Philosophy and Social Criticism, V7, N1, 1980.

CHAPTER 13

FREEDOM OF SPEECH
AND MASS MEDIA

A well-organized community will exhibit a certain structure of rules. The foundational set of rules, i.e., the rules that override and have priority over all other rules, one may term the "basic structure" of the community. Basic structure here means the fundamental principles which specify the basic rights and duties for all members of the community. The basic structure is an expression of a set of ultimate values that define the community and the central institutions of that community.[1]

The basic structure that concerns us here is that of a representative democracy. For our purposes, a democracy is a political system where the members of the community freely decide who will possess political authority and on what terms. Political authority is distinguished from other forms of authority in that those individuals that have it have the authority to make rules for the community as a whole and have a monopoly of power in a geographic area to apply those rules. The supreme authority of political institutions is the power correlative to the supreme role of the basic structure for the community. Political leadership in a democracy is decided on the basis of a competition between various candidates for power. This competition is a part of an electoral process, i.e., a set of rules whereby members of the community vote to determine who will receive political power or decide questions of public policy directly as in a referendum.

If the election process is to achieve its goal, i.e., select the best qualified individuals and/or decide referenda, it should be conducted in a rational manner.   A rational electoral system would have to meet several conditions.[2] First, one must have a clearly defined goal one is attempting to achieve. Here, the general goal is the maintenance and adaptation of the basic structure to new circumstances and needs. Secondly, one should have all the relevant information with which to decide between candidates and policy questions. Candidates and policies are means by which a community achieves its goals. In order to choose means and goals rationally, the electorate must be aware of all the relevant alternative goals and means and then choose the optimum goals (the goal(s) that will best maximize the values of the basic structure) and the most efficient means to achieve them. Central to this rational electoral process is availability of impartial, complete and relevant information concerning means and ends, the character and views of candidates and the existing conditions of the society as it impinges on the basic structure.

Impartiality and completeness of information are distinct notions. Impartiality concerns the unbiased and objective manner of presentation of information and facts. That is, the type of communication that presents information in the manner that the facts actually impinge on the basic structure.[3] Of course, information may be impartial but incomplete. It is incomplete if it fails to communicate the totality of relevant information on an issue as it relates to the basic structure, i.e., the totality of facts needed to make a rational decision. It is at this point that the right to free speech plays a crucial role.

The right to free speech is a moral right; a right one has simply because one is a person. A moral right is a justified claim that others act or refrain from acting in a certain way toward the possessor of the right. As such, a right is a normative structure that specifies the correct moral relation between persons and provides a degree of autonomy for persons to determine events in some specified domain.

A discussion of any right, whether it is free speech or some other right, must include four separate questions. The first question is that of the definition of the right in view; it is necessary to specify the meaning of the concept so as to distinguish it from other right concepts. Secondly, the justification for the rational and moral acceptability of the right must be addressed. Assuming the right is justified, one must ask what relation it has to the other preexisting rights of the basic structure. That is, rights can be related to one another in several ways. One right, for example, can be a presupposition of another, as the right to life is to all others. Or a right can expand the value of another as privacy may maximize that of autonomy.   Finally, implementation concerns the institutional arrangements necessary to make the right actual in the social and legal structure. The analysis of free speech can best be understood by following this structure.

The definition of free speech seems to involve four components. First, it means that there is no legal restriction on the content of the speech. That is, no point of view or subject matter is forbidden by law. Secondly, free speech must mean that there is no legal limit on the scope of one's speaking, i.e., no restriction to the size, timing or location of the potential audience. In addition, speech can be direct or indirect. In direct speech the individual speaker expresses himself while in indirect speech the individual gives some form of support to someone else's speech.

The moral justification for free speech can be framed in utilitarian or non-utilitarian terms. A non-utilitarian defense of free speech grounds it in some conception of individual autonomy and dignity. On this view, freedom of expression is seen as essential to the humanity of individuals who structure their lives and achieve self-understanding through rational dialogue. For the purposes of this essay, however, the utilitarian approach, such as that of J. S. Mill is more useful.

Mill's utilitarian justification views free speech as a necessary condition for the rational growth of knowledge which he saw as utility maximizing.[4] Knowledge can increase, Mill argued, only if all individuals can criticize the existing beliefs and propose new ones which are accepted on their ability to survive public debate on their merits. On Mill's view, the survival of true beliefs can best be promoted in this open free debate.

The relation of free speech to other rights of the basic structure suggests how free speech can be limited or expanded. It can be argued, for example, that the right not to be harmed can restrict speech as in libel or by falsely yelling 'fire' in a crowded place. Additionally, the scope of speech may be limited in order to protect minors as in the case of pornography. Free speech may be enlarged by, for example, providing persons with an education so as to increase their ability to communicate as well as expand their access to ideas, or, as will be argued here, by providing individuals with access to mass media. This concerns the implementation of the right to free speech.

Democracy, as suggested above, is a *form* of government where distribution of political power is decided by the informed consent of the governed. A necessary condition for democracy, therefore, is the existence of the rights to free speech, press and communication. Without these freedoms acquisition of political power could not occur in a competitive and rational manner nor would the electorate be able to hold accountable individuals who already possess political power. That is, speech must be independent of the existing political power structures if it is to objectively evaluate and criticize these structures.[5]

Traditionally, free speech was seen as potentially threatened primarily by government censorship. However, modern communication technology has created a new threat to the impartiality and rationality of speech and communication. At the time the Constitution was written, it was relatively easy for individuals with modest economic means to enter the marketplace of ideas and have some chance at having an impact on public policy issues. Today, the private concentrated ownership of mass media seriously limits access to the marketplace of ideas and thus the scope of speech of most individuals. It also raises questions about the objectivity and completeness of the ideas that do achieve publicity.

Mass media here means the total set of institutions (television, radio, newspapers) using complex technology to transmit messages and programs to a large audience. These media have informational and entertainment components. The informational component includes news programs, public debates, educational and community programs; entertainment includes all other programming (e.g., sports, films, game shows, etc.). Clearly the politically more relevant aspect of media is the information component (though, of course, entertainment programming also has a less obvious but nevertheless indirect and real relevance). It is the objectivity and completeness of this dimension that primarily concerns us here.

Several realities of contemporary mass media are sources of concern. First, there are the concentration and increasing monopolization and conglomerization of major media. For example, in 1972 only 4% of cities had more than one newspaper, and 60% of newspapers were owned by chains.[6] In many cities, newspapers own radio and TV stations; of the top 25 TV markets, 28 of the 69 newspapers published had ownership interests in the TV station in the same community. In addition, about 70% of radio and TV news comes from the AP and UPI news wires.[7] The three major networks, ABC, CBS, NBC, together receive 52% of total revenues of all TV stations in 1978 and they control the majority of programming of the affiliated tv stations they do not own.[8] These three networks produce 95% of all prime-time programming. In a recent poll, 64% said they relied on TV as their only source of news. The networks news programs have daily viewership of about 50 million persons.[9] Furthermore, many tv critics believe tv news is too brief, lacks depth and emphasizes the visually spectacular and melodramatic.[10] Finally, the networks are, in turn, part of larger corporate conglomerates (NBC is owned by RCA and CBS has 39 major subsidiaries).[11]

The economic concentration of media is problematic for essentially three reasons. First, the private ownership of media presents a condition of potential conflict of interests, i.e., the need for objective and complete information may conflict with the economic interests of those who own the media or those who sponsor programs through advertising. Commercial advertising links the media with the corporate sector and establishes a source of influence over programming. Just as the press must be economically and legally independent of political power in order to evaluate and criticize government, so too it must be autonomous with respect to economic interests. Secondly, the increasing concentration of media conglomerates exacerbates the first problem for it reduces the condition of pluralism Mill saw as necessary for progress to knowledge and preventing the entrenchment of status quo ideas. Concentration of media increases the possibility of the concentration of political power by reducing the diversity of ideas and by limiting the agenda of the scope of public debate. Thirdly, the profit orientation imposes an imperative on the media for maximally large audiences (higher advertising rates) which again tends to exclude controversial ideas and presents a substantial economic barrier to those who may wish to enter broadcasting since the costs are often prohibitive. This economic imperative for maximum viewers also tends to reduce the intellectual and aesthetic quality of most programming, thus ignoring the interests of substantial segments of the population.

The press has often been referred to as the "fourth estate" or the fourth element of the tripartite division of federal power among the executive, legislative and judicial branches. The press has this crucial role for if a government is to maintain its democratic character it must function within the parameters determined by the electorate and be held accountable through the objective reporting and criticism by the press. But what provides for the fairness and accountability of the press? Several Supreme Court cases and federal regulations have sought to respond to this question. Government regulation as administered primarily by the FCC provided for the orderly assignment of wavelengths for broadcasting on the limited electromagnetic radio spectrum through a renewable licensing procedure. Later developments created the "fairness doctrine" which requires that broadcasters provide reasonable opportunities to present conflicting views on controversial issues. It also provides for "equal time" to legally qualified candidates for public office to use the stations if the station has given time to other candidates for the same office.[12]

The fairness doctrine suggested broadcasters are public trustees of essentially public property (the airwaves). This view was upheld by the Supreme Court in Red Lion Broad. Co. v. FCC (326,US,1969). The court ruled that the fairness doctrine is not an attack on the freedom of speech or editorial autonomy of broadcasters. On the contrary, the fairness doctrine is not only consistent with the First Amendment but is an application of it. This is a repudiation of the traditional laissez-faire approach to free press, i.e., freedom as absence of legal restraint.

Justice White ruled that the right to access to media has priority over claims of editorial autonomy for several reasons. First, the scarcity of frequencies requires that on property rights be limited by the public's right to know. Broadcasters are trustees of the channels of representative community views, not just their own views. The right of the viewers and listeners have priority over the rights of broadcasters.

The fairness doctrine goes some way to enlarge public access to media, but it is limited. The doctrine allows access only as a response to what the broadcasters have already addressed, but it does not allow for positive and initial access. If controversial topics are ignored by the media, the public has no right to initiate debate on it. The media's power to set the agenda is crucial here.[13] Furthermore, the government theoretically provides for the accountability of the media by the threat of revoking licenses, yet in the history of the FCC, fewer than five stations were denied renewal.[14]

Other sources of press accountability have been suggested. Mass media receive the bulk of their revenue from advertising paid for by corporations, other groups or individuals. Clearly, advertisers may influence broadcasters by deciding whether or not to support programs with commercials, but their basic concern is with profit, which is based on the size and demographics of viewers, not the objectivity or completeness of the programs. Editors, directors, producers can serve as gatekeepers whose conscience may provide a more unbiased media, yet they are critically limited in their influence due to their dependency on the station for employment. External media critics again rely on other media and there is a reluctance to seriously challenge individuals who are members of the same profession. The only remaining group which can offer the possibility of accountability, objectivity and completeness is the viewer, the public, the actual consumer of programming.

The right of public access to mass media on the part of the general public can take either a positive or negative form. Positive access means the right to airtime or page space regardless of whether the broadcaster has raised the issue. *Negative* access occurs only if the broadcaster has initiated discussion as provided by the Fairness Doctrine. Clearly, positive access is necessary if the media are to be fully accountable for what they say and don't say.

The argument for public access to mass media is based on the role media play in a democratic society and the nature of the property structures comprising the media. As has been indicated above, the objectivity and completeness of information presented on the media are crucial if the media is to perform its function. To do this it must be independent of political and corporate influence. To provide for this it must be structured to include built in monitoring and self-criticism to ensure that those influences do not occur. Positive public access would provide this institutional mechanism to promote objectivity of the media by providing a forum for criticism of the media on its own programming time.

The present private ownership of mass media overlooks some characteristic features of media. A necessary condition for the private ownership of anything seems to require the possibility that many individuals who may, at least potentially, own similar properties and thus through competition, in a properly regulated market, protect the interests of non-owners, the consumers. However, ownership of non-media enterprises is distinct from media because of the scarcity of wavelengths for broadcasting. This scarcity places media more within the realm of a public utility. Public utilities are often considered natural monopolies because a plurality or utilities in the same geographic area would be prohibitively costly. To compensate for this lack of competition, a public regulatory commission monitors its performance. Since several wavelengths are available in a geographic area, the media need not be monopolistic (though de facto, it is in many areas), yet the scarcity of these wavelengths and the role of the media in the political process puts it closer to the domain of a utility than that of a factory. Since media are in the middle ground on the spectrum of ownership between a public utility on the one end and a competitive private enterprise on the other, then it seems plausible its institutional structure should borrow elements from both. Namely, the media should be profit oriented especially in its entertainment role (given sufficient plurality and de-concentration) and public participation in its informational programming.

Public access, if it is to have any significant impact on the media, must mean access to segments of prime time on a regular basis. This access would take the form of a public forum to evaluate the past performance of the station and initiate discussion concerning future programming. This forum would correspond roughly to the "letters to the editor" column of newspapers. The public forum should be complemented by a permanent institutional structures including significant participation of the public on the boards of directors of mass media to allow input on the overall planning of informational programming. Greater media accountability would also be enhanced by expansion of the independence of editors and producers from their employers. Employee rights should be guaranteed so that these individuals cannot be fired or punished for disobeying orders in order to serve the public interest by protecting the objectivity of the media. These considerations should be combined with de-concentration of the media, prohibiting the ownership of more than one medium in a geographic area and restrict, or preferably eliminate, media enterprises combining with other economic interests.

Applying these ideas to newspapers would involve several reforms. Positive public access to newspapers would mean a portion of the paper is set aside and is controlled by an independent community group which would decide how to fill the pages. Simply expanding the letters to the editor column would not be sufficient for this again is at most negative access and is under the control of the editors and therefore publishers of the newspapers. Public representation on the board of directors and expansion of employee rights as in the case of TV and radio would also be required.

In an importantly relevant case (Miami Herald V. Tornillo, (418US241,1974) the Supreme Court ruled that newspapers cannot be compelled *by law* to publish replies to editorial opinions with which some individuals may disagree. The Court argued that editorial autonomy, i.e., the right to decide what to print and how to editorialize, is protected by the First Amendment. To require a newspaper to publish certain material would diminish the freedom of the press and possibly result in self-censorship of the press by ignoring controversial issues to avoid having to give access to others to reply.

The Miami decision is logically weak and inconsistent with Red Lion. The court did not distinguish between content and scope of speech. A ruling in favor of Tornillo would have in no way restricted the content of the Miami Herald, but it would have greatly expanded the scope of Tornillo's speech. Furthermore, the First Amendment would seem to prohibit the state from restricting what papers may print, not in requiring that they expand their coverage in the interest of an informed citizenry , which has priority according to Red Lion. Justice Burger noted that "It is correct . . . that a newspaper is not subject to the finite technological limitations of time that confront a broadcaster, but it is not correct to say that, as an economic reality, a newspaper can proceed to infinite expansion of its column space to accommodate the replies that a government agency determines or a statute commands the readers should have available."[15]

Burger's logic is dubious for several reasons. In Red Lion, the court allowed the right to reply on radio and tv where the limitations of time are absolute, whereas the page limitations on newspapers are a minor economic factor. For Burger to say the number of pages "are not subject to infinite expansion" is irrelevant hyperbole. Furthermore, the right to reply does not mean that a government agency dictate content; a democratic community based committee could make these decisions. Finally, the concern over the possible self-censorship of the press can be dealt with by requiring positive access to the press, not merely a negative access based on the press taking the initiative on an issue.

It is true that a distinction does exist between broadcast and print media.

The government regulates access to the finite broadcasting spectrum, whereas no such regulation exists for the print media since no physical limits exist for the number of newspapers that may be published. However, the economic limits for starting a newspaper are almost as inexorable. The logic of the Red Lion decision is more compatible with the actual realities of mass media and the need for public access.

Finally, the decision of the court is implausible because it assimilated the right to free speech to the right of a free press. Of course, these rights are closely related, but they are distinct. The right to free speech is a basic moral right since it is an integral part of the basic structure and allows the basic structure to continue to exist as a democracy. As basic, it is strongly and inextricably tied to our conception of what a person is and what is essential to human welfare.

The right to a free press, on the other hand, takes on a different character when applied to broadcasting and newspaper publishing. As such, the right to a free press is an instrumental right, i.e., a right defined and protected in a certain manner in order to maximize some other basic right(s).[16] Instrumental rights can be viewed as part of the implementation of the basic right to free speech. In this case, a free press is necessary to maintain the integrity of the basic structure of democracy. The fairness doctrine is morally correct as it applies to broadcasting since the rights that define broadcasting are instrumental rights to provide for an informed public. If the right to free press were synonymous with the basic right to speech, then the fairness doctrine would require that each individual and unassisted speaker also advocate the contrary point of view whenever he spoke in an issue of community importance. But this would clearly be a violation of basic rights to free speech and autonomy.

The structure of instrumental rights is more flexible than that of basic rights. Developments of new technology, or changes in economic conditions may require an alteration of an instrumental right in order to maintain or increase its ability to protect its corresponding basic rights. Instrumental rights are open to cost/benefit analysis and subject to modification to ensure an appropriate balance of instrumental and basic rights to enhance the basic structure. Editors and producers, as persons, have the basic right to free speech, but as controllers of technology and media resources, they enjoy instrumental rights known as "editorial autonomy." This autonomy, is not identical with personal autonomy; it concerns control over property (technology, paper, etc.) not persons. As such, it does not enjoy the same right to non-interference as the right to free speech.

Some have argued that mass media should be totally independent of private ownership and be more like a public college or museum.[17] *Only* then, the argument proceeds, will intellectual and aesthetic integrity be possible in broadcasting. This argument would be valid if it could be shown that properly regulated marketplace forces, have no capacity to meet human needs in an efficient manner. The above argument only requires the independence of the informational component of media from economic influence. To totally ignore market forces, at least in the entertainment sector of media, opens up the possibility of a worse tyranny *by* a small group that controls media to serve only their own narrow interests.[18]

Certain of the above proposals have already been implemented into the cable TV system. In 1971, the FCC required that cable systems in the top 100 markets have a channel for free public access on a first come first served basis. Productions of less than five minutes are to be paid by the cable company, those more than five minutes by the user. New cable systems must have a two-way communication capacity. There must also be a channel for access by local and government political candidates.

Unfortunately, these proposals are not enforced and are limited even if they were enforced. Further development of cable systems could be a source of greater pluralism in broadcasting that adds competition to the industry. However, the concern here is not just with the number of broadcasters but their accountability and responsiveness to viewers, and their relationship to political and economic realities. Pluralism without genuine dialogue does not ensure objectivity and completeness of information; accountability requires positive access for this is the *only way* in which a full dialogue can be established between the viewer and the broadcaster; without it we simply have parallel monologues.

The present public broadcasting corporation is a valid component of broadcasting, but it is inadequate by itself to deal with all the significant problems of media. Namely, as a government agency, it is unduly influenced by political forces and does not give direct positive access to or criticism of the other media or itself.

This proposal for public access can be valid morally only if it can be implemented in a reasonable manner. The central question is, "Who decides who has access?" Should extremists, racists and other marginal groups be allowed to spread hatred and prejudice? Who speaks for the community? These and similar questions must be addressed.

The only group justified in deciding who speaks for the community is the community itself. Democratic elections can determine who will be on committees to decide who speaks and/or presents alternative informational programs. Essentially all groups should have access on a first come first served basis with the only restriction on the time certain programs may be broadcast to protect minors if the material is inappropriate for them.

Finally, it is reasonable to suggest that granting public access to 'hate' groups will in fact decrease their appeal and diminish the influence they enjoy today.[19]

Public access to and criticism of mass media may remedy some problems, however, will it *mean* even greater mediocrity? Does a more democratic media *mean* more game shows, sports, soap operas?[20] If it did, it would be a serious flaw in this proposal since, as indicated above, these programs ignore the needs of significant and large minorities. The airwaves are a public asset that must serve the needs of all significant segments of the community. Positive public access and greater representation of viewers on the boards of directors cannot but give greater voice to groups that may not have received enough attention thus far by mass media. Public access will provide a forum for the re-structuring of mass media and make it more responsive to the needs of a pluralistic society. A more democratic media can protect the rights of minorities and thereby provide a more pluralistic programming, whether it will depends on the details of the actual legal implementation of public access.

Conclusion

Modern communication technology, for the first time in history, enables mass participation in political processes. Yet, the present economic embodiment of mass media has created an industry that is over concentrated which places control over information in a few corporate hands. Control over information is tantamount to control over political and social institutions. This weakens democracy and what weakens democracy allows some individuals to dominate and exploit others. Public access to media strengthens democracy and allows for new possibilities in self-government and cultural expression.

NOTES

I am indebted to Michael Bayles, R.M. Hare and Jim Sterba for their insightful suggestions on a previous version of this manuscript. This essay also benefitted from discussion following presentation to the International Association for Philosophy of Law and Social Philosophy (Amintaphil) meeting at the University of Pennsylvania in Philadelphia on Oct. 31-Nov. 2, 1986; the Florida Philosophical Association meeting at Stetson University in Deland, Florida on Nov. 21, 1986 and the Philosophy Department of the University of Florida. A version of this essay appeared in *The International Journal of Applied Philosophy*, 4, 1988.

1. cf. Rawls, John. 1971. *A Theory of Justice*. Cambridge: Harvard University Press, p.7; "Basic Structure as Subject" *American Philosophical Quarterly*, V14, N2, April 1977, pp. 160-161.

2. Cf. Brandt, Richard. 1979. *A Theory of the Good and Right*, Oxford: Clarendon Press, pp.10-14.

3. Cf. R.M. Hare.1981. *Moral Thinking.* Oxford: Clarendon Press, pp.129,135-40.

4. Mill, J.S., *On Liberty.* Bobbs-Merrill Co. 1956, pp. 20-25.

5. Cf- Meiklejohn, Alexander, *Political Freedom*, Oxford UP, 1965, PP8-29; Scanlon, Thomas, "A Theory of Freedom of Expression," *Philosophy and Public Affairs.* l,2, 1972, pp.204-26.

6. Bagdikian, Ben H. *The Media Monopoly*, Boston: Beacon Press, 1983, Pp.3-25; "Right to Access: A Modest Proposal," *Columbia Journalism Review.* Spring 1969, pp. 10-13.

7. Barron, Jerome, *A Freedom of the Press for Whom?* Bloomington: Indiana UP, 1973, p. 337-8; "Access to the Press: A New First Amendment Right," *Harvard Law Review.* v.8o, May 1967, pp. 1641-1680.

8. Schmidt, Benno C. *Freedom of the Press vs. Public Access*, New York: Praeger, 1976, p. 43.

9. Ibid., p.42.

10. Ibid., p.60.

11. Ibid., pp.63-4.

12. Ibid., p.43.

13. Barron, 0p. Cit., pp.127-8.

14. See J. Klapper, *The Effects of Mass Communication*, Glencoe: Free Press, 1960.

15. Ibid., p.235.

16. cf. Dworkin, Ronald, *Taking Rights Seriously*, Cambridge: Harvard UP, 1977, pp. 22-8, 90-100, & "Is the Press Losing the first Amendment?" *New York Review of Books*, n.19,v.27, Dec. 1980, pp. 49-57; Murphy, Jeffrey, & Coleman, Jules, *The Philosophy of Law.* Totowa: New Jersey; Rowman & Allanheld, 1984, pp. 88-91.

17. Barrett, Edward L., Cohen, William, *Constituional Law*, 6th edition, Mineola: New York: The Foundation Press, 1981, p. 1432.

18. Held, Virginia, "Advertising and Program Content," *Business and Professional Ethics Journal*, v.3, nos.3&4, 1984, pp.67-9.

19. cf. Marcuse, Herbert, "Repressive Tolerance" in *Critique of Pure Tolerance*, Boston: Beacon Press, 1970.

20. Barron, op. cit., p. 290.

21. Bowie, Norman, E., "Commentary on Held," *Business and Professional Ethics Journal.* v. 3, nos. 3&4, pp. 89-90.

CHAPTER 14

JUSTICE AND THE LEGAL PROFESSION

There are many ways in which a society can be unjust. The most radical injustice would exist if the basic structure of the society, the fundamental distribution of rights and duties, were itself unjust, as a slave or sexist society, for example, would be. Even if the basic structure were just, the specific laws and acts of the legislative body could be inconsistent with the basic structure. This could be due to the ignorance, incompetence or bias of the legislators. Though laws may be fairly drafted, the lack of proper enforcement or implementation can also result in injustice. For example, the police, judges and courts may themselves be incompetent or prejudiced or structured so as to unfairly discriminate against a certain individual or group. Because of the type of society we live in, our legal system has become so vast and complex that it requires experts to understand and use it effectively. Hence, even if the laws are formulated fairly and even if the judges and jury are impartial and competent, the lack of legal counsel of sufficient competence and integrity can result in an unjust decision by the court. If a defendant lacks legal representation or has representation of a significantly inferior caliber vis a vis the opposing attorney, then the guilt or innocence may not be correctly determined or the prescribed penalty may be unfair. It is at this point that the chain of justice may have its weakest link.

The legal profession, thus, plays a pivotal role in the determination of justice. As understood here, lawyers constitute a profession in that they are a group of persons whose function in society presupposes a substantial period of formal education consisting of significant theoretical content. In addition they largely regulate themselves and enjoy material affluence and social prestige usually accompanying individuals who meet the essential needs of persons, e.g., health, knowledge and justice.[1] In their professional capacity, lawyers perform several roles in society.[2] They may counsel others in drafting various documents such as leases, wills, contracts, etc. Attorneys may also serve as intermediaries in negotiations between various parties in disputes as in labor/management discussions. However, next only to the actual formulation of laws, the role that is most crucial in matters of justice is that of trial advocacy in an adversarial judicial proceeding. In this context, lawyers represent their client in a court of law when their client is involved in some dispute with one or more persons. It is obvious that the nature of this legal representation can have significant impact on whether the rights of individuals are protected.

The legal profession as it exists today in the U.S. is a profession that sells its services in the marketplace to those who can afford to pay. Furthermore, the profession, as all professions, consists of members who are not equally well trained or experienced or competent in their knowledge and application of the law. This is due to basically two factors, individual and social: individual differences in terms of intelligence, experience or personal moral characteristics such as dedication and honesty and differences in socioeconomic background that gives individuals differential entry into colleges and law schools of varying quality and prestige.[3] Putting it bluntly, affluent and well connected individuals have access to the best lawyers with an extensive staff of specialists to defend their clients in court, whereas the poor have no similar access or no access at all.[4]

Beyond this socioeconomic factor, there are certain institutional realities of the courts that give the affluent special advantages.[5] Attorneys representing wealthy individuals have occasion to use the court system more frequently than others and as such develop informal relations with court personnel which often facilitates their transactions. In addition, the advantaged often have long term lawyer-client relationships that solidifies the lawyer's loyalty to the client as opposed to individuals who use lawyers on an episodic and isolated manner. Furthermore, the present court system is overloaded with cases which cause delays which, in turn, raises costs which the poor are less able to bear. Finally, given the present political realities, the financial resources of lawyers of the well-to-do provides the opportunity by way of lobbying and campaign contributions to influence the making of substantive rules that decide outcomes.[6] This kind of long term strategy is useful to the social elite but usually unavailable to the disadvantaged and infrequent user of the courts.

Procedural Justice

Procedural justice consists in the implementation of certain principles of justice (as specified by the basic moral framework) to the exercise of political authority. Procedural justice in the form of due process is a set of rights whereby one's other rights and duties are determined by the court according to a specified mechanism, the trial in this case. The mechanism is established to ensure that the state acts justly, i.e., consistently with the basic structure, in abridging the rights of the accused. As such, due process is grounded in those moral principles that give legitimacy to the exercise of political power.

The right to due process is not a right like the right to life, liberty or property. The right to liberty, for example, does not imply that every reduction of individual liberty is unjust; the incarceration of criminals is not obviously unjust. The right to due process is unique in that there seems no just way by which the state can deny a person due process.[7]

The issue before us then is: what are the necessary conditions and structures to correctly and fairly determining the guilt, innocence or liability of individuals in a class stratified society and profession? ('class stratified' here means that certain individuals have certain advantages and disadvantages simply because they are born into a certain family in a certain social and economic situation, not that there is no mobility between classes.) These structures will, in part, consist of what is termed 'procedural justice'.[8] These procedures consist of several rules. First, there must be a particular dispute where specific individuals are involved. Secondly, a third party, such as a judge or dispute settler, is present; no one is to be judge in his or her own case. In addition, the dispute settler must not have a private interest in the outcome, only to objectively determine the guilt or innocence of the parties involved. The settlement of the dispute takes place in a forum where information about the dispute is heard, the courtroom. The dispute is settled according to substantive legal principles and rules based on all the relevant information presented. Procedural justice is constructed so that only the guilt or innocence of the parties involved is used as a basis for determining justice.

The nature of procedural justice in the context of a trial can best be clarified by comparison with other types of procedures. Rawls' discussion is helpful here.[9] He contrasts pure, perfect and imperfect procedural justice. Pure procedural justice occurs when there is no criterion for the correct outcome independently of applying the procedure correctly. Examples of this are found in certain games of chance as in tossing dice. In this game there is no way to determine who wins or loses except by throwing the dice and seeing the result (assuming the dice are fair, of course). Perfect procedural justice is characterized by as a situation where there is an independent criterion for the correct outcome prior to the procedure being carried out. An illustration of this would be the equal division of a cake among two or more persons. Here the person who cuts the cake takes the last piece, thus ensuring a fair division. By contrast, imperfect procedural justice is exemplified by a trial. Here, the outcome desired is that the accused be found guilty if and only if he or she has committed the crime. The trial is the mechanism to determine this but no trial procedure is infallible so as to guarantee the correct outcome each time. Hence, a trial is an example of imperfect procedural justice for there is an independent criterion for the correct outcome, i.e. the guilty should be found so and the innocent, found innocent; but no procedure can ensure this absolutely. This may be due to the unavailability of sufficient and impartial information concerning the alleged action or the veracity, impartiality or competence of the individuals involved. The goal of justice, then, is to design procedures that are more likely to give us the correct outcome; the more reliable the procedures the more one is warranted in believing the punishment decided upon by the court is justified and deserved.

The adversary trial system is an instantiation of procedural justice. The structural features of this model are based on the assumption that truth concerning guilt will emerge from the struggle between two contesting parties who present their side in an impartial tribunal. One maximizes the probability of arriving at the correct outcome to the extent one can insulate this tribunal from irrelevant conditions and factors. That is, one should not be found guilty or innocent simply because one is of a certain race or sex or of a certain economic status. Furthermore, if one's economic status prevents one from having a lawyer or from having a lawyer of sufficient and comparable competence to that of the opposing attorney, then too the trial process is adulterated by an external and irrelevant factor.

These procedures must be carried out within certain economic and moral constraints.[10] One should, for example, strive to minimize the cost of the legal procedure in terms of reducing cost of personnel and materials. However, this minimum must not be so low as to unreasonably increase the probability of error, i.e., convicting the innocent or acquittal of the guilty. These moral costs must be minimized to the degree possible within certain economic parameters.

In addition to the instrumental value of procedural justice described above, these procedures also have an intrinsic value.[11] The instrumental value rests on the procedures as means to determining guilt or innocence; the intrinsic values are values the procedures have independently of the correctness of the outcome. These "process benefits" involve values such as dignity, fairness, participation and social harmony. Procedural justice is founded on the peaceful resolution of conflict as opposed to dueling or some violent conflict resolution based on brute strength and as such it promotes communal harmony. The dignity of the participants is promoted if they are given some sense that they have some control over their lives and destiny. This cannot take place if individuals are not able to participate meaningfully in the trial. This means the presence of competent legal counsel is crucial. If the parties involved cannot understand the process they are less likely to accept the settlement as correct and fair.

The argument presented here thus far is as follows: if there exists a society where there are widespread inherited privileges of status and wealth that are passed down from one generation to the next and if these privileges often allow one to attain a quality of education superior to that of others in lower socioeconomic levels and if these differential levels of professional training give the privileged advantages in the courts through better legal representation, then that society, to that extent, is unjust. It is unjust because the only relevant factors in determining a correct decision in a court of law are the facts of the case and the law, not whether one is able to afford a Harvard law professor as an attorney.

These theoretical considerations are supported by substantial empirical data. As Bedau and others have argued with respect to capital punishment, racial and economic factors play a significant role in who is found guilty and how severely he or she is punished. It seems clear from the evidence that poor black male rapists were more likely to get the death penalty (when it was constitutional to do so) than white male rapists, thus reaffirming the street saying "Those without the capital get the punishment."[12]

Equal Opportunity

In addition to the above argument based on procedural fairness there is also the argument based on equal opportunity. The general conception of equal opportunity holds that individuals must not be prevented from being considered for positions or denied certain rights on the basis of traits that have no relevance to the ability to perform adequately in those positions. In other words, equal opportunity means the absence of certain obstacles in pursuit of some goal.[13] These obstacles could be natural (lack of innate ability), socioeconomic (lack of education or wealth) or legal (the law prevents one from attaining it, e.g., women prohibited from voting). The full meaning of equal opportunity varies with respect to the overall political theory one accepts, yet most political theorists would accept that, minimally, equal opportunity means the absence of legal impediments to attaining one's goal. For example, if there is no law that specifies that women cannot vote, then men and women have equal opportunity to influence the election by voting. Of course, this formal equality can be undermined by certain background social and economic conditions such that, say, women do not have an equally good education or the leisure time to pursue political affairs. These background injustices of the past (racism, sexism) live on in the present perhaps not in the formal legal sense but socially and economically so that certain individuals cannot take full advantage of their rights and opportunities. It is clear from the preceding argument that even this formal understanding of equal opportunity is vitiated in the manner it is implemented in a judicial system that does not provide equal chance to equally competent legal counsel to protect one's rights as specified by the law.

The formal sense of equal opportunity is related to the 'rule of law'. The rule of law means individuals are judged impartially as dictated by the written law, not according to the whims and caprice of those in power. The rule of law means the consistent administration of laws. However, consistent administration of laws cannot occur when administration involves legal advice of radically different value and competence arising from the background social circumstances of economic and educational inequality.

If the argument given above is correct, then one must consider possible reforms to address the problem. One possible answer would involve the government regulation of fees that trial lawyers can charge making sure that everyone can afford legal counsel. This would include free legal services for the most indigent. In fact, this last proposal has been implemented by Congress in 1974 when it founded the Legal Services Corporation to provide free legal services for the poor.[14] This proposal would enable everyone to have legal representation but it would not provide equal legal representation since the best lawyers would still be inaccessible to the disadvantaged.

Another approach would allow full laissez-faire market mechanism to apply to the legal profession with advertising and competition. This would probably significantly lower the cost of legal advice compared to the present system of minimal advertising and minimal competition. Again, this would not provide equally good legal counsel for all, since there would still be price differences that would put the affluent on the advantage. Nor would increasing "pro bono" services adequately address the problem since it would not eliminate the advantages of those who have access to superior legal advice on a consistent basis.[15]

Other proposals have included various insurance schemes or the requirement of mandatory service to the disadvantaged for a few years after graduation for all lawyers.[16] These suggestions are helpful but, again, they do not provide for equal legal services across social strata.

The only solution to this problem is the socialization of the trial lawyers as a profession.[17] Trial lawyers would be government employees available to the public free of charge. Lawyers would be assigned cases on the basis of expertise and availability. If more than one lawyer is qualified to defend or prosecute a client, then a lottery would be used to decide. It is not necessary to socialize those lawyers that do not serve as trial lawyers for the question of justice is primarily and finally decided in the courts.

It is clear that reform of the legal profession must address the problem at every level of the architecture of the legal system.[18] This means reform must take place throughout the various roles that lawyers perform in society. As mentioned above, these roles are adjudication, negotiation and counseling. As suggested above, adjudication is solved by socialization. To address the needs of negotiation and counsel an office offering free legal advice in non-trial cases would also be necessary. To further improve the position of the poor would mean their organization into groups of like interests such as tenant unions. Organization enables the group to act in a coordinated fashion and make long term strategies for mutual benefit.

Finally, the issue of equal access to legal aid has a political dimension. The courts are institutional facilities for the implementation of authoritative legal norms promulgated by Congress. Given the present system of campaign contributions, lobbying and prevailing class origins of the legislators (many of whom are lawyers themselves) requires that we consider the possibility of whether the formulation of these norms may themselves be slanted to favor the affluent. The partial solution here would involve the public financing of campaigns and increased lobbying by the organized poor to promote and express their needs and perspectives.

A just society is one where the justice of the basic structure is fully implemented into every level of society in a consistent and thorough manner. If the basic structure does not permeate the structure of law from legislation, enforcement, adjudication and legal representation, then, to that degree, the society is unjust. A just society must be one where, as Rawls puts it, the "lottery of birth" should not reduce one's chances in a court of law.

NOTES

This paper benefitted from comments after its presentation to the Florida Philosophical Association meeting in St. Petersburg in 1987. A previous version of this essay appeared in *The International Journal of Applied Philosophy*, 5,1, 1990.

1. Wasserstrom, Richard, "Lawyers as Professionals: Some Moral Issues" in *Ethics and the Legal Profession,* Davis, Michael; Elliston, Frederick eds., Buffalo: Prometheus Books, p. 131.

2. Abel, Richard, "Socializing the Legal Profession," *Law and Policy Quarterly, Vol. 1,* No. l, January, 1979, pp. 13-17.

3. Auerbach, Jerold S. *Unequal Justice,* New York: Oxford UP, 1976, pp. 4-12, 40-60; Larson, Magali S. *The Rise of Professionalism,* Berkeley U. of California Press: 1977, pp. 166-177; Jencks, Christopher and Riesman, David, *The Academic Revolution,* New York: Doubleday, 1968, pp. 150-3.

4. Abel, op. cit., pp. 5-35.

5. Galanter, Marc, "Why the 'Haves' Come out Ahead: Speculations on the Limits of Legal Change," *Law and Society Review,* 9, Fall 1974, pp. 98-104.

6.Grcic, Joseph, "The Ethics of Financing Elections" *The Southern Journal of Philosophy,* Vol. 25, No. 3, 1987.

7. Resnick, David, "Due Process and Procedural Justice" in Pennock, J. R., & Chapman, J.W., eds. *Due Process,* Nomos 18, New York: NYU Press, 1977, p. 208; Ibid., Scanlon, T.M., "Due Process," pp. 94-97.

8. Bayles, Michael, "Principles for Legal Procedure," *Law and Philosophy, 5, 1986,* pp. 33-57; Golding, Martin, *Philosophy of Law,* Englewood Cliffs: Prentice Hall, 1975, pp. 108-122.

9. Rawls, John. A *Theory of Justice,* Cambridge: Harvard UP, 1971, pp. 83-7.

10. Bayles, op. cit. pp. 41-50; Baker, C. Edwin, "The Ideology of the Economic Analysis of Law," *Philosophy and Public Affairs,* Fall 1975, pp. 6-48.

11. Bayles, op. cit., pp. 50-53.

12. Bedau, Hugo Adam, Radelet, Michael L. "Miscarriages of Justice in Potentially Capital Cases," 197.

13. Hare, R.M., *Moral Thinking,* Oxford: Clarendon Press, 1981, pp. 1 56-7; Westen, Peter, "The Concept of Equal Opportunity," *Ethics, 95,* July 1985, pp. 838-841; Barry, P*olitical Argument,* New York: Humanities Press, 1965, chap. 6; Nelson, William, "Equal Opportunity," *Social Theory and Practice, Vol.* 10, No. 2, Summer 1984, pp. 168-70; Plamenatz, John, "Diversity of Rights and Kinds Of Equality," in *Equality,* Pennock, J. Roland, Chapman, John W. eds., New York: Atherton Press, pp. 87-93.

14. Luban, David, "Political Legitimacy and the Right to Legal Services," *Business and Professional Ethics Journal, Vol.* 4, Nos. 3-4, pp. 43-68.

15. Rosenfeld, Steven B., "Mandatory Pro Bono" in Davis, op., cit., pp., 391-427.

16. Bayles, Michael, *Professional Ethics,* Belmont: Wadsworth Publishing Co., 1981, pp. 43-50.

17. Abel, op. cit., pp. 12-23.

18. Galanter, op. cit., pp. 135-45; Laski, Harold, *A Grammar of Politics*, New Haven:Yale UP, 1931, pp. 565-7.

CHAPTER 15

THE RIGHT TO PRIVACY

Any adequate discussion of moral rights must consider at least four separate but related questions. These questions concern the definition, justification, relation and implementation of the right under consideration. Definition is basic since one must first specify the meaning of the concept in question. In this case, one must ask whether the right to privacy is a distinct right-concept or whether it is subsumable under some other category of right. If privacy is indeed a separate right conceptually understood, the next logical step is to determine whether there is in fact such a moral right and what reasons can be given for and against such a claim. Once this has been established, one should show how the right to privacy is related to other well-established rights, e.g. liberty and property. Finally, no discussion of rights would be complete without some mention of the legal and political institutions needed to implement, maintain and secure this right. Let us consider these questions in turn.

1. Definition

We cannot enter here into a detailed discussion of the nature of rights, but a brief characterization is necessary. A moral right, as understood here, is a human right; a right one has simply because one is a human being. As such, it specifies the correct moral relation between persons which requires that individuals act and refrain from acting in certain ways with respect to one another. A moral right is a valid claim justified by reference to some objective moral principle (such as Kant's categorical imperative). More specifically, a right is a normative element that provides for a certain degree of autonomy or freedom of action for an individual that cannot be restricted simply to maximize social utility or some collective goal (except in clear and present emergencies). Moral rights, then, are complex normative structures that provide the autonomy to determine events in some specified domain. In order to specify this domain, the right must be defined so as to distinguish it from other rights.

In 1890, two lawyers, Samuel D. Warran and Louis D. Brandeis (who later became Justices of the United States Supreme Court) co-authored an article in which they attempted to specify the meaning of privacy. They argued that the right to privacy is the right to be let alone or the right not to be bothered.[1] As important as this may be, still it doesn't seem specific to privacy. For example, A, could be spied upon by B by having special video and audio devices hidden in one's apartment and yet in no way is B interfering with A's right to be let alone in the sense that his actions are not interfered with. Hence, the right to be let alone is more akin to the right to liberty, to non-inference with one's actions or the absence of coercion or externally imposed constraints.

Judith Thomson has argued that there is no unique right to privacy but rather there are rights associated with privacy which are subsumable under other rights.[2] She supports her argument with several examples. In one instance, A owns a pornographic picture which he keeps in a safe. B has a special viewing device which allows him to see A's picture. B has violated A's right to privacy, but more fundamentally, A's right to property in the picture has been violated. In another example, A does not want his face viewed and so he keeps it covered. B uses his special video technology to look at A's face through his veil. B has thus violated A's right to privacy or the right not to have his face looked at. This right, however, Thomson claims, is part of the more basic right over one's person.

How successful is Thomson argument that the right to privacy is not a distinct right? Not very. Her argument that we acknowledge several rights whose status as rights is extremely questionable. Do we have a right not to be looked at or does a property right mean the right not to have that property seen? Thomson's approach is dubious because it is extremely ad hoc and her invocation of the right over our person is too vague to be helpful.

Some have suggested that the concept of privacy is related to the acquisition and dissemination of personal information. Elizabeth Beardsley and Richard Wasserstrom have argued that privacy is the right to decide and control when and to what degree information about oneself is communicated to others.[3] On this view privacy does not consist in control over all information about oneself for this is impossible since each time one walks on the street others have some information about one's height, weight, sex, etc. Rather, privacy concerns control over personal information about oneself, even though what is construed as 'personal' may vary with individuals in a society and across societies.

W.A. Parent and Thomson have objected to this definition because of its use of the term 'control.' Thomson gives the example of A having an x-ray device which allows him to look through walls into B's home. B has thereby lost *control* over who can look at him, but B's right to privacy is not violated unless A *actually uses* the device to look at B.[4] Parent argues along the same lines in his example of the comatose patient case. If A is in an irreversible coma and his wife refuses to let anyone see A to protect his privacy, A's right to privacy is not violated even though he has no *control* over the personal information about himself. The point is that control over information is distinct from the *knowing* of that information.

Parent suggests his own definition of privacy as the right "of a person's not having undocumented personal information about himself known by others."[5] 'Personal information' is defined as "information that most people in a given society at a given time do not want widely known about themselves."[6] In America today this would include information about ones marital happiness, drinking and sexual habits, income, and wealth. Parent specifies "undocumented" information for some information may have somehow entered the public record in the form of, for example, a newspaper article. Once the information is in the public domain, the dissemination of it is not a violation of privacy. Parent believes this definition captures the core meaning of ordinary usage of 'privacy' and excludes shades of meaning which are more properly part of the meaning of such rights as liberty, autonomy, and property.

Parent's definition shows the category of privacy is distinct from liberty, yet it is too narrow. The problem concerns the 'undocumented' condition. If some personal information has somehow made its way into a newspaper twenty years ago and that information is discovered by someone today, it seems plausible to argue that *further* publication and dissemination of that information is a violation of the right to privacy for privacy is a right that allows for *degrees* of violation. Privacy is violated in the degree of the *quantity* of personal information publicized and in the *scope* or extent of this publicity. Hence, further communication of documented information is a further violation of the right to privacy.

It is further unclear as to what constitutes 'documentation.' Clearly publication in the print or video media is documentation, but what of information, about one's health stored in hospital computers or credit data stored in a bank's computer, or academic grades filed in a school file? All such information can be considered private, yet it can be considered documented and in the public domain. Yet, clearly, the further dissemination of this information would be a violation of privacy. If this is correct, the right to privacy should be defined as the right of a person not to have personal information about himself known by others. This definition seems to capture the core of ordinary usage and yet avoid its vagueness.

2. Justification

Granted the definition is correct, there is still the task of justifying the right by reference to some moral theory or principle. Some have argued that privacy is essential for intimacy, for intimacy involves the sharing of personal information not shared with others where intimacy is essential for a healthy and satisfying life.[7] But it is not clear that privacy is necessary or sufficient for intimacy. Intimacy it seems, is based on sharing and caring, not only on the exclusivity of information revealed. One may confide one's most private thoughts to a psychoanalyst, thoughts one might even withhold from a spouse or lover, and yet not be intimate with the analyst. Further, it seems two strangers may be intimate and yet continue to be essentially unknown to one another. In fact, a person may choose not to be intimate with anyone, such as a hermit, and yet, he still has a right to privacy.[8] Finally, it might plausibly be argued that privacy stifles intimacy for privacy ceates barriers between persons who might otherwise become intimate.

Others claimed that the right to privacy is based on the principle of respect for persons as choosers.[9] Unwanted observation of one may change the choice situation and thus preclude the possibility of a free choice. Free choice, in turn, is interpreted as essential for developing one's identity. However, this seems more an argument for autonomy which is the right to self-determination or the making of unhindered choices, than an argument for privacy.

I believe a better justification of privacy can be made if we refer back to our definition and examples of personal information. These examples were one's marital circumstances, drinking and sexual habits, income and wealth. We can see that these all concern past behavior, present tendencies of behavior, and the results of one's behavior. The right to privacy then, concerns who knows what our behavior has been, what it resulted in, and how we are presently disposed to behave. Behavior can be construed as a function of our body: how we act is based on the physical and mental disposition of our body in a given environment. Thus, as John Locke argued for private property on the basis of our ownership of our body and the labor thereof, so an analogous argument can be made for privacy: Recall Locke's words in his *Second Treatise:* "...every man has property in his own person, this nobody has any right to but himself. The labor of his body and the work of his hands we may say are properly his. Whatever, then, he removes out of that state that nature hath provided and left it in, he hath mixed his labor with, and joined to it something that is his own, and thereby makes it his property."[10]

Anyone who believes slavery is wrong believes a person owns and has an exclusive right to his or her body. Our actions, inactions, relations or behavior is a function of our physical body and as such we can be said to own this expression of the body. But how can one own behavior? The way one can own anything, by having the right to determine who has access or use of it. To determine who has access to our behavior means to determine who has information about our behavior and the right to determine this is the right to privacy.

Of course, some of our behavior takes place in a public context, e.g. walking in the street, and as such is not private. As has been said above, what fragments of one's behavior are considered private will vary with individuals and in cultures.

Locke's theory of property has, of course, been subjected to substantial criticism, but these criticisms do not touch the argument here presented. A look at some of these critiques will make this apparent.

Some have charged Locke with using 'property' in an equivocal manner.[11] 'Property' in its paradigm use refers to objects or land or the like, not one's hands, legs or body. It is true that the term is primarily used for things external to one's body, yet Locke's argument merely claims that one has distinct and inalienable rights over one's body with the correlative duty upon others to forebear the use of our body in specified ways. Does, however, the ownership of one's body mean one owns one's children who are, in some sense, the product of one's body? Locke would certainly reject this implication since children, when they reach adulthood, attain the moral status equal to their parents and thus come to have full rights in their body. Or, to put it another way, the right to life overrides the right to property so that the child's right to life has priority over any property rights the parents may have in the child.

Still others have pointed out that Locke does not clearly state why mixing one's labor with land makes the land mine, rather than simply losing my labor. Locke may have an answer to this when he suggests that labor increases the value of land and as such one is morally more entitled to that value than those who have not contributed to its value. In any case, this point does not impinge on my thesis concerning privacy for behavior is not mixing one's labor with some public or common substance but is, as it were, labor unmixed. It is true, that, in a sense, behavior is interaction with one's social and physical environment which may be " public" in that it is not owned by anyone, yet to conclude that one's behavior thereby becomes public, would be premature. Arguing analogously to Locke on private property, one can say that, though one's behavior is an interaction with a 'public' domain, through behavior one restructures it in a distinctive manner thereby transforming it into one's 'private' domain. If one's behavior were a pure epiphenomena caused by the environment, then this argument for privacy would indeed be problematic, but this type of extreme behaviorism is implausible from the start. More importantly, the issue is not what is the complete descriptive causal nature of behavior, but the normative issue of the moral implication of holding that one owns one's body; the 'public' dimension of behavior merely points out that total privacy is an impossibility which, at the same time, one may add, is also morally and psychologically undesirable.

The consequences of denying that one owns one's body, and therefore one's behavior, would involve allowing for the possibility of gross violations of something like Kant's second formulation of the categorical imperative: "Act so that you treat humanity ... always as an end and never as a means only."[12] It would be to go beyond the scope of this essay to defend Kant's principle, yet most ethicists would agree that to reject it totally, vague though it may be, would be to reject morality itself. The violation of privacy, in the most severe sense, can involve the use of another person as a means of entertainment or diversion or worse, with the voyeur as an extreme example.[13] The love for gossip shows how prevalent is our curiosity about the private lives of others, yet there must be limits to this tendency, or persons will be reduced to objects of amusement without any of the privileges of thespians. As MacIntyre has said in *After Virtue,* the unity and identity of an individual life consists in "The unity of a narrative embodied in a single life."[14] My life is a "story that runs from my birth to my death," and since I am the author of that story, I have the right to tell it, publish it or keep it private.

In any case, the right to privacy is not absolute but may be overridden by some more basic right or normative consideration. For example, one's privacy may be transgressed to save one's own life or an innocent third party. Additionally, a distinct and significant danger to social welfare, as in the event of someone contracting a deadly communicable disease, is a sufficient reason for violating a patient's privacy. Privacy, as most if not all rights, is a *prima facie* right that can be negated by other more compelling rights. Unfortunately, due to the open texture or indeterminacy of our moral concepts the exact conditions for the defeasibility of a right cannot be given.

3. Relation

A discussion of the traditional rights to life, liberty and property will clarify the relation privacy has to them. Rights can be related to one another in several ways, two of which are relevant here. A condition can be a necessary condition in the sense that without it the other cannot exist or a maximizing condition in the sense that it allows for the greater scope and expression of something else.

The right to life may be said to be the necessary condition for any other right since without it no other right can be meaningfully maintained. The right to privacy seems at first to be unrelated to the right to life and it is unrelated if one understands the right as the right not to be unjustifiably killed. It is also unrelated if one means by it the positive right to be provided with necessary means in order to continue living such as food and shelter. It is, however, related to more extended meaning of the right to life, the right to a distinct individual life. That is, if one has a valid claim not only to live, but to live in some degree of uniqueness, then privacy is necessary. It is necessary for, without privacy, the opportunity to develop one's own specific character and life-style would be significantly reduced due to fear of disapproval and various other social pressures. Understood in this way, privacy allows a society to avoid the homogeneity it may wish to escape for reasons of the sort Mill refers to in his *On Liberty.*

The right to privacy is related most closely to the right to liberty as a maximizing condition. Information about one's personal life can be used as a weapon (as in the case of black-mail) and thus a means of restricting one's legitimate right to liberty. The right to privacy is a condition that safeguards and promotes the right to liberty, for as others have pointed out above, unwanted publicity can alter the choice situation and thus limit one's freedom.[15]

As privacy is a maximizing condition for liberty, so some degree of property is a necessary condition for privacy. Since the right to privacy is the right to determine who has information about oneself, to control access to this information requires controlling access to some of the space around one. One's house, apartment or car can be seen as a way of defining the space one needs to protect one's privacy. This of course is only an argument for some minimal right to property, not at all an argument for unrestricted right to ownership.

Some have argued that the right of privacy is incompatible with our need for community and as such, it contributes to modern urban alienation and loneliness.[16] Though one may grant alienation and isolation are serious social problems, they are not related to the question of privacy. A true community, in the sense of shared values and goals, cannot exist without the recognition of an individual right to privacy and freedom. Though intimacy is not part of the definition of privacy, it is made possible through respect for privacy, which enables in turn the formation of the core community, the family.

4. Implementation

The implementation of a right concerns the legal and governmental measures needed to protect and enforce the right. Although the U.S. Constitution does not explicitly state that privacy is a right, it has been invoked as a right in some Supreme Court decisions. The Third (quartering of soldiers in private homes), Fourth (freedom from unreasonable searches), Fourteenth (right to due process) and Ninth Amendments ("The enumeration in the Constitution of certain rights, shall not be construed to deny or disparage others retained by the people.") have been cited as a constitutional basis for the right to privacy. The actual use of privacy as a right was introduced into constitutional law in the case of *Griswold v. Connecticut* (1965) concerning the Connecticut law prohibiting the use of artificial contraception. Justice Douglas argued that this statute was a violation of the privacy of marriage, which he held was sacred. Similarly in the abortion decision, of Roe v. Wade (1973), the Court held that the right to an abortion is allowed under the right to privacy.[17] Yet, the Court has never clearly defined this right and future cases will likely necessitate a more precise determination.

As we come to find ourselves living in an increasingly technological age where information about our health, income, credit rating, phone calls, etc., is stored in vast computers, the law must anticipate possible violations of privacy in this arena. Clear definitions of who has rights to what information must be determined. This requires the categorization of information into classes based on levels of privacy involved. Though, as our earlier discussion shows, *control* over information is logically distinct from the having of the information, yet practically speaking, control is sufficient for the having and as such who has control over what information is crucial to the protection of privacy. It would seem that a right such as privacy, which is so closely related to liberty and individuality, would be considered significant enough by the state to offer it the protection that only the force of law can provide.

NOTES

A version of this essay appeared in *The Journal of Value Inquiry*, 20, 1986.

1. Warren, Samuel D., and Brandeis, Louis D., "The Right to Privacy," *Harvard Law Review* 4 (1890), p. 56.

2. Thomson, Judith, "The Right to Privacy," *Philosophy and Public Affairs*, Vol. 4 (1975), pp. 295 315.

3. Beardsley, Elizabeth, "Privacy, Autonomy and Selective Disclosure," in J. Pennock and J. Chapman (Eds.), Nomos 13: Privacy (New York: Atherton Press, 1971), pp. 50-70; Wasserstrom, Richard, "Privacy: Some Assumptions and Arguments," in R. Bronaugh *(Ed.), Philosophical Law*, pp. 148-167.

4. Thomson, J.J., op.cit., pp. 295-315.

5. Parent, W.A., "Recent Work on the Concept of Privacy," *American Philosophical Quarterly* 20 (4) (Oct. 1983), p. 346

6. Ibid., p. 346.

7. Fried, Charles, "Privacy," *Yale Law Review* 77 (1968), p. 477.

8. Reiman, Jeffrey, "Privacy, Intimacy and Personhood," *Philosophy and Public Affairs* 5 (1976), p. 34.

9. Benn, Stanley I., "Privacy, Freedom and Respect For Person," in R. Wasserstrom (Ed.), *Today's Moral Problems* (New York 1975), p. 8.

10. Locke, John, *Second Treatise on Government* (New York: Macmillan, 1956), p. 59.

11. E.g., Proudhon, P.J., in *What is Property?* (New York: Howard Fertig, 1966), p. 61.

12. Kant, I., *Foundations of the Metaphysics of Morals* (Bobbs-Merrill, 1959), p. 47.

13. An existential perspective of a similar situation is presented by J.P. Sartre in his phenomenological description of "The Look" in *Being and Nothingness* (New York: Washington Square Press, 1966), p. 352.

14. McIntyre, A., *After Virtue* (Notre Dame Press, 1983), pp. 202-203.

15. Benn, op.cit., p. 4.

16. Boone, C. Keith, "Privacy and Community." *Social Theory and Practice 9* (1) (1983), pp. 1-25.

17. Cf. Grey, Thomas C., *The Legal Enforcement of Morality* (New York: Knopf, 1984), pp. 40-55.

CHAPTER 16

EQUALITY AND THE FAMILY

Human social and political structures are in part a reflection of certain fundamental biological facts. The first of these facts is that mankind is sexual in nature and the second is that human offspring need a lengthy period of care in order to survive. This in part explains why man is a social creature and why some version of the institution of the family has existed in all known societies. This is not to say that the nuclear monogamous romantic form of this institution is universal, for it is not. Human history has witnessed an immense array of variations in meeting the basic biological facts of our nature. Everything from 'promiscuous' communal marriages, to polygyny, polyandry, lifelong monogamy, serial monogamy etc. have existed. Why different societies at different times have different forms of marriage and family structures is partly due to economic, scientific and technological evolution, political and religious ideologies, social and ecological circumstances and changing assessments of what constitutes an ethical relationship between spouses and offspring.

Western philosophical discourse has been occasionally preoccupied with the relationship of the family to political institutions and social justice. Some, such as Plato and Marx, saw the family unit consisting of husband, wife and children as incompatible in some respects with their understanding of community, individual development and autonomy. Others, such as Hobbes and Aquinas, however, understood the monogamous patriarchal family as an appropriate model on which to fashion the political superstructure. Underlying these disagreements are conflicting visions of social justice and morality.

Traditionally, one function of the family has been to offer individuals security and protection from external attack and harm. To harm someone means to act contrary to their interests and make them worse off than they would have otherwise been. This obligation applies to governments as formulated by Mill "...the only purpose for which power can be rightfully exercised over any member of an civilized community, against his will, is to prevent harm to others."[1] as well as individuals. Mill goes on to say "to bring a child into existence without a fair prospect of being able, not only to provide food for its body, but instruction and training for its mind, is a moral crime, both against the unfortunate offspring and against society; and that if the parent does not fulfill this obligation, the State ought to see it fulfilled..."[2]

Clearly, a person can be harmed in many ways. One can harm another physically (as in bodily injury, mutilation, or genetic abnormality) or psychologically (producing mental anguish, personality disorders or indoctrination), or economically (stealing or damaging one's property or assets) or politically by restricting one's liberty and opportunity. Individuals are susceptible to some harms more at certain times of their lives and from some sources more than others.   For example, psychological harm may arise from one's disordered family background and the loss of liberty may originate from the state. As long as an individual is alive he or she is subject to possible harm, but how early in one's life can one be harmed; can one be harmed by being conceived or by not being conceived?

Many laws, such as those providing for genetic screening, seem to be designed to prevent harm to as yet unconceived individuals. There are cases where a child born blind, deaf and retarded sued her doctor for delivering her and another where a child sued a hospital for not allowing her to be aborted and still others involve illegitimate children suing their parents for the disadvantages of illegitimacy.[3] These wrongful life cases as they are called, pose puzzling conceptual problems.

In most wrongful life cases the courts have refused to accept the claims of the offspring for several reasons. The court argued that these cases seem to require one to compare existence and nonexistence and to conclude nonexistence is better in some cases.[4] In the illegitimacy case, the child's mother was raped by an inmate in a state mental institution and the child sued the state arguing the state was negligent in preventing her mother from being raped. But if her mother was not raped the offspring in question would never have existed. Therefore, this child would never have been harmed for this child would never have been conceived. How can the harm principle be applied in these cases?

One way to apply the harm principle is to consider the impact a genetically deformed child has on others. One can say that such a child harms society in general in that the society must provide for extra resources necessary to meet his or her needs, resources that could be used to enhance the life of the genetically normal. If this is not sufficient one could supplement the harm principle, which is a principle of nonmaleficence, with a general principle of minimal beneficence. This principle would require that only genetically normal persons or persons with at least some minimal capacity to have a meaningful life or a life of well-being be brought into existence.[5] What this minimal capacity is and what a meaningful life is will, of course, vary with time and place. This principle of minimal beneficence may be grounded through some version of a Rawlsian hypothetical contract or average utility.

These conditions of well-being are many and encompass the full spectrum of needs persons have in order to enjoy a life worth living. The wrongful life cases suggest the need of an adequate and normal genetic inheritance to avoid retarded and otherwise deformed persons. Beyond this, of course, the proper rearing of children must meet certain conditions. The parents must have sufficient knowledge about the nutrition and health of children to ensure biological health. They also must be psychologically healthy in order for their children to have a greater chance of mental health. They also must have sufficient economic resources to provide the child with clothes, shelter, nutrition and education. These requirements are justified on the basis of the moral duty to prevent harm or provide some minimal benefit.

The present institution of the family presents substantial obstacles in preventing harm to and meeting the needs of children. Sociological evidence and ordinary experiences reveals that some parents are not genetically, psychologically, educationally or economically fit to have or raise children. Besides the obvious physical harm that poor nutrition, economic exploitation and abuse can cause, the issue of psychological well-being means, among other things, a sufficient degree of self-esteem so that the child has a belief in his or her own self-worth which is necessary for success and achievement throughout life. The sense of self-worth usually arises from the affection, care and support of some individual or group, but it is obvious parents often do not provide this.

An important component of well-being and genuine personhood is individual autonomy.[7] One has autonomy or self-determination when certain obstacles to one's actions are absent and when certain conditions are present.[8] To have freedom of action certain external impediments must be missing such as lack of physical barriers of coercive threats or the lack of resources. Internal conditions for autonomy include the absence of such conditions as obsessions, compulsive habits and the presence of sufficient knowledge and rationality. For a person to be autonomous he or she must not only be free of external impediments but also free of a mindless parroting of the beliefs and values of others. However, this is exactly the danger when offspring go through the process of socialization, i.e., the process of taking on the customs, values and beliefs of the culture and family into which they are born. To be sure, all children must be socialized one way or the other, but it is crucial how this process of enculturation takes place. What seems to be required is socialization that includes the inculcation of sufficient rationality so that the child will eventually become aware just what his or her process of socialization was and critically evaluate it, accept some and perhaps reject other beliefs and customs.

Proper socialization, then, means to be educated and trained so that one can eventually achieve a degree of self-knowledge to objectively scrutinize one's culture.[10] Families, however, in their present form, often seek to perpetuate through their children their own political, moral or religious dogmas in a manner that the offspring may not be able to rationally evaluate or discard without emotional trauma at a later time. This socialization as indoctrination creates children who are intellectual slaves by weakening their autonomy and self-determination as well as perpetuating various immoral and false belief systems and attitudes.

This view of socialization goes against the traditional view as supported by Charles Fried and others. He contends that "The right to form one's child's values, one's child's life plan and the right to lavish attention on that child are extensions of the basic right not to be interfered with in doing these things for oneself."[11] He goes on to say that the parents must do this "in the child's best interests" and that "society has no special right to choose [a child's values] since society, after all, is only the hypostasis of individual choosing persons."[12] But, surely the right not to be interfered with ends when one is harming another, child or adult. Secondly, if, as Fried says, the parents must socialize in the `best interests' of the child, how can these interests not include autonomy? This does not mean that an Amish community, for example, would not be able to present its values and way of life to its own offspring, only that the alternative values and life plans be also presented in their socialization in an overall context of critical rationality to enable the child to choose his or her own identity.[13]

Besides being harmed genetically, physically and psychologically one can also be harmed politically. If one's liberty and opportunity are unjustifiably limited, to that degree one is harmed. The present institution of the family poses serious obstacles to equality of opportunity of children. For our purposes, equality of opportunity means the absence of certain obstacles in the pursuit of some goal. These obstacles can be natural (genetic defect, handicaps, lack of innate ability) socio-economic (lack of wealth, social status or education) or legal (the law prohibits it).[14] If we accept some version of human moral equality such that persons are entitled to equal chances or some degree of equal access to social resources just because they are persons, then a certain conception of equal opportunity follows.[15] It is obvious that persons are born into families and social classes of widely unequal wealth, education and status. It is further obvious that these inequalities have an impact on the life prospects and opportunities of individuals, even though there are no legal impediments present. This is why Rawls suggests the right to what he terms "fair equality of opportunity" points to the abolition of the family in order to provide all offspring with equal starting social and economic conditions.[16] However, Rawls refuses to go this far but his reasons are not clear except that, given the full implementation of his two principles of justice, he believes the inequalities of the family would "more easily be accepted."[17] This may be true, but that they are accepted does not mean they are justified. It is also interesting to note that the family is not mentioned by Rawls as one of the "primary goods" crucial to the reasoning of the hypothetical individuals in the original position.

Rawls suggests at one point, as have others, that the family cannot be abolished because it alone can provide the necessary affection the child needs to be psychologically healthy and have a sense of self-worth. However, it is not all obvious that the status quo family arrangement actually provides such necessary affection for most children. Other social arrangements for raising children may do better than the nuclear family.[18] A more communal raising of children, with the parents and community sharing in the nurture of offspring, would provide greater equality and opportunity by making the resources of the community more equally available to every child. It has been further suggested that the traditional monogamous family limits the sources of affection for children and deprives them of the security and richness of the larger community group.[19]

The arguments suggested above entail the restructuring of the traditional family and reproductive rights. Reproduction involves several distinct and independent processes. First, there is conception whereby one contributes one's genetic material. This is normally followed by gestation or the development of the fetus which could take place in an artificial womb or in someone other than those who provided the genetic material. Finally, rearing of the offspring means providing the proper social and psychological environment for the offspring. A person or persons may be fit in all, some or none of these aspects of reproduction. Couples that are genetically, psychologically, educationally or economically likely to cause harm to potential offspring must not be allowed to have children. Individuals who are only fit genetically can conceive and possibly carry the child to term, but must then give it up to a child raising institution or to foster parents who are deemed fit in all of the above mentioned respects.

This recommendation, of course, goes against the prevailing traditional view that there is a right to have children.[20] The question of rights must be analyzed into four distinct elements: definition, justification, relation and implementation. In terms of definition, the alleged right to have children is normally construed as a negative right i.e., a right that others not prevent one from conceiving and rearing children, not that one has a positive right that a child be provided one. It is true that the 1968 UN Declaration of Human Rights did include the right to procreate as a basic right. But how does one in general determine whether a given moral right exists or not? This is the problem of justification.

One can define a moral right as a justified claim based on some moral principle.[21] The principles one might invoke concerning the right to have children would probably be autonomy, privacy, natural law or some version of the general principle of utility. The argument from autonomy is based on the claim that persons have the right to act and exercise their bodily capacities without interference from others. Of course, this right is legitimately expressed only within the limits that exclude harming others unless they consent to the harm. Clearly children cannot consent to be conceived, born or reared. Those individuals that cannot validly consent to a certain treatment, whether the mentally retarded, insane etc., are generally protected by the state which sets guidelines to protect their interests. In this respect children are an analogous case. Consequently, prospective parents cannot claim to have such a right if it entails harm to the possible offspring or does not meet a certain level if beneficence to ensure the offspring's well-being. The right to privacy suffers from the same difficulty.

A Kantian argument can be used to clarify this further. Kant's first formulation of the categorical imperative states: "Act only on that maxim whereby you can at the same time will that it should become a universal law."[22] It would be beyond the scope of this paper to discuss this complex statement fully, but it seems plausible to say that Kant believes this principle is a necessary condition for moral action, i.e., it must be logically possible for all persons to do likewise under the same circumstances. However, by using the concept 'will' and through his examples, especially of the rich man, Kant is also suggesting that a moral action is one where one would be willing or find it acceptable to be the recipient of such an action in the future. The categorical imperative then is a form of the Golden Rule (Do unto others as you would that they do to you.) a principle based on the equality of persons which implies reciprocity and equal consideration of interests.[23] We can apply this imperative as follows: If we approve to the degree that we are genetically normal, autonomous, benefitted from a good familial and social environment and we believe these are important goods to have, then we must act to ensure them in our offspring.

Kant's second formulation of the categorical imperative reinforces the above argument. It reads: "So act as to treat humanity whether in thine own person or in that of any other in every case as an end in itself and never a means only."[24] To claim one has a right to bear and rear children even though one cannot meet the minimal standards of nonmaleficence and beneficence then one can be said to use children as a thing in violation of their dignity as persons. To bring children into the world for one's own ends, whether status, social acceptance, companionship, emotional satisfaction, to perpetuate one's genes (genetic immortality) race, ethnic group or family name, without regard to the necessary conditions for a morally proper upbringing is to use the child as a mere means to an end.

The natural law argument presents a different kind of approach. Proponents of this approach such as Thomas Aquinas claim that those ends persons are by nature inclined are good.[25] Since people are inclined to sexual intercourse and since the purpose of sexual intercourse is reproduction, there is a right and, indeed, a duty, to reproduce. This argument suffers from some well-known defects. It is not clear one can argue that the end of a natural inclination is good unless one also assumes that nature and humanity were created by a good creator. Without this assumption we cannot show that every natural inclination or process is good; nature may be indifferent or even detrimental to human welfare. Even if one could show this, it would not follow that everyone must reproduce (Aquinas considered celibacy a higher calling than matrimony) or reproduce under all circumstances. Or, put in purely naturalistic terms, one could plausibly argue that not life but a certain kind or life (one on balance, worth living, i.e., containing more good than evil, however this is understood is not relevant here) should be brought into existence.

The general point so far is that no right can be legitimately exercised under all conditions. Rights exist as a set of impinging powers; to extend one right inordinately may reduce the value of another right. Similarly, one right may enhance another as privacy and knowledge expand freedom. One may grant that there is a right to conceive and rear children if one grants that the right is contingent on the ability of the potential parents not to harm the progeny in the ways specified above.

The justification of the right to have children based on the principle of utility poses a different challenge. The duty to maximize utility can be understood as the obligation to maximize total or average utility. If one were to require that one maximize total utility, there would be an obligation to expand the human population to the point where one more person would make the total net happiness of the planet less than it would be without that person. Average utility requires that one increase the population until the overall utility of life of the next possible person would be lower than the average utility of the population without that person. If the population is constant, maximizing total utility would also maximize average utility. To adopt the total utility principle would have the repugnant consequence of a planet teeming with persons with lives just barely worth living.[26] The principle of average utility is plausible and consistent with the argument presented here.

Having considered the issues of the definition, justification, and relation of the right to procreate, there is still the matter of implementation. There are several ways in which the state could carry out this policy of controlling reproduction. Governments have at their disposal several options: education, regulation, monetary incentives and prohibition. To prevent the birth of severely defective offspring the state could offer financial inducements that the relevant potential parents choose sterilization. As Supreme Court Justice Oliver Wendell Holmes wrote when he upheld the sterilization of a retarded mother, herself an offspring of retarded parents,: "Three generations of imbeciles are enough."[27] This would involve a very small percentage of the potential parents. However, couples unfit to procreate may be fit to adopt and raise children. A couple that is genetically fit but psychologically unfit due to severe mental retardation, incorrigible and incapacitating mental illness or other disqualifying personality trait would also be encouraged to undergo sterilization. This again would be an exceedingly small percentage of the population.

The largest group to be affected by the suggested restructuring of the family would be those who are educationally and economically unsuited to raise children. Economic conditions can be alleviated through government subsidy, adoption or the communal raising of children but educational standards can be met in two ways. One would require mandatory classes of all prospective parents in the nurture of offspring. Those who are otherwise fit and have completed the requisite educational training would receive a license to have children.[28] Of course, unless some reversible sterilizing agent could be introduced into the general population, persons cannot be totally prevented from conceiving, but the combined effect of a general educational program on the virtues of responsible procreation, regulation (licensing after education for procreation, genetic screening) incentives (for sterilization, limiting offspring) and penalties (removal of offspring from parents clearly unsuited to rear children, as is done today, loss of certain tax advantages, etc.) would go some distance in reducing harm to offspring. The state presently licenses potentially harmful activities in other areas of life including driving a car or practicing medicine; procreation and rearing can clearly be dangerous to offspring, it too should be regulated for the same reason.

These suggestions for radical reform of the family might be resisted because of the belief that the nuclear family consisting of husband, wife and children are a natural and universal expression of human nature.[29] On this view the family fulfills vital functions that cannot be fulfilled by other groups. These functions include the satisfaction of sexual needs, the propagation of the species, mutual economic support and socialization of the children. However, these patterns are not universal and even if they were there would be no need to perpetuate a given social arrangement when morally superior alternatives become available. The growth of scientific knowledge about genetics and the development and education of children as well as the obvious socio-economic changes in the contemporary family (increased divorce, both spouses working full-time), a different conception of children which rejects the notions of offspring as mere sources of cheap labor or security in old age, require a rethinking of the traditional family. It is of course true that children are an element of human happiness for many, but to what extent this happiness is a product of socialization, a substitute for unmet needs, a product of ignorance and poverty or an attempt to live vicariously through one's offspring is not clear.

Would licensing parents violate the right to privacy and lead to excessive intrusion into the family?[30] As suggested above, the right to privacy cannot be interpreted as the right to harm someone in the home, especially a child who is not there by his or her consent. Undoubtedly there would be some intrusion into the lives of prospective parents, but how can this be compared to the benefit of preventing harm to future persons? This interference is in fact practiced today by adoption agencies investigating prospective adoption parents and surely these kinds of inquiries are justified.

Licensing certain activities as practiced today presumes there is a body of knowledge one must master before one can engage in a certain activity. Is there such a body of knowledge concerning parenting? Can we accurately predict who will be a qualified parent? Genetics is a science that can be used to predict with a great deal of accuracy the possibility of genetic defects. Also, it seems clear, that there is a substantial amount of objective knowledge concerning nutrition and child development. It is true that present day psychological knowledge cannot fully predict who will be a fit parent, still it can at least be used to exclude some who are clearly unfit and future psychology will presumably do better. Nor is absolute accuracy in the licensing procedure necessary to justify licensing. All that is necessary is that licensing do better than no licensing. And finally, the potential harm that comes from being raised in an inferior socio-economic class in terms of loss of opportunity is not based on controversial body of knowledge but on realities fairly objective and obvious in most cases.

Will licensing be fairly used or will it discriminate against the poor and the minorities? As argued here, only those genetically unfit will not be allowed to conceive children, all others can have children but may not necessarily be allowed to raise them. If they lack the proper education, psychological make-up or economic means (unless government provides subsidy) then their children will be raised by adoptive parents or communally.

Some might argue that to provide equal opportunity in terms of equal starting conditions entails bringing down those offspring who might otherwise have received a superior socialization thus resulting in social inefficiency or overall mediocrity.   However, equal opportunity as understood here means providing each person sufficient resources to develop his or her abilities; those with greater abilities would have access to greater resources in order to achieve their limit for reasons of self-development as well as to make a larger contribution to social welfare. Furthermore, bringing the lower socio-economic class up means gaining talents that were previously undeveloped and made no social contribution. As Mill pointed out with respect to a society that systematically denied women equal chances as men, such a society was inefficient in that it politically excluded half the population from competition for jobs and positions of power thus reducing the pool of applicants from which these individuals were chosen.[31]

The question of equal opportunity for children raises the related issue of equal opportunity for women. Traditionally in almost all cultures women were denied the same rights as men; their destiny was to be pregnant and housewives. This almost universally assumed inferiority of women included a double standard concerning sexual behavior with men given liberties in pre and extra-marital sex usually denied women. It was not until the industrial revolution that the social position of women began to improve and only at the beginning of this century did women begin to get the same political rights as men. This greater political equality combined with the development of artificial contraception greatly increased the freedom of women. This freedom has meant increased opportunities for education and careers which increased the need for limiting reproduction. The argument presented here for greater limitation on procreation and a more communal rearing of children will add momentum to the continued liberation of women.

The approach presented here has focused on the potential parents and the possible harm to the offspring that may result. This micro perspective is complemented by the macro approaches to limiting population as a public good which others have argued. Here the claim is that limiting population growth is a public good that is necessary to ensure a decent standard of living for the present and future generations. What these approaches seem to lack however is a sufficient awareness of the urgency and full ramification of the population problem. This issue is not just providing a decent minimum for all but to increase the level of self-actualization and the achievement of human excellence. Due to the scarcity of human resources, the level of human fulfillment and development will always be in reverse proportion to the size of the population. Human history is filled with appalling masses which hardly reach an infinitesimal fraction of their potential as persons and in fact most have and still live today on the edge of existence and in degrading misery. Why perpetuate this grotesque panoramic spectacle of global human suffering and borderline existence through the uncontrolled growth in the population? Why not strive for the actualization of human excellence in knowledge, virtue, artistic expression and personal happiness; potentialities that have barely been tapped. To create excess number of persons is a kind of adulteration of collective human existence.

This is not an argument for the development of some Ubermensch or master race which thrives at the expense of others. The creation of human excellence must take place in a framework of equal respect for the potentialities of all persons. Whether or not all can achieve the same level or not, all deserve an equal opportunity to do so.

To be sure, many of these recommendations for restructuring the family are in a sense not new (Plato and Marx have endorsed something like it) but in another sense, they are futuristic in nature. Futuristic to the extent that they are contingent on future developments in the field of psychology and its ability to provide an objective body of knowledge concerning child development and good parenting. Nevertheless, if we are genuinely committed to autonomy, equal opportunity for children and women, and human excellence, then the traditional rights of parents must give way eventually to licensing and a more communal and equal raising and socialization of offspring. This is not an argument for the violation of rights but for the possibilities of transforming procreation from an act of careless passion to an act of enlightened reason.

NOTES

A version of this essay appeared in *Perspectives on the Family,* Moffat, R., Grcic, J., & Bayles, M., eds., Mellen Press, 1990.

1. John Stuart Mill, *On Liberty* (New York: Bobbs-Merrill, 1956), p. 13.

2. Mill, *Liberty*, p. 128.

3. I will not consider in any detail whether there is an obligation to conceive and bear offspring that would be genetically normal and have, on balance, a good life. See Derek Parfit, "Future Generations: Further Problems," *Philosophy and Public Affairs* 11 (1982): 113-72; James Sterba, "Explaining Asymmetry: A Problem for Parfit" and Parfit's reply, *Philosophy and Public Affairs* 16 (1987): 188-92 and 193-94; R.M. Hare, "Abortion and the Golden Rule," *Philosophy and Public Affairs* 4 (1975): 201-22.

4. Michael Bayles, "Harm to the Unconceived," *Philosophy and Public Affairs* 5 (1976): 293-95.

5. Bayles, "Harm," pp. 300-03; Bonnie Steinbock, "The Logical Case for 'Wrongful Life'," *Hastings Center Report* 16 (April 1986): 15-20; Thomas Foutz, "Wrongful Life: The Right Not to be Born," *Tulane Law Review* 54 (1980): 480-99; John A Robertson, "Procreative Liberty and the Control of Conception, Pregnancy and Childbirth," *Virginia Law Review* 69 (1983): 405-64.

6. According to the available evidence, every year in the U.S. as many as a million children are abused and over one thousand killed by their parents; 80% of incarcerated criminals were abused as children; see Saad Nagi, *Child Maltreatment in the U.S.* (New York: Columbia University Press, 1997).

7. Karl Marx and Friedrich Engels, *Communist Manifesto,* in *Marx-Engels Reader,* ed. Robert C. Tucker (New York: Norton, 1978), p. 490; Karl Marx and Friedrich Engels, *Critique of the Gotha Program,* in *Marx-Engels Reader,* p. 541; and Friedrich Engels, *The Origin of Family, Private Property and State,* in *Marx-Engels Reader,* p. 746.

8. Robert Young, "Autonomy and Socialization," *Mind* 79 (1980): 565-66.

9. Joel Feinberg, *Social Philosophy* (Englewood Cliffs, N.J.: Prentice Hall, 1973), p. 13.

10. Kenneth Henley, "The Authority to Educate," in *Having Children,* ed. Onora O'Neill and William Ruddick (New York: Oxford, 1979), pp. 254-61; Jeffrey Blustein, *Parents and Children* (Cambridge: Harvard University Press, 1978), pp. 154-56.

11. Charles Fried, *Right and Wrong* (Cambridge: Harvard University Press, 1978), pp. 152-54; Aristotle seems to hold a similar view: *Nicomachean Ethics,* bk. 8:12 and *Politics,* bk. 1.

12. Fried, *Right and Wrong,* p. 154.

13. Wisconsin v. Yoder, 406 U.s. 158 (1972); Amy Gutman, "Children, Paternalism, and Education: A Liberal Argument," *Philosophy and Public Affairs* 9 (1980); 340-49.

14. Peter Westen, "The Concept of Equal Opportunity," *Ethics* 95 (1985): 838-41.

15. Bernard Williams, "The Idea of Equality," in *Philosophy, Politics and Society* (Second Series), ed. Peter Laslett and W. G. Runciman (New York: Barnes and Noble, 1962), pp. 124-27.

16. John Rawls, *A Theory of Justice* (Cambridge: Harvard University Press, 1971), pp. 74, 301, 511; James S. Fishkin, *Justice, Equal Opportunity and the Family* (New Haven: Yale University Press, 1983), pp. 35-44; Plato, *Republic*, bk. 5.

17. Rawls, *Theory of Justice*, p. 512.

18. Benjamin Beit-Hallahm and Albert I. Rabin, "The Kibbutz as a Social Experiment and as a Child-Rearing Laboratory," *American Psychologist*, July 1977, pp. 532-35; Graham B. Blaine, *Are Parents Bad for Children?* (New York: Coward, McCann & Georghegan, 1973), pp. 147-48, 150-57; Bruno Bettelheim, *Children of the Dream* (New York: Macmillan, 1969); Christopher Jencks and David Riesman, *The Academic Revolution* (New York: Doubleday, 1968), pp. 147-48.

19. John McMurtry, "Monogamy: A Critique," in *Occasions for Philosophy*, ed. James C. Edwards and Douglas MacDonald, (Englewood Cliffs, N.J.: Prentice Hall, 1979), p. 282.

20. S. L. Floyd and D. Pomerantz, "Is There a Natural Right to Have Children?" in *Morality and Moral Controversies*, ed. John Arthur (Englewood Cliffs, N.J.: Prentice Hall, 1981), pp. 131-38; Hugh Lafollette, "Licensing Parents," *Philosophy and Public Affairs* 9 (1980): 186; Kenneth Boulding, "Marketable Licenses for Babies," in *Population Evolution and Birth Control*, ed. Garrett Hardin, 2d ed. (San Francisco: Freeman, 1969), pp. 340-41; Garrett Hardin, "The Tragedy of the Commons," in *Population, Evolution and Birth Control*, pp. 374-75.

21. Joel Feinberg, "The Nature and Value of Rights," *Journal of Value Inquiry* 4 (1970): 243-57; Carl Wellman, *Morals and Ethics* (Englewood Cliffs, N.J.: Prentice-Hall, 1988), pp. 236-39.

22. Immanuel Kant, *Foundations of the Metaphysics of Morals*, trans. L. W. Beck (New York: Bobbs-Merrill, 1969), p. 22.

23. See R. M. Hare, *Moral Thinking* (Oxford: Clarendon Press, 1981), pp. 21-23, 107-116.

24. Kant, *Foundations*, p. 53.

25. Thomas Aquinas, *On the Truth of the Catholic Faith, Summa Contra Gentiles*, trans. V.J. Bourke (Garden City, N.Y.: Doubleday, 1956), bk. 3, pt. 2.

26. See Parfit, "Future Generations."

27. Buck v. Bell, 274 U.S. 200 (1927).

28. Lafollette, "Licensing," pp. 183-85; Anthony Graybosch, "Parenting as a Profession: Children's Rights and Parental Responsibility," *Cogito* 2 (Sept. 1984): 95-98.

29. Rustum Roy, "Is Monogamy Outdated?" in *Marriage and Alternatives*, ed. Roger Libby (Glenview, Ill.: Scott, Foresman, 1977), pp. 29-30; Richard Wasserstrom, "Is Adultery Immoral?" in *Philosophy and Women*, ed. Sharon Bishop and Marjorie Weinzweig (Belmont, Calif.: Wadsworth, 1979), pp. 120-27; Marvin Harris, *Cultural Anthropology* (New York: Harper & Row, 1983), pp. 84-93; Suzanne Keller, "Does the Family Have a Future?" in *Family in*

Transition, ed. Arlene S. Skolnick (Boston: Little Brown & Co., 1977), pp. 578-92.

30. Lawrence Frisch, "On Licentious Licensing: A Reply to Hugh Lafollette," *Philosophy and Public Affairs* 11 (1982): 1975; Ferdinand Schoeman, "Rights of Children, Rights of Parents, and the Moral Basis of the Family," *Ethics* 91 (1980): 6-19.

31. John Stuart Mill, *On the Subjection of Women* (Greenwich, Conn.: Fawcett, 1971); Virginia Held, *Rights and Goods* (New York: Free Press, 1984), pp. 191-206.

32. I am grateful to the late Michael Bayles and R. M. Hare for their helpful comments on an earlier version of this paper.

CHAPTER 17

ACADEMIC FREEDOM
AND DEMOCRACY

Recent discussions about the quality of American education have sparked renewed debate about the question of tenure. To address this problem adequately, one must consider the role of educational institutions, especially colleges and universities, in the political and social context in which they are defined and structured. For the purposes of this essay, we will assume the political system of a representative democracy as the relevant political context for our discussion. Let us briefly consider this system.

A democracy is a political system in which individuals of that community freely decide who shall have political power and on what terms. The role of those persons who have political power is to make decisions (laws) for the community as a whole. These persons are chosen through an electoral system where candidates for power are selected by citizens casting votes according to their preferences. For these preferences to be rationally expressed, the electorate needs complete and impartial information about the character and policies of the candidates, the existing conditions of the community, the appropriate ends to be pursued and the most efficient means to achieve them. This is where free speech and academic freedom are crucial.

The type of democracy that is assumed here places a special importance on the right to free speech. A systematically complete discussion of free speech or any complex concept should consist of five distinct aspects:

definition, history, justification, relation and implementation. Definition, of course, is central for specifying the exact nature of the concept under discussion, ideally giving necessary and sufficient conditions for the use of the concept. The historical aspect is simply a survey of the temporal evolution of the concept; this usually provides suggestions for its justification. Justification refers to the arguments or reasons necessary to rationally assent to the validity of the alleged right, which, in normative discourse is usually made in terms of some moral theory from which the right is presumably entailed. The notion of relation concerns the role the right under discussion plays with respect to other rights or moral categories. Finally, implementation addresses the problem of the proper institutional or legal structures necessary to apply and protect the right in actual social circumstances. Let us consider these questions in turn.

As a first approximation, the right to free speech will be defined here as a right that others refrain from restricting the **content** of speech. That is, there is no idea or opinion that is forbidden by law. In addition, there must be no limit on the **scope** of speech, i.e., no restriction on the size, timing or location of the potential audience. This first approximation which presents the right to free speech as absolute and totally unrestricted is modified when its relation to other rights and interests is brought into the discussion. It will be assumed that free speech can be limited in order to prevent harm to others. Traditional examples of justified limits on speech include such cases as falsely yelling "fire" in a theater, libel, to protect minors, as against pornography, etc.

Historically, the right to free speech has had a long if checkered career. It's origins probably go back to Socrates' defense of the freedom of thought in Plato's *Apology*. There, Socrates argued, among other things, that he had a higher duty to the gods to pursue knowledge which he believed would ultimately benefit Athens as well benefit him. Liberal thinkers such as Locke and later Mill use various arguments to justify free speech as a human right. However, it is generally agreed that special protection for the right to free speech for faculty members as academic freedom (see below) was first fully implemented in Germany in the nineteenth century.

For our purposes, the justification of the right to free speech can be based on the necessary conditions for the growth of knowledge and the nature of democracy. This justification can be made in utilitarian or non-utilitarian terms. A non-utilitarian defense of free speech grounds it in some conception of individual autonomy and dignity. A utilitarian approach such as that of J. S. Mill views free speech as a necessary condition for the rational growth of knowledge.[1] Mill argued that only if all individuals can criticize existing beliefs and propose new ones can knowledge increase.

Free speech is also a necessary condition for democracy. For persons to rationally choose their representatives, they must have access to the most complete and objective information, especially if political power is to be distributed by the informed consent of the governed. Without the right to free speech, political power could not be acquired in a competitive and rational manner, nor would the electorate be able to hold accountable individuals who already possess political power. The right to free speech, then, has a double foundation: as a necessary condition for rationality and the growth of knowledge, and for the maintenance of a democratic government.

The right to free speech, like any other crucial right, must have an institutional implementation. That is, it must have social structures that define and interpret it (e.g. courts), expand and publicize it (e.g. the press), as well as promote and nourish it (e.g. educational institutions). Educational institutions perform at least four central functions in a democratic society: the socialization (inculcating of the community's beliefs values and customs) of new members, the training and certification for the various roles and professions, the development of individual potential and knowledge and the development of a critical perspective. That is, in a democratic society, educational institutions do not merely passively transmit the existing beliefs and values but also seek to evaluate and criticize them and to promote the development of more adequate ideas and a more rational society.[2]

It is assumed here that rationality is a desirable trait for any society to have, but it is especially desirable in a democracy. Rationality is desirable, first, in that it means partly to take the most appropriate means to achieve the given goals (instrumental reason). This sense of rationality would seem to be of cross-cultural value. The other aspect of rationality involves a general critical attitude and questioning of means and ends. A community that accepts both aspects of rationality should be called an 'open society' or one based on free inquiry. Such a society is typified by the assumption that no society is perfect in knowledge or moral virtue and that this fallibility and imperfection are corrigible by rational inquiry and criticism.[3] Some communities, however, may be typified by obtaining and maintaining beliefs by appeal to what they consider a sacred and infallible person, or text, or tradition. These communities would value rationality in its instrumental dimension (means-ends) but not in its overall critical dimension. The question of academic freedom is relevant only in a society that accepts rationality in both senses.

The institutionalization of the promotion and development of free speech and free inquiry occurs primarily in the context of educational institutions. The socializing and training function is performed at every level of education, but the development of the critical attitude, which is necessary for an open and free society, is primarily performed at the college and university level. Because of the knowledge of the faculty and their role as educators of new generations, institutions of higher learning are the logical loci of systematic and open inquiry and of the initiation of social reform. To be sure, not all colleges and universities have the overriding dedication to the pursuit of knowledge; some are committed to political, religious or other ideologies in a dogmatic or noncriticizable way. Undoubtedly, such institutions have a right to exist in a free society, but if all educational institutions were of this type, a free society would cease to be free.

Open and free inquiry in academia has traditionally been protected by the development of what is termed "academic freedom." Academic freedom means that tenured professors cannot be terminated or penalized in any way for exercising their right to free speech and inquiry, inside or outside the college (including research, teaching and publication). This is a privilege distinct from the general civil right to free speech that citizens of a democracy have, since other citizens working in the private sector may be legally fired or penalized in some way for expressing opinions displeasing to their employers. A direct implication of this understanding of academic freedom is that decisions concerning an academic's work can only be made on the basis of competence as understood in that profession, not whether one agrees or disagrees with his or her ideas. If agreement were a condition for hiring, tenure and promotion, new ideas and free inquiry would be stifled. Decisions concerning the appointment, tenure and promotion of professors must be made by their peers; peer evaluation is crucial if authority over academics is to be exercised in a manner consistent with free inquiry and the growth of knowledge. However, as it exists presently, only 'tenured' professors have this protection: let us consider this concept of tenure.

Academic freedom has been institutionalized through the practice of tenure. Tenure means that once a teacher has served a probationary period (usually no more than seven years), he or she is granted guaranteed employment until retirement and can be dismissed only for failing to perform specified duties, or for moral turpitude, for financial exigencies which require the elimination of a tenure slot in the department, or because of the elimination of the department itself. The idea of tenure is related to the nature of the responsibilities of professors. These responsibilities include the function of socialization, professional training, the development of critical reason (teaching), and the growth of knowledge (research), as well as the support and maintenance of the educational institution itself (service). Hence, tenure has been usually decided by determining to what extent one has successfully promoted the goals of teaching, research and service to the university. The American Association of University Professors also claims that tenure serves the purpose of providing economic security which in turn will attract qualified individuals to the profession.[4] Academic freedom, then consists of three essential concepts: the commitment of educational institutions to the pursuit of knowledge per se (not the propagation of some dogma or ideology), the exercise of authority over academics must be only by peers, and the security against termination or tenure.

Though the theory of tenure as sketched above may not seem obviously problematic, in practice, several problems seem to have emerged.[5] Firstly, tenure does not protect junior faculty during their probationary period. This is a significant factor for it seems plausible that junior faculty are at least as likely and probably more so to introduce new and unpopular ideas than older and more established colleagues. However, since untenured faculty usually seek to achieve tenure there will be a tendency to avoid controversial issues that might alienate and antagonize older members of the department who will later make the tenure decision. Consequently, the present system of tenure may filter out the very individuals and ideas it was meant to protect. In addition, it creates a high level of anxiety in junior faculty who must function at their best under this same stress. Secondly, the brief probationary period puts pressure on individuals to publish quickly and in quantity which may reduce the quality of the publications. Thirdly, once a professor has been denied tenure, universities usually do not help in finding alternate employment. Fourthly, to the extent the present system under protects junior faculty it may overprotect the tenured faculty in the following way. In theory, tenured professors can be terminated for failing to adequately carry out their duties, but in practice, the present system allows individuals to continue teaching while meeting only minimal standards of competence. This is the problem of so-called "deadwood" which many feel exists because of the difficulty of removing individuals who are tenured because the security of guaranteed employment removes incentives for a high level of performance. Tenure also reduces the financial and academic flexibility of colleges and universities since it is difficult to terminate individuals for economic reasons or for reasons of new staffing and teaching needs.[6]

Some have argued for the abolition of tenure and its replacement with a system of renewable contracts.[7] This would involve the right to due process by peers with the burden of proof not to renew a contract resting with the institution. Contracts could not be denied renewal if it meant the violation of academic freedom. In addition, contracts must specify the exact terms of employment and conditions for renewal.

This proposal is problematic for several reasons. First, the theory of the present system of tenure does not preclude the termination of any individual who is failing to perform his or her duties, whether teaching, research or service. Short of termination, of course, other measures can be used to provide incentives for better performance, measures such as raises, promotions, sabbaticals, and course load variations. More importantly, one must ask "Incentives for what?" To amass a long bibliography of mediocre value or to publish only if one has something of importance to say? True, in the past there may have been a reluctance on the part of universities to terminate professors, but this is an institutional weakness, not an intrinsic problem with tenure.[8] Tenure will not be abused if steps are taken by faculty, administration and students to protect their rights and ensure that teachers live up to their responsibilities. All teachers should have their teaching evaluated on a regular basis by peers and students. Professors who are strong in teaching but weak in publications should have their teaching schedule reflect this, and conversely for strong researchers who are weak teachers. All professors should also be encouraged to participate in paid summer institutes on a regular basis to keep abreast of developments in their field.

The renewable contract idea would at the very least have a chilling effect on professors' speech and research. All forms of subtle pressure could be used by the administration and faculty to remove someone with whom they are uncomfortable or for financial reasons. In addition, a flood of costly litigation would likely result from non-renewed professors. Finally, and perhaps most importantly, there is the possibility of conflict of interest given that all faculty would be equally nontenured. When a colleague came up for renewal there may be a tendency to be lenient since this would increase the chances of one's own renewal in the future. In the tenure system which exists today at most schools, tenured faculty do not have reasons to be lax on junior faculty, in fact, quite the contrary may often occur.[9]

A related argument contends that professors should not be singled out for the special protection that tenure provides, but employee rights for all should be expanded. On this view, all employees should have expanded rights in the workplace including the right to due process if disciplinary action or discharge is recommended. This means the employer must specify a just cause for terminating or penalizing an employee, base promotions and raises on public and fairly applied standards, and uphold employee rights. These rights involve, in addition to the right to due process, the right to "blow the whistle" or go public with immoral or illegal company activities, the right to privacy, and the right to strike.[10] It may well be true that all employee rights should be extended, yet this point ignores the special status of the teaching profession. The academic profession is, in a sense, a foundational profession in that all other professions depend on it for their training and education. It is foundational in the sense that it helps to inculcate through the process of socialization the basic or foundational values of democracy. As such, it seems clear that the excellences of the teaching profession in terms of teacher skills, liberties and moral integrity would permeate the breadth of society. Consequently, a lack of independence on the part of teachers would contaminate with dogmatism and stagnation the entire gamut of educational and professional training and cultural life.

As suggested above teachers play a pivotal role in the preservation of liberal democracy a role which, say, plumbers and bus drivers do not. Furthermore, though the right to "blow the whistle" is an important right that should be protected, it is not clear that a private corporation should tolerate free speech to the degree of allowing an employee to publicly insult, ridicule and denigrate his own employer and his products or services and advocate those of a competitor. The general consideration that suggests itself here is whether the behavior of the employee is consistent with the assigned function of the employee. That is, it seems one cannot have the most extensive set of rights in the workplace, since this may conflict with efficiency or adequate job performance.[11]

However, in academia there is no conflict between freedom and efficiency since freedom is precisely one of the goals and defining characteristics of the professor. It is this type of wide-ranging freedom and independence that tenure guarantees and that the academic profession needs if it is to be capable of criticizing the status quo. In most cases, the function of the non-academic individual is more narrowly defined as performing a certain task within a corporate structure, whereas the academic's role is not fully defined within the narrow confines of his or her institutional affiliation but involves the role of critic in the larger context of the society itself. Just as judges must be independent of political pressures in order to decide cases fairly, so professors must be independent of political, economic and administrative control. It is this role which gives academics special status that merits special protection which tenure, properly applied, provides. Again, this is not to suggest that non-academic employees should not have greater rights in the workplace, for they should. The point has been to define their different roles and functions from which flow differential rights and duties.

The problem of junior or non-tenured faculty must be addressed if tenure is not to be used as a reward for timid conformists. To deal with this problem, some have suggested that junior faculty not be terminated for exercising their right to express new and perhaps unpopular ideas. The institutionalizing of due process for these professors would protect their freedom, if they are competent, of course.[12] This does not mean that junior faculty should have tenure from the start, but it does mean that they cannot be terminated for reasons tenure is meant to guard against. Since a probationary period seems to be necessary to evaluate the competence of new employees, junior faculty cannot have the same protection as senior faculty since the idea of tenure is to protect those who can best perform the function of a teacher, education and criticism; to give it to others would be detrimental to the advancement of these basic purposes.[13]

The argument presented here has been in terms of the social and institutional structures necessary to maximize freedom and knowledge. In order for elections to be rational and government to be accountable, democracy requires free speech and a properly socialized new generation that is rational and critical. Free speech and knowledge are maximized if those most knowledgeable have the freedom of free inquiry without fear of reprisal. Teachers and professors are in the vanguard of scientific, cultural and political progress through their own field-related research, teaching (socializing students to think critically and rationally), and general role as social critics. This vocation can be fulfilled only if professors can question every aspect of the status quo, whether it concerns the university, the profession, the community or the political system as a whole. Tenure, properly understood, protects teachers in their performance of these functions and thus preserves an open and free society.

NOTES

A version of this essay appeared in *Terrorism, Justice and Social Values*, Peden, C., Hudson, Y., eds., Mellen Press, 1990.

1. Mill, J.S., On Liberty, Bobbs-Merrill Co., 1956, pp. 20-5.

2. Cf., Dewey, John, *Democracy and Education*, New York: Macmillan Co., 1963; Lovejoy, Arthur, "Academic Freedom," *Encyclopedia of the social Sciences*, V.l, New York Macmillan Co., 1937, pp.384-387; Strike, Kenneth, *Liberty and Learning*, Oxford: Martin Robertson, 1982, pp. 54-8, 75-8.

3. Mill, op. cit., pp. 30-34.

4. AAUP: Policy, documents and Reports, 1977, p.2; Passmore, John, "Academic Ethics" *Journal of Applied Philosophy*, V.l, N.l, 1984.

5. Sartorius, Rolf, "Tenure and Academic Freedom," in Pincoffs, Edmund, ed., *The Concept of Academic Freedom*, Austin: University of Texas Press, 1972, pp. 141-155; Jaggar, Alison, "Tenure, Academic Freedom and Professional Competence," *The Philosophical Forum*, V.X, N.3-4, 1978-9, pp.360-363.

6. Hare, R.M. "Tenure" unpublished manuscript, p.l; Robinson, George; Moulton, Janice, *Ethical Problems in Higher Education*, Englewood Cliffs: Prentice Hall, *pp.45-7.*

7. Sartorius, Rolf, op. cit., *pp.150-5.*

8. Cahn, Steven, *Saints and Scamps: Ethics in Academia*, Totowa, NJ,: Rowman & Littlefield, 1986, pp.76-9.

9. Sartorius, Rolf, op. cit., p.155, Atherton, Margaret, Morgenbesser, Sidney, and Schwartz, Robert, "On Tenure," *The Philosophical Forum* V. X. N. 2-4, 1978-9, pp.349-50.

10. Ladenson, Robert, "Is Academic Freedom Necessary?" *Law and Philosophy*, 5, 1986, pp.69-75; cf., Werhane, Patricia, *Persons, Rights and Corporations*, Englewood Cliffs, NJ: Prentice-Hall, 1985, pp. 110-22.

11. Ways, Max, "The Myth of the Oppressive Corporation" in Donaldson, Thomas, Werhane, Patricia, eds., *Ethical Issues in Business*, Englewood Cliffs, NJ: Prentice-Hall, 1983, pp. 312-4.

12. Atherton, Margaret, et al., op. cit., p.344.

13. Schneewind, J.B., "On 'On Tenure'" *The Philosophical Forum*, V.X, N.2-4, 19789, pp. 355-6; see "The Part-time Problem: Four Voices" by Elizabeth Flynn, John Flynn, Nancy Grimm, and Ted Lockhart, *Academe*, Jan-Feb. 1986, pp.12-8 and "The Status of Part-time Faculty," *Academe*, 67, N.l, Feb.-Mar. 1981, pp. 29-39, for a discussion of why tenure should be available to part-time instructors. For an analysis of the state of American education today, see *College: The Undergraduate Experience*, Report of the Carnegie Foundation for the Advancement of Teaching, by Ernest L. Boyer, New York: Harper & Row, 1987; *Nation at Risk*, Report of U. S. Dept. of Education, April 1983; Hacker, Andrew, "The Decline of Higher Learning," *The New York Review of Books*, Feb. 13, 1986, pp 35-42.

ABOUT THE AUTHOR

Joseph Grcic is a professor of philosophy at Indiana State University. He was born on the island of Olib in Croatia, grew up in New York City, attended Stuyvesant High School and graduated from City College of the City University of New York (Phi Beta Kappa). He received his Ph.D. from the University of Notre Dame and was a Post Doc Fellow at the Center for Applied Philosophy at the University of Florida. He has presented invited talks to the American Philosophical Association, the World Congress of Philosophy (Moscow), The International Association for the Philosophy of Law and Social Philosophy, Florida Philosophical Association, Indiana Philosophical Association and other groups. His published books include *Moral Choices* and *Perspectives On the Family* (co-edited) and articles in various journals.